The Balance of Night

The Balance of Night

Elara Nightsong

Contents

Act 1: The Path of the Priestess

1

The Eclipse of Faith

The air inside the temple was heavy with incense and ancient whispers, the flicker of crimson torches casting long, ominous shadows across the black marble floors. Eve stood at the center of the ritual chamber, her gaze fixed on the towering effigy of Lord Asmodeus. His menacing figure, carved from obsidian, loomed over her like a watchful god, a reminder of the power and authority that ruled this infernal domain.

The priestess carried an ethereal beauty that defied the expectations of those who beheld her. Once a celestial being of light, her transformation into a fallen angel had left her appearance hauntingly captivating. Her black hair cascaded down her back like a waterfall of shadows, shimmering faintly in the dim torchlight of the sanctuary. It framed her pale, delicate face - a face that seemed as if it had been sculpted from marble, smooth and cold to the touch, yet strangely alluring.

Her eyes, once radiant with the light of the heavens, had turned into deep pools of darkness, as black as the void itself. They held a hypnotic quality, drawing in those who dared to look into them too long, as if they could see through the very soul of a person. There was a quiet, unspoken power behind her gaze, a force that could command armies or silence a room with a single glance. It was said that no one could look into her eyes and not feel the pull of something ancient and mysterious, something beyond mortal comprehension.

Eve's thin, lithe frame only added to her otherworldly appearance. She moved with a grace that seemed almost unnatural, her steps silent, her gestures precise and deliberate. Her body, while slender, exuded a strength that belied her fragile appearance. She wore the robes of a priestess, dark and flowing, adorned with infernal symbols that marked her as a servant of Asmodeus. The fabric clung to her frame in a way that accentuated her femininity without diminishing the power she projected.

Her skin was alabaster, pale as the moonlight that she so often invoked in her rituals. It gave her a ghostly presence, as though she were not entirely of this world. And yet, despite the coldness of her exterior, there was an undeniable beauty in her form - a beauty that spoke of her former life as a being of light and grace. Though she had fallen, that celestial elegance remained, twisted now by the dark power she wielded.

But it was her wings that truly captured attention - a pair of immense, black wings, both majestic and foreboding, stretching out from her back with the elegance of night itself. Once the pristine white of the heavens, they had become symbols of her descent, transformed into the very embodiment of darkness. The feathers, impossibly dark, almost seemed to absorb all light, casting a deep shadow around her wherever she went. Yet, it was not the blackness of her wings alone that stirred awe, but the veins of dark red energy that pulsed along their edges.

The energy swirled like liquid fire, tracing the feathers in serpentine patterns of barely contained fury. This dark red aura seemed alive, accentuating the otherworldly beauty of her wings, glowing faintly as it rippled through the air. It wrapped around her wings like molten veins of magma, casting flickering reflections of crimson light throughout the room, as if she held within her the heart of the abyss itself. These wings, once symbols of purity, were now a vivid reminder of her power and allegiance to the Dark Prince, Asmodeus.

Despite her outward appearance of fragility, Eve was a force to be reckoned with. Her beauty was not soft or gentle; it was fierce, almost dangerous. She embodied the balance between creation and destruction, light and dark, and it was this duality that made her both feared and revered in the temple. To look upon her was to see the embodiment of Asmodeus' will, a creature both captivating and terrifying, a reminder of the beauty and power that could be found in darkness.

She approached the altar and knelt before it, lighting a candle as an offering to Asmodeus. The flickering flame danced in front of her, casting long shadows on the walls of the sanctuary. She closed her eyes and let herself slip into a deep meditation, feeling the presence of her Lord. But as the power of the temple surged through her, she felt something else - a familiar darkness stirring within her.

In her early days in the second circle of hell, Eve had been a figure of serene poise, a priestess whose dedication to Asmodeus was unquestionable. She performed her duties with an almost ethereal grace, her prayers and rituals a balm for the tormented souls who sought solace within the temple's shadowed walls. Her role was to guide and comfort, to bring the wisdom of the Dark Prince to those who needed it. Her presence was calming, her demeanor one of quiet strength and unwavering faith.

But as the celestial forces encroached upon their realm, seeking to subvert the balance and impose their own vision of order, Eve's world changed irrevocably. The conflict intensified, the stakes grew higher, and the temple's sacred grounds became a battleground. It was during these dark times that Eve's latent potential began to reveal itself, not merely through her resolve but through the physical manifestation of her inner strength.

When the call came for warriors to stand against the invasion, Eve stepped forward with a determination that belied her peaceful past. The transformation from a priestess to battle priestess was not an easy one; it demanded more than mere physical prowess. Eve had to harness the arcane knowledge she possessed, blending it seamlessly with the brutal art of combat. She trained tirelessly, her once-soft voice now commanding legions and her graceful movements evolving into a dance of destruction.

Her ascension to battle priestess was marked by trials that tested her limits. She faced adversaries who were once her celestial kin, beings she had known as allies but now stood against her as enemies. The transition was brutal; the battlefield was unforgiving, and the weight of leadership bore heavily upon her shoulders. Yet, Eve rose to the challenge, her spirit unyielding.

In battle, Eve was a tempest. Her prayers became incantations of power, her rituals transformed into strategic maneuvers. She wielded both divine and infernal magic with a precision that astonished her allies and struck terror into the hearts of her foes. Her black wings, once symbols of purity, became banners of fear, their dark red energy crackling with every commanding sweep.

Her reputation as a battle priestess grew as quickly as her mastery over combat and magic. The temple's forces rallied behind her, and her tactical brilliance turned the tide in numerous skirmishes. She was not just a warrior but a beacon of hope and a symbol of Asmodeus's wrath against those who dared to challenge his domain.

Despite her success on the battlefield, Eve's journey was marked by a deepening internal struggle. Each victory came at a cost, and the bloodshed left an indelible mark on her soul. Yet, she remained steadfast, driven by an unshakable belief in her cause and a profound sense of duty.

But tonight, as she knelt before the altar, her thoughts were not of the power she held. They were of the nature of the universe itself, of the duality that governed everything in existence. For as long as she could remember, Eve had questioned the rigid lines drawn between good and evil, light and dark. Asmodeus taught that the light was weak, that it sought to control and subdue. But Eve saw something more - something Nietzsche had whispered to her in her darkest dreams: there was no true good, no true evil. Only will, only strength, only the eternal dance of forces beyond mortal comprehension.

As the ritual began, she recited the incantations that called forth Asmodeus' power, but her mind drifted to deeper, more forbidden thoughts. "What if", she pondered, "the light and the darkness were two sides of the same coin? What if balance, not dominion, was the true path to power?"

"Eve," a voice echoed from the shadows. "Lost in your musings again, Priestess?"

She recognized the voice immediately. Lord Vesperion. His presence was always accompanied by a palpable shift in the air, a sense of power that could not be ignored. He stepped forward, his black robes flowing like smoke as he approached her. Eve turned to see the towering, armored figure of Asmodeus' mightiest general, standing in the archway. His presence commanded both respect and fear. Though he was brutal in battle, his strategic mind was second only to Asmodeus himself.

"You honor me, Lord Vesperion," Eve said, rising from her kneeling position, but keeping her gaze respectfully low. She could feel his eyes on her, sharp and assessing. "I was reflecting on the nature of power. It is not simply force. It is something more. Balance... harmony between what we can see and what we cannot."

Vesperion's gaze narrowed, his glowing red eyes studying her intently. "You speak as though you've begun to doubt our Lord's teachings. Asmodeus rules through domination, not balance."

Eve smiled faintly, masking the thoughts stirring inside her. "No, I do not doubt Him. I only seek to understand deeper truths."

Vesperion approached her, his massive figure dwarfing hers. "Deeper truths? You walk a fine line, Eve. Be careful not to stray from the path. I have heard much of your recent works, Priestess,"

Vesperion's voice rumbled like distant thunder. "The angels who once dared to defy us now fall to their knees at your command. You have proven yourself not only in faith but in battle. A rare combination indeed."

Eve looked up, meeting his eyes. There was no fear in her, only a deep resolve. "My devotion to Asmodeus guides me, my lord." Eve's eyes flickered with a faint crimson glow.

Vesperion studied her for a long moment before nodding. "Very well, Eve, but remember this: in the realm of Asmodeus, strength is everything. Those who falter are consumed by the darkness they wield."

Eve nodded solemnly. "I will not falter, my lord." She had strayed long ago, and there was no turning back. Her path would be one of discovery - of unraveling the duality that governed not just the realms of Hell and Heaven, but the entire universe. Nietzsche's words echoed in her mind: "There are no facts, only interpretations."

She was the living embodiment of that philosophy, torn between the world she had pledged herself to serve and the truths she had yet to fully uncover.

As the night deepened, Eve's thoughts grew darker. She would explore these truths, even if it meant stepping beyond the boundaries of Asmodeus' teachings. Because to wield true power, she had to understand the universe in all its complexity - its light and darkness, its order and chaos, its endless cycles of creation and destruction.

For now, she would play the role of the faithful priestess, but in time, the balance she sought would reshape everything.

The Second Circle of Hell, often known as the Circle of Lust, is a realm of intense, turbulent passions and unfulfilled desires. It is a domain marked by ceaseless storms and whirlwinds, where the souls of the damned are condemned to be swept away by the powerful gales that mirror the uncontrollable nature of their earthly sins. The winds themselves are a manifestation of their desires, which perpetually toss them about, never allowing them to find rest or solace.

This circle is characterized by its harsh, unrelenting environment. The air is thick with a heavy, oppressive heat that stings and scorches, amplifying the torment of the souls trapped within. The landscape is barren and desolate, with jagged rocks and sharp, craggy outcroppings that contribute to the unending agony of its inhabitants. The ground is uneven and treacherous, reflecting the unstable and chaotic nature of lustful passions.

In this infernal realm, the damned are subjected to relentless punishment that mirrors their earthly sins. Their souls are forever entwined in the stormy winds, continuously battered by gusts that symbolize their insatiable cravings. This eternal storm forces them into a state of perpetual disarray, never allowing them to settle or find peace. Their attempts to grasp at fleeting moments of respite are thwarted by the ever-present winds that drag them back into the turmoil.

The visual and auditory landscape of the Second Circle is stark and haunting. The sky is perpetually overcast, cloaked in dark, roiling clouds that obscure any trace of light. Occasional flashes of lightning illuminate the desolate terrain, casting eerie shadows and creating an atmosphere of dread and despair. The howling winds create a constant, wailing noise that echoes through the void, adding to the torment of the souls who are trapped there.

The Second Circle of Hell serves as a stark reminder of the consequences of unchecked desires and the eternal nature of sin. It is a realm where the passions and lusts of the damned are manifest in their suffering, creating a vivid, unending representation of their earthly failings.

Hell is also marked by the presence of grotesque, demonic entities that serve as both tormentors and overseers. These beings are twisted and malformed, their forms a grotesque amalgamation of various animalistic and infernal features. They prowl the circle, their eyes glowing with a malevolent light as they ensure that the damned receive their just punishments. These demons are both sadistic and efficient, their presence a constant reminder of the power and cruelty of the infernal realm.

Overall, it is a place of ceaseless suffering, where the damned are tormented by their own sins and the very elements of their environment. It is a realm where desires are twisted into instruments of pain, and the very fabric of the landscape is a reflection of the inner torment of its inhabitants. It is a stark reminder of the consequences of succumbing to one's base desires and the inescapable nature of eternal punishment.

The Temple of Asmodeus stands as a solemn yet majestic sanctuary amidst the relentless chaos of the Second Circle. It is a rare bastion of order and purpose, offering a beacon of refuge from the otherwise ceaseless torment of the realm. This sacred space, carved from the very bedrock of Hell, exudes an aura of dark grandeur and power, a stark contrast to the stormy desolation that surrounds it.

The architecture of the temple is both imposing and awe-inspiring. Massive, obsidian pillars support a vaulted ceiling that seems to stretch into the abyss, adorned with intricate carvings depicting the twisted yet divine symbolism of Asmodeus. These carvings come to life in the flickering, infernal light of the temple, casting shifting shadows that dance across the walls. The air within the temple is cooler and less oppressive than outside, imbued with an otherworldly calm that provides a semblance of peace to those who enter.

Within its vast, shadowy halls, the atmosphere is thick with the scent of burning incense, a blend of rich, dark fragrances that soothe

the weary souls and demons alike. The floor is paved with smooth, dark marble, veined with veins of crimson and gold that catch the light in mesmerizing patterns. The central altar, where the faithful gather to offer their devotion, is a grand, ornate structure of black stone, its surface etched with runes of power and protection. Here, sacrifices and offerings are made, and the ritualistic practices of worship are performed with meticulous reverence.

The temple serves not only as a place of worship but also as a sanctuary for those who serve Asmodeus. The souls who have dedicated themselves to his service find respite from their eternal torment here, their sins and sufferings momentarily alleviated as they engage in devotion and rituals. The soothing chants and prayers offered in this sacred space provide a brief escape from the relentless winds and chaotic passions of the outside realm.

In this haven, demons and mortal souls alike can partake in communal gatherings and study the esoteric teachings of Asmodeus. The temple's libraries hold ancient tomes and scrolls that reveal the dark wisdom and secrets of the Dark Prince, accessible to those who seek to deepen their understanding and commitment. The echoes of ritualistic music and the hum of demonic energy create a harmonious environment where the faithful can renew their strength and focus their resolve.

This shrine stands as a critical point of connection and support within the Second Circle - a place where the devout can momentarily escape their torments and find purpose and solace in their devotion. It is a testament to the power and influence of Asmodeus, a dark sanctuary where faith and suffering intertwine to create a unique, albeit fleeting, sanctuary from the eternal chaos.

The church stood tall, its darkened spires twisting into the heavens like skeletal fingers clawing at the fading light of day. Eve, a priestess of unyielding faith, walked through the grand halls, her steps silent but purposeful. Her long, dark robes swept the stone floors, a contrast to the flickering crimson torches that lined the walls. There was a weight in the air today - something beyond the usual pull of demonic energy.

Eve had just finished her meditation and was preparing to retire for the evening when a sudden, hushed murmur reached her ears. The disturbance was subtle but noticeable, like the faint ripple of disturbed waters in an otherwise calm pool. Her gaze shifted towards the entrance of the temple, where a figure was now making their way through the grand, obsidian doors.

The visitor was a mortal, a young woman with an aura of desperation and resolve. Her name was Seraphina; a name ironic for someone who had fled from a life entangled in the webs of celestial contemplations. Her turmoil in life had led her to seek solace in the temple in death, hoping that the dark wisdom of Asmodeus might offer her some respite.

Seraphina was clad in a modest, travel-worn dress that hung loosely on her slender frame. Her dark hair, disheveled from her journey, framed a face marked by exhaustion and fear. Her eyes, however, held a glimmer of hope as she entered the temple, guided by the palpable presence of divine energy that radiated from within its walls.

Eve observed Seraphina from her position at the altar, her curiosity piqued. The mortal's aura was not one of the usual condemned souls seeking redemption, but rather one of someone in desperate need of guidance - a situation Eve was well-equipped to handle.

The mortal approached the altar, her gaze lowered in reverence and uncertainty. Eve, rising from her seated position, approached her with graceful, measured steps. The flickering light of the torches highlighted the ethereal beauty of Eve's dark, flowing robes and the dark red energy that pulsed along the edges of her wings.

"Welcome to the Temple of Asmodeus," Eve said, her voice smooth and calming. "I am Eve, Priestess of the Dark Prince. How may I assist you?"

Seraphina lifted her gaze, her eyes meeting Eve's with a mixture of awe and relief. "I-I need help," she stammered, her voice trembling. "I am Seraphina. I've come from the mortal realm seeking... guidance. My family - my family demanded so much from me, and I could not meet their expectations. I'm lost."

Eve's eyes softened with empathy. She could sense the weight of Seraphina's burden - a conflict of faith and self-worth that was as heavy as any infernal torment. "Please, take a seat," Eve gestured towards a nearby bench. "Tell me more about what troubles you."

Seraphina sat down, her hands clasped tightly in her lap. "I was raised in a deeply religious family. They believe in absolute piety and adherence to their faith. From a young age, I was taught that any deviation from their strict principles would condemn me to eternal damnation. I've lived my life trying to please them, to live up to their impossible standards. But no matter how hard I tried, I always fell short. And now, here I find myself, in Hell."

Eve listened intently, her expression contemplative. "And what is it that you seek from this place? What do you hope to find in the teachings of Asmodeus?"

Seraphina's eyes glistened with unshed tears. "I don't know anymore. I'm tired of the constant pressure instilled within me to be perfect, of living in fear of failure. I thought... I thought maybe here, in this place of darkness, I might find a different perspective. Something that might help me understand what I truly want, beyond what my family demands."

Eve nodded, her gaze thoughtful. "It is common for mortals to seek solace in the face of overwhelming expectations. The teachings of Asmodeus offer a perspective that is often contrary to the rigid doctrines you are accustomed to. In the eyes of Asmodeus, power and self-determination are paramount. There is no inherent value in suffering under the weight of unattainable standards if they lead only to internal strife."

Seraphina's brow furrowed. "But how can I reconcile this with my family's beliefs? They have drilled into me that deviation from their path was considered sin, and I fear that in rejecting their expectations, even now, will lead to their disapproval and further suffering."

Eve's expression grew serious. "Understand this: Asmodeus teaches that existence itself is a struggle for power and dominance. This struggle is not merely physical but also existential. It was not the rejection of your family's beliefs that brought you suffering, but the attempt to conform to an ideal that is not your own. True power lies in understanding and embracing your own desires, not in fulfilling the expectations of others."

Seraphina absorbed Eve's words, her fingers loosening from their tight grip. "But what if I disappointed them? What if they still see me as a failure even now? I don't know how to separate their expectations from my own sense of self-worth."

Eve leaned forward slightly, her gaze piercing yet reassuring. "Consider this: the expectations placed upon you by others are a form of control, seeking to dominate your will and dictate your actions. True strength comes from within, from asserting your own will and choosing your path based on your desires and values. To be free from such expectations, you must recognize that you have the power to define your own worth, independent of external judgments."

Seraphina's eyes widened as a flicker of understanding crossed her face. "So, you're saying that I should... reject their expectations? Embrace what I truly want?"

Eve nodded. "Not merely reject, but understand and redefine your own desires. Embrace the power to shape your own destiny. If your family's expectations caused you suffering and conflict, then their influence over your life was an obstacle to your personal growth. By asserting your own will and finding what truly matters to you, you can transcend their control and find a path that brings you genuine fulfillment. And from this place, perhaps you can finally reconcile your sins, find peace within yourself, and ascend."

Seraphina's expression began to change from one of despair to tentative hope. "I... I see now. It wasn't about pleasing them or conforming to their ideals. It's about understanding my own desires and making choices that align with who I truly am."

Eve smiled gently, her own eyes reflecting a glimmer of approval. "Precisely. The teachings of Asmodeus offer a path of self-empowerment and self-discovery. It is a journey of asserting your own will and embracing your true nature. In doing so, you free yourself from the constraints of imposed expectations and find a deeper, more authentic sense of purpose."

Seraphina's shoulders relaxed, and she took a deep breath, as if a weight had been lifted from her. "Thank you, Priestess Eve. I feel... lighter. I think I understand now what I need to do."

Eve placed a reassuring hand on Seraphina's shoulder. "You are welcome. Remember, the power to shape your own path lies within you. Trust in your own desires and have the courage to follow them."

As the session drew to a close, Seraphina rose from the bench with renewed resolve. She bowed to Eve in gratitude before making her way towards the exit of the temple, her steps lighter and more determined than when she had arrived.

Eve watched her leave, a sense of quiet satisfaction settling over her. The night's work had reaffirmed her role as a guide and counselor, bridging the gap between the mortal and infernal realms. In the sanctuary of the Temple of Asmodeus, amidst the flickering light and shifting shadows, she had once again demonstrated the profound impact of understanding and embracing one's true desires.

The ritual chamber fell silent once more, the ambient glow of the torches casting a warm, flickering light on the dark marble floors. Eve took a deep breath, allowing herself a moment of reflection before returning to her own thoughts, her mind still touched by the deeper truths she sought to uncover.

As the night wove its eternal tapestry of shadows and storm, Eve stood resolute, a beacon of guidance and wisdom amidst the relentless chaos of the Second Circle. Her role as Priestess of Asmodeus felt more vital than ever, a steadfast presence in a realm of unending tumult. Satisfied with the night's work and the serenity she had cultivated within the temple's hallowed walls, she returned to her chambers. With a deep sense of fulfillment and inner peace, Eve settled into her bed, reflecting on the harmony she had achieved amidst the storm.

2

The Ritual of Shadows

The Temple of Asmodeus stood as an ancient sentinel amidst the relentless turmoil of the Second Circle of Hell, its stone walls imbued with an ageless power that defied the chaos surrounding it. As a storm raged outside, darkened clouds roiled and winds howled in a cacophony of fury, the temple remained an oasis of serenity. This sanctuary, shielded from the tempest by ancient enchantments and sacred wards, served as a beacon of stability and control amidst the tumultuous landscape of Hell.

Tonight was of particular significance: it marked the annual observance of "The Ritual of Shadows," one of the temple's most revered ceremonies. This ritual was more than a mere tradition; it was a profound declaration of their dominion over the dark forces that sought to unravel the order of their realm. The Ritual of Shadows was designed to strengthen the temple's protective barriers, renew the bonds between its inhabitants and the powers they worshiped, and reaffirm their mastery over the forces of chaos that continuously threatened their existence.

The importance of this ritual stemmed from the cosmic balance it sought to maintain. In the grand scheme of the infernal hierarchy, the balance between order and chaos was crucial. The storm outside, an embodiment of the relentless chaos that perpetually threatened their world, was a reminder of the necessity of this ritual. By performing the Ritual of Shadows, the temple sought to reclaim control over the chaotic elements that sought to infiltrate their sanctum, ensuring that the equilibrium between darkness and order remained intact.

The ceremony itself was a complex and esoteric process, steeped in ancient traditions and arcane practices. It was designed not only to bolster the temple's defenses but also to channel and direct the raw, untamed energies of the shadows. This involved intricate preparations and a performance that demanded both precision and profound spiritual engagement from those who performed it. The ritual was a demonstration of their ability to harness and manipulate the dark forces that pervaded their realm, a testament to their unwavering faith in Asmodeus and their mastery over the shadowy aspects of existence.

This was all painfully clear to Eve as she prepared to lead the night's ritual proceedings for her very first time, and accordingly, she could sense the gravity of the occasion. The storm outside seemed to reflect the turbulent energies that were to be channeled and controlled within the temple. Each flicker of the candlelight in the ritual chamber cast dancing shadows that grew longer and more intricate as the ceremony approached. The air was thick with anticipation and the scent of incense, which mixed with the faint tang of sulfur and myrrh, creating a heady aroma that heightened the ritual's mystical atmosphere.

Tonight, the Ritual of Shadows was not just a ceremonial duty but a vital expression of their resilience against the forces that sought to disrupt their carefully maintained order. The storm outside was a symbolic reminder of the chaos they faced daily, and the ritual was their means of asserting control over it. The intricate patterns drawn on the floor, the ancient incantations spoken, and the ceremonial tools used were all part of a grand design to reaffirm their strength and their commitment to Asmodeus.

As the hour of the ritual approached, Eve moved with practiced grace through the corridors of the temple, her dark robes flowing like liquid night. The temple was abuzz with activity as temple acolytes and priests prepared the sacred space for the ceremony.

In the main ritual chamber, the central altar stood adorned with dark crimson and onyx, the colors of shadow and mystery. Ritualistic tools, obsidian daggers and scrolls etched with ancient sigils, were meticulously arranged on the altar. Heavy tapestries draped the walls, depicting scenes of celestial warfare and infernal realms, their imagery both awe-inspiring and daunting.

Mortals and demons began to gather, filling the pews and surrounding the chamber. The faithful came to witness the Ritual of Shadows, drawn by its significance and the promise of its power. The air was thick with anticipation as these diverse beings, ranging from demons of various ranks to mortal souls seeking favor, took their places. Their murmurs and shifting movements created a low hum of collective reverence.

At the front of the chamber, the High Priest and High Priestess of the Temple of Asmodeus stood side by side, their presence commanding the reverent attention of the assembled followers.

The High Priest, clad in deep crimson robes adorned with intricate gold embroidery, stepped forward. His voice, deep and resonant, echoed through the chamber as he began the opening sermon. "Beloved followers," he intoned, "tonight we gather to perform the Ritual of Shadows, a sacred ceremony that honors the balance between light and dark. This ritual is a testament to our devotion and our mastery over the forces that shape our existence. As we prepare to channel the energies of the abyss, let us remember the importance of our commitment to Asmodeus and the divine order he represents."

Beside him, the High Priestess, draped in flowing black and silver robes, raised her hands to address the congregation. Her voice, melodic and soothing, complemented the High Priest's tones. "This ritual is not merely a display of power, but a profound act of unity with the forces that govern our realm. Through the shadows, we seek to understand the deeper truths of our existence and our place within the grand design. Let the coming hours be a time of reflection and revelation, as we honor our patron and embrace the mysteries that lie within the darkness."

The High Priest and High Priestess exchanged a solemn nod, their eyes meeting with a shared sense of purpose. As the followers listened intently, their hearts and minds aligned with the sacred intent of the ritual. The opening sermon set the tone for the evening's proceedings, reinforcing the significance of the ceremony and the collective dedication of all present to the will of Asmodeus. As they stepped back and took their seats at either side of the altar, they gave Eve a nod to proceed with the ritual.

Eve took her place at the altar now, her presence commanding attention and respect. Her hands moved deftly, arranging the ritualistic items with precision. She drew a complex pattern on the floor around her using a mixture of salt and sacred ash, creating a protective barrier designed to channel the ritual's power and keep malevolent forces at bay. The ritual was not only an act of devotion but also a demonstration of control over the chaotic energies of the Second Circle.

As the final preparations concluded, the acolytes gathered in a semicircle around the altar, their eyes fixed on Eve with reverent anticipation. The chamber's atmosphere grew charged with palpable energy, the air thick with expectation. The rhythmic drumming of ceremonial gongs began, their sound resonating through the temple like the heartbeat of an ancient beast.

Eve took a deep breath, centering herself. She raised her arms, and the chamber fell into a hushed silence. Her voice, clear and commanding, began the incantation. The words, spoken in an ancient tongue, blended guttural sounds with melodic phrases that conveyed deep power and the eternal balance of light and dark.

The incantation flowed through the chamber:

"Umbrae velum, potestas tenebris,
Adsum nos in misterium, lux et umbra,
Voce nocturnae et pacto inferni,

Exaudi nos, sanctus deorum."
Translated, it meant:
"Shadows veil, power of darkness,
We gather in mystery, light and shadow,
By the voice of night and infernal pact,
Hear us, sacred gods."

The ritual unfolded with a series of intricate steps. Eve performed a sequence of movements, her gestures graceful yet purposeful, as she chanted the sacred verses. The shadows on the walls seemed to come alive, shifting and swirling in response to her commands. The candles flickered wildly, casting long, sinuous shadows that intertwined and separated, reflecting the dance of the ritual's energies.

As Eve's incantation reached its crescendo, the air seemed to ripple with a dark, shimmering force. The protective barrier she had drawn on the floor began to glow with a faint, eerie light, signifying the activation of the ritual's power. The chamber's temperature dropped slightly, and a deep, resonant hum filled the space, echoing the ritual's growing intensity.

Eve's movements became more deliberate now. The shadows on the walls converged, forming abstract, shifting patterns that mirrored the sacred geometry she had inscribed on the floor. The interplay of light and dark grew more dynamic, illustrating the ritual's influence over the chaotic energies of the Second Circle.

Throughout the ritual, Eve's followers observed with a blend of awe and reverence. The acolytes, draped in their own dark robes, mirrored her movements with precision, their faces etched with deep respect for their leader. Whispers of prayers and expressions of devotion drifted through the chamber, as their eyes remained fixed on the central figure of their worship.

Among them was Liora, a dedicated young acolyte known for her unwavering commitment to the temple. As the ritual progressed, Liora cast frequent glances at Eve, her admiration palpable but tempered by a flicker of concern. Her eyes, reflecting both reverence and an underlying worry, followed Eve's every gesture, hoping for a sign of reassurance amidst the intensity of the ceremony.

As Eve conducted the Ritual of Shadows, her mind wrestled with more than just the ceremonial precision. Her focus, while outwardly composed, was marred by a profound inner conflict. The ritual, meant to showcase her mastery over chaos and her unyielding devotion to Asmodeus, became a crucible for her own existential doubts.

The dichotomy of light and dark, a theme central to the ritual, mirrored Eve's internal struggle. She had embraced the darkness since her fall, wielding it as a means to achieve balance and power. Yet, as she chanted the ancient incantations and manipulated the shadows, she questioned if the shadows she controlled were merely a manifestation of her own inner discord. Was her power a true reflection of control, or was it an attempt to conquer the turmoil within her?

The ceremonial blade she held was both a symbol of her authority and a stark reminder of her past. It represented her role as a mediator between light and dark, but it also evoked memories of her celestial origins and the fateful fall that led her to her current path. Each movement of the blade, each spoken verse, stirred reflections on her dual nature - torn between her role as a priestess and the remnants of the celestial being she once was.

The Ritual of Shadows, while demonstrating her control over the chaotic energies, also brought her personal conflicts into sharper focus. As the shadows danced and twisted in response to her commands, Eve's thoughts lingered on the philosophical implications of her actions. Was she merely directing the chaos, or was she grappling with the very essence of her own identity and purpose? The ritual became a mirror, reflecting not only her mastery over the darkness but also the enduring battle within herself.

As the ritual reached its zenith, Eve was suddenly engulfed by a vivid and unsettling vision. The walls of the chamber dissolved into a swirling vortex of darkness, and she found herself standing on the edge of an abyss, gazing into a vast, shadowy void. Within this abyss, fleeting images of future events flashed before her eyes - battles, betrayals, and moments of pivotal choice.

Among these visions, one stood out with a striking intensity. She saw herself not merely as the Priestess of Asmodeus but in a form of immense power, commanding the very essence of the night and shadows. This vision of herself, wielding control over the darkness with an authority that transcended her current role, was both alluring and ominous. It hinted at a potential future marked by extraordinary power and responsibility.

The vision faded, leaving Eve with a profound sense of foreboding. The prophecy suggested that the shadows she manipulated in the ritual were not just symbols of the past but harbingers of significant challenges yet to come. The duality of her existence, her public role as a Priestess and the hidden depths of her being, had never seemed more relevant.

Eve drew forth the obsidian dagger, holding it aloft. The blade gleamed ominously in the candlelight, its edge reflecting the raw power of the ceremony. With a decisive motion, she made a ceremonial cut through the air, creating a breach that allowed the ritual's energies to flow through with a rush of cold wind. The chamber was illuminated by a brilliant, pulsating light, and the shadows seemed to respond in a tumultuous dance.

As the ritual concluded and the chamber settled back into its serene calm, Eve took a moment to center herself. The weight of the vision and the prophecy was heavy on her shoulders, but she resolved to face whatever lay ahead with the strength and wisdom bestowed upon her by Asmodeus. The shadows had spoken, offering a glimpse into the path that lay before her, and it was now up to her to interpret their message and prepare for the trials to come.

Addressing her followers now, Eve's voice was steady and reassuring. "The shadows have shown us glimpses of what may come. We must remain vigilant and steadfast in our devotion. The darkness is not to be feared but embraced and understood. Together, we shall navigate the path that lies before us and honor the will of Asmodeus."

As the echoes of the ritual's energy began to subside, Eve stepped to the center of the chamber, where the shadows still danced in the candlelight. With a deep breath, she raised her arms, the ceremonial dagger held high. The chamber fell silent, every eye fixed on her with a mix of reverence and anticipation.

Eve's voice, rich and resonant, filled the room as she began the Closing Benediction. Her words were a blend of ancient incantations and heartfelt blessings, weaving together the threads of the ritual's power and purpose.

"Great Lord Asmodeus, Sovereign of Shadows and Keeper of the Balance, we stand before you, humbled by the power and wisdom you have bestowed upon us tonight. The Ritual of Shadows has drawn forth the energies of the abyss and channeled them to reveal the truths hidden in darkness.

By your will, we have embraced the shadows, not as a force to be feared but as a testament to our strength and our understanding of the eternal balance between light and dark. We have witnessed visions that guide us towards the future, and we acknowledge the lessons they carry.

May the shadows that have danced before us be a reminder of your omnipresence, a symbol of the strength and clarity we draw from your presence. As we depart from this sacred space, let us carry forth the resolve to face the challenges ahead with unwavering faith and courage.

In the name of Asmodeus, we bless this temple and all who dwell within it. Let the darkness that surrounds us be a shield and a guide, illuminating the path we must walk. May our hearts remain steadfast, our spirits resilient, and our devotion unshakable.

As we return to our daily lives, let the power of the shadows we have embraced remain with us, guiding us, protecting us, and reminding us of the divine balance that governs our existence.

With these words, we conclude our ritual, but our commitment to you, Lord Asmodeus, endures. We are your instruments, your faithful servants, and we shall honor your will in all that we do.

So it is spoken, so it shall be. Ave Asmodeus."

With a final sweep of her arms, Eve lowered the dagger and stepped back, her gaze sweeping over her followers. The chamber resonated with a sense of completion and peace as the followers offered their silent prayers of gratitude and reverence. The ritual was complete, and the night's work had drawn them closer to their purpose.

After the ceremony concluded, Liora approached Eve, her voice barely above a whisper. "Priestess Eve, your guidance has always been a beacon for us. But... I sense a growing darkness in the air. Are we truly prepared for what lies ahead?"

Eve placed a reassuring hand on Liora's shoulder, her gaze softening. "The darkness you sense is a reminder of the balance we must maintain. Our preparation and devotion keep us strong. Trust in the ritual and in the power of Asmodeus. We face the shadows not with fear, but with the knowledge that we hold the strength to overcome them."

As the final echoes of the Ritual of Shadows faded into the night, the atmosphere within the Temple of Asmodeus shifted from the intense focus of the ceremony to a more relaxed and celebratory ambiance. The chamber, once dominated by the dramatic interplay of shadows and light, now hosted a gathering of temple followers who had come to share in the afterglow of the ritual's energy.

Candles had been relit around the chamber, casting a warm, inviting glow that softened the edges of the room and bathed it in a sensual light. The air was thick with the mingling scents of incense and the intoxicating aroma of rich, spiced wines. Plush cushions and low tables were set up around the chamber, laden with an assortment of decadent treats and libations.

The followers, a mix of demons and devoted mortals, began to mingle with a sense of liberated excitement. Conversations flowed easily as the sense of community and shared experience created an atmosphere of openness and connection. Laughter and lighthearted banter filled the room as they indulged in the pleasures of the evening, their inhibitions dissolved by the communal celebration.

As the mood became more intimate, the space transformed into a setting for sensual and erotic play. The congregation, guided by the temple's traditions, engaged in group activities that explored their deepest desires and connections. The sensuality of the evening was both a manifestation of their devotion and a celebration of their shared commitment to the tenets of Asmodeus. The interactions were marked by a mixture of playful exploration and profound connection, their movements reflecting the primal energies released during the ritual.

In one corner of the chamber, a group of followers engaged in a sensual dance, their bodies moving in synchronized harmony, their touches both tender and electrifying. Nearby, others gathered around a table, their conversations turning to more intimate and exploratory themes, their laughter punctuated by soft, sensual touches.

Amidst this atmosphere of indulgence and pleasure, Eve observed the interactions with a mixture of satisfaction and contemplation. Her role in the ritual had been central, and now she could see the fruits of her labor manifesting in the form of a liberated and joyful congregation. As she watched, her thoughts drifted back to the ritual's intensity and the profound experiences it had elicited.

The High Priest and High Priestess, having watched the celebration from their own vantage point, made their way toward Eve. Their expressions were a blend of pride and warmth, their movements purposeful as they approached her amidst the ongoing revelry.

The High Priest, his robes flowing with each step, was the first to speak. "Eve," he began, his voice carrying the deep resonance of genuine admiration, "tonight's ritual was a testament to your dedication and skill. The way you commanded the shadows and guided the energies was nothing short of exceptional."

Eve, still attuned to the lingering vibrations of the ritual's power, met his gaze with a look of quiet pride. "Thank you," she replied, her voice steady. "The Ritual of Shadows is a profound experience, and I am honored to have been able to facilitate it."

The High Priestess, her presence exuding a calm and reassuring energy, nodded in agreement. "Indeed, you handled the ritual with both grace and authority. Your ability to channel the energies and maintain the balance was truly impressive. The followers are deeply appreciative of the experience you provided."

As they spoke, Eve could feel the sincerity in their words, a reflection of the deep respect they held for her role within the temple. Their praise was not just for her skill but also for the way she had embodied the essence of the ceremony.

The High Priest continued, "The way you navigated the complexities of the ritual and maintained the focus of the congregation was exemplary. Your performance not only fulfilled the ceremonial requirements but also elevated the experience for everyone present."

The High Priestess added, "Your role as the central figure in the ritual was crucial in setting the tone for the evening. The followers were deeply moved by your command over the shadows and the balance you maintained. It's clear that you are truly dedicated to the path of Asmodeus."

Eve felt a sense of fulfillment as they spoke. The ritual had been both a personal and collective journey, and the acknowledgement from the High Priest and High Priestess was a testament to the success of the evening.

With a warm smile, the High Priest concluded, "We are proud to have you as a pillar of this temple, Eve. Your dedication and skill have strengthened our community and deepened our connection to the divine. Thank you for your outstanding contribution."

As the High Priest and High Priestess offered their praise, Eve felt a renewed sense of purpose and commitment. The Ritual of Shadows had been a significant moment in her journey, and the recognition from her peers only reinforced her dedication to the path she had chosen.

As the night continued with the followers' celebrations and the ongoing sense of camaraderie, Eve took a moment to reflect on the evening's events. The ritual had been a powerful affirmation of her role within the temple, and the connections forged and deepened through the shared experience were a reminder of the community's strength and unity.

The High Priest and High Priestess left her with a final, reassuring nod before joining the celebration themselves. Eve watched as they mingled with the followers, their presence adding to the sense of joy and fulfillment that permeated the room.

In the midst of the ongoing revelry, Eve found solace in the knowledge that her efforts had made a meaningful impact. The Ritual of Shadows had been a profound experience, and the support and recognition from the High Priest and High Priestess were a testament to the success of her role.

As the night unfolded, Eve embraced the sense of connection and celebration that surrounded her. The journey of the evening had been both a reflection of her inner strength and a manifestation of the collective devotion to Asmodeus. With the ritual complete and the followers enjoying the fruits of their shared experience, Eve felt a deep sense of contentment and pride in her contribution to the temple's sacred traditions.

As the followers dispersed and the candles dimmed, Eve retreated to her private quarters, her mind still abuzz with the revelations of the night. The Ritual of Shadows had not only demonstrated her power but also revealed the depth of her inner conflict and the challenges she would face. The path ahead was uncertain, but Eve was resolute. She would continue to serve Asmodeus with unwavering dedication, even as she grappled with the shadows within herself.

3

Echoes of the Past

The night after the ritual was not kind to Eve. Despite the ceremony's success and the reassurance of her fellow priestesses, she found herself unable to rest. She lay on her bed, the shadows of the temple cast long and twisting on the stone walls. The faint hum of infernal magic still lingered in the air, but it did little to soothe her. Instead, her mind churned with thoughts she couldn't quite place, an unease crawling under her skin like an itch she couldn't scratch.

When sleep finally overtook her, it came in fits, dragging her into a whirlpool of vivid dreams and restless visions. It wasn't the kind of peaceful slumber that rejuvenated the body - it was something darker, deeper. The memories came first, familiar yet distant, flashing through her mind like fragments of a life she had tried so hard to forget.

She stood on a radiant plane, the golden skies of Celestia stretching endlessly above her, the air heavy with the scent of flowers and the soft glow of purity. The soft winds carried the songs of other angels, their voices intertwining in harmonious praise for the Creator. It was a place of endless beauty, untouched by the shadows she would come to know all too well. Eve, once a Virtue of Pudicitia, an angel of chastity, had soared through these skies with grace and dignity, her every movement imbued with divine purpose.

Her wings had been vast and shimmering, an extension of her will to uphold virtue and purity in the cosmos. She had been revered, not just among her fellow angels, but by mortals who looked to her as a beacon of self-restraint, devotion, and the very embodiment of innocence. There was no greater honor, she had once believed, than to be the symbol of chastity in a world teeming with temptation and sin.

In the dream, she could still feel the weight of her celestial wings, pure and white, though the memory of them had long since dimmed in the waking world. Yet here, in this vivid echo of her past, they were as vibrant as the day she had first soared through the heavens, radiant with divine light, untarnished by the sins she would later embrace.

But even in the midst of this divine splendor, a sense of isolation had begun to creep into her heart. As Pudicitia, her role was clear: she was to remain untouched, unsullied by desire or indulgence. To her fellow angels, she was the paragon of restraint. To mortals, she was the unreachable star, the virtue they were told to aspire to but could never truly attain. The reverence she received came at a price - the cold distance that others maintained in her presence, as though her purity were something fragile, easily corrupted by the mere proximity of warmth.

She had lived among angels, but a chasm had always existed between her and them. Unlike the others, who embodied virtues such as kindness, charity, or justice - things that allowed for connection and interaction - Pudicitia's virtue required solitude. Purity demanded separation. She could not love; she could not desire; she could not even be tempted, lest the very thing she represented be called into question. And in time, the very thing that had once been her pride began to feel like a cage.

Though she had carried out her duties without question, a seed of doubt had quietly taken root within her heart. It began as a whisper, a subtle yearning for something more than the sterile existence of purity. The weight of her role, the burden of perfection, had started to feel suffocating. How could she truly understand the mortals she was meant to guide when her existence was so far removed from their experiences? How could she know the struggle of resisting temptation when she had never been allowed to feel it?

Her doubt did not go unnoticed.

A figure of great wisdom had once stood by her side - Laziel, an angel who embodied the virtue of humility. He had been one of the few who spoke to her not with reverence, but with gentle understanding. Laziel had often counseled her in the gardens of Celestia, his voice soft but filled with the weight of ages.

"You carry a heavy burden, Pudicitia," he had said to her one day, his golden eyes reflecting the endless light of Celestia's skies. "But burdens shared are burdens lightened. You need not be alone in this."

"I am never alone," she replied, her voice steady, yet distant. "I walk with virtue, with purity. It is enough."

Laziel had tilted his head slightly, his expression unreadable. "Virtue without understanding becomes rigid, inflexible. You are pure, yes, but purity that is not tested cannot truly know its strength. Be cautious, Pudicitia. Questioning your path is natural, but be mindful of where those questions lead."

His words had lingered with her, but she had pushed them aside. What could Laziel know of the burden she carried? His humility allowed him to walk among mortals, to understand their flaws and failures without being consumed by them. Her chastity, by contrast, required isolation, a purity so pristine that it could not afford even the slightest crack.

Yet, cracks had begun to form.

It was during one of her rare visits to the mortal realm that her doubts came to a head. She had been sent to observe a temple dedicated to her virtue, a shrine where men and women knelt in supplication, praying for the strength to resist temptation. As she watched them from above, she felt something strange - envy. These mortals, though flawed, were allowed to experience the very desires they sought to overcome. They struggled, yes, but they were allowed to feel, to want, to yearn. And in that yearning, there was something she could never touch - a connection to life that she had been denied.

The fall began not with a grand rebellion, but with a quiet, internal revolt. Eve had begun to question the very nature of her existence. Why should she remain pure when purity itself felt like a lie? How could she guide mortals if she had never experienced what they did? She wanted to understand - to feel desire, to know temptation, to taste the very thing she had been taught to avoid.

The moment she gave in to those thoughts, her fall was inevitable.

The irony was bitter. When the heavens cast her out, it was not to a realm of purity or repentance, but to the Second Circle of Hell - Lust. For the angel who had once represented chastity, there could be no crueler fate. She had fallen, not for indulging in lust, but for daring to question her place in the divine order. And now, she found herself in a realm where desire ruled, where indulgence was not only accepted but celebrated.

Laziel's final warning echoed in her mind as she lay broken on the infernal soil, her once-pristine wings singed and blackened. "Be mindful of where those questions lead."

But it was too late for caution. The path had been set.

Her new life in Hell was one of torment and adaptation. At first, Eve fought fiercely against the hellish reality she had been thrust into. Every fiber of her being still clung to the memory of the celestial purity she had once embodied, the light that had once filled her heart. The memory of her wings, now charred and broken, haunted her. Each night, as she lay in the dark corners of the Second Circle, the echoes of her fall whispered through her mind. The once-revered angel of chastity was now cast into a realm ruled by lust, desire, and indulgence.

The first few years were the hardest. Eve had wandered through the Second Circle, lost and confused, trying to hold onto the last vestiges of her former self. The sights and sounds of lustful revelry surrounded her at every turn, demons reveling in the excesses of their sins, indulging in pleasures she had never allowed herself to feel. She had tried to block it out, to resist the temptation that whispered to her like a constant hum in the air. But the pull of Hell was strong, and with each passing day, her resolve weakened.

In time, Eve came to a painful realization - there was no going back. The Eve that had once soared through the skies of Celestia, the angel who had carried the virtue of chastity, was gone. The moment she had questioned her place in the celestial order, the moment she had allowed herself to feel envy for the mortals' desires, her fate had been sealed. There could be no redemption for her here.

Her resistance to the ways of Hell only delayed the inevitable. The demons around her sneered at her attempts to maintain her purity, mocking her as a relic of a world that no longer had any use for her. The harder she fought, the more they taunted her, until she found herself isolated, alone in her struggle.

It was in the depths of her despair that she met the one who would change everything: Lysandra, the powerful archpriestess whose presence commanded reverence. Lysandra had seen Eve from a distance, watching with cold amusement as the fallen angel clung to her former virtue, refusing to give in to the pleasures that surrounded her. But Lysandra was not one to leave potential unrecognized, and she saw something in Eve that the other demons did not - a fire that had not yet been fully ignited.

One day, as Eve sat by the banks of the River Styx, her head lowered in exhaustion, Lysandra approached her. The demon priestess was tall and regal, her skin a deep crimson that glistened in the dim light of the underworld. Her eyes, sharp and piercing, seemed to see through Eve's very soul.

"Why do you resist?" Lysandra's voice was a low purr, smooth and commanding. "You've fallen, angel. Your purity is nothing more than a memory. There is power in this place, if you are willing to take it."

Eve lifted her head, meeting Lysandra's gaze. "I don't want this. I didn't ask for any of this."

Lysandra smiled, a knowing look in her eyes. "Ah, but you did, didn't you? You questioned your place in the heavens. You longed to feel desire, to understand the very thing you were sworn to resist. Now you are here, in the heart of desire itself. Denying what you've become will only make you weaker."

Eve frowned, her heart heavy with the weight of Lysandra's words. She wanted to argue, to push the demon priestess away, but deep down, she knew Lysandra was right. There was no going back to Celestia. There was no reclaiming the purity she had once held so dear. She had already fallen, and the only path left was the one before her.

"You don't have to fight this," Lysandra continued, her voice softening slightly. "There is power in embracing who you are now. You may have fallen, but that doesn't mean you're powerless. In fact, here, you can become something far greater than you ever were in Celestia."

Lysandra extended a hand to Eve, her crimson fingers gleaming in the darkness. "Come with me. I can show you how to turn your fall into your greatest strength."

Eve hesitated for a moment, the weight of her decision pressing down on her. But the more she thought about it, the more she realized that Lysandra was offering her something no one else had - an opportunity to reclaim her agency. She was no longer bound by the rigid expectations of Celestia, no longer confined to the cold pedestal of chastity. Here, in Hell, she could rewrite her own destiny.

Slowly, Eve reached out and took Lysandra's hand.

Under Lysandra's guidance, Eve began to embrace her new reality. The demon priestess became her mentor, teaching her the ways of Hell and helping her to understand the power that lay in her fall. Lysandra was patient but firm, pushing Eve to confront the parts of herself she had always denied. Desire, lust, indulgence - these were not weaknesses, but strengths that could be harnessed, weapons in a world that thrived on passion and excess.

At first, it was difficult. The remnants of Eve's celestial nature still clung to her, pulling her back toward the purity she had once embodied. But Lysandra was relentless, urging Eve to break free of those chains. She showed her the power of seduction, not as a mindless indulgence, but as a tool for control, a way to bend others to her will. Eve learned how to use her fallen nature to her advantage, how to turn her angelic beauty into something dark and alluring, something that drew others in and made them powerless before her.

As Eve grew more comfortable in her new identity, she began to rise through the ranks of the Temple of Asmodeus. Her once-weak and broken wings, now strong, radiating with lust energy, became symbols of her transformation. No longer a fallen angel struggling to hold onto her past, Eve had become a force to be reckoned with, a demoness who wielded her fall as a weapon.

Her rise was not without challenges. There were those who doubted her, demons who saw her as nothing more than a failed angel clinging to remnants of her old life. But Eve was relentless. She embraced the teachings of Lysandra, proving time and again that her fall had only made her stronger. She learned the sacred rites of the temple, memorized the ancient texts, and dedicated herself to the worship of Asmodeus.

Lysandra watched with pride as Eve grew into her new role. "You see?" she said one evening as they stood atop a high spire, looking down at the temple grounds. "You've become something far greater than you ever were in Celestia. Here, you are free. Here, you are powerful."

Eve nodded, her black wings unfurling behind her. She had embraced her fall, and in doing so, she had found her true strength. As she looked out over the temple, she knew that her journey was far from over. There was more power to be gained, more battles to be fought, but with Lysandra's guidance, she was ready for whatever lay ahead.

And so, Eve rose, not as Pudicitia, the angel of chastity, but as Eve, the priestess of lust, a demoness who had found power in her fall and who would rise even further in the ranks of Hell.

The dream twisted, the once-bright skies darkening as storm clouds gathered above. She felt the tremors beneath her feet, signaling the upheaval that was to come. The war was on the horizon, the balance between Heaven and Hell about to shatter. And with it, her carefully constructed world.

The storm in the dream mirrored the chaos that had once engulfed Hell - the Celestial invasion. It had been a time when the heavens, in their arrogance, dared to breach the borders of Hell, hoping to reclaim what they saw as lost. Eve had not been newly fallen when it all began, struggling to find her place among the demons she now called kin. She was a Priestess of Asmodeus by this time, and felt a sense of peace with her new life. The angels, her former brothers and sisters, had descended like a blinding light, their radiance piercing the dark realm of Asmodeus.

Eve remembered it vividly: the first breach of the heavenly forces. It had been on the outskirts of the Second Circle, where she had been wandering aimlessly during some down-time at the temple. The sky had torn open with a thunderous crack, and from it, a legion of angels poured forth, their golden armor gleaming, their swords aflame with holy light. The sheer brilliance of it had been both terrifying and awe-inspiring. For a brief moment, she had felt a pang of nostalgia - these were the beings she had once stood beside, beings she had fought for. But that moment of weakness was short-lived.

Hell's forces had rallied quickly, demons of all ranks surging forward to meet the heavenly threat. Yet, amidst the chaos, Eve had hesitated. She had been neither wholly angel nor fully demon, lost between two worlds, unsure of where she belonged.

It was then that she met Lord Vesperion.

He had appeared in the thick of battle, his presence so powerful that it had stilled the air around him. Vesperion, a demon lord of Hell, had been a towering figure of shadow and flame, his dark wings spreading wide as he cut through the angelic forces with a cold, calculated precision. His eyes, burning with an intensity that could rival the fires of Hell itself, had locked onto Eve, recognizing something in her that even she hadn't fully understood.

"You don't belong on the sidelines," Vesperion had said, his voice a deep, commanding growl that resonated through her very bones. "You're no ordinary demon, and you're certainly no angel anymore. It's time you understood what you are."

Eve had been taken aback by his words. There had been no mockery in his tone, no condescension - only a cold truth. Vesperion had seen her for what she was: a fallen angel, but one with untapped potential, something far more dangerous than she had realized.

"I... I don't know how," Eve had admitted, her voice faltering. The truth of it stung - she had no idea how to be what Hell required of her.

Vesperion had stepped closer, his towering form casting a shadow over her. "That's because you're still clinging to what you were. You need to let go of the angel within you and embrace the power of the demon you've become."

From that moment on, Vesperion had taken her under his wing. He had become both a mentor and a ruthless taskmaster, teaching her not only the ways of Hell but also how to wield the darkness that now resided within her. Under his tutelage, Eve had learned how to fight - not with the grace and purity of a celestial being, but with the brutal efficiency of a demon. Vesperion had shown her the art of warfare in Hell, where strength, cunning, and ruthlessness were the only means of survival.

The training had been grueling. Vesperion had spared her no mercy, pushing her to her limits and beyond. Every day was a battle, both within and without. Eve had struggled to reconcile the angel she had been with the demon she was becoming. But Vesperion had been relentless, breaking her down, forcing her to confront the truth she had been avoiding: she was no longer a servant of light. She was a creature of darkness, a weapon to be honed in the fires of Hell.

"You're holding back," Vesperion had growled during one of their many sparring sessions. They had been training in the infernal fields, the heat from the lava flows around them making the air thick and suffocating. Eve had been struggling, her movements sluggish, her strikes lacking the power they needed.

"I'm not -" Eve had started to protest, but Vesperion had cut her off with a sharp backhanded strike that sent her sprawling to the ground.

"Don't lie to yourself," Vesperion had hissed, his eyes blazing with fury. "You're afraid. You're still clinging to the light. Let. It. Go."

Eve had laid there for a moment, panting, her body aching from the blow. But it hadn't been the physical pain that had hurt the most - it had been the truth in Vesperion's words. She had been holding back. She had been afraid to fully embrace the darkness within her, afraid of what it might mean, of what she might become.

But as she lay there, something had shifted within her. She had realized that Vesperion was right - she couldn't continue to fight this battle half-heartedly. She couldn't cling to her former self and expect to survive in this world. If she was going to fight, if she was going to survive, she had to let go of the angel within her and become what Hell needed her to be.

Slowly, Eve rose to her feet, her wings unfurling behind her. No longer the pristine white feathers of her past, they had transformed into dark, shadowy appendages, shimmering with a crimson aura. Power surged through them, raw and undeniable. In that moment, she had finally relinquished the light, embracing the darkness that now coursed through her soul.

From that day forward, Eve had fought not as a fallen angel, but as a demon. She had become a warrior of Hell, a battle priestess who wielded both the sacred rites of the temple and the raw, brutal power of a soldier. Under Vesperion's guidance, she had learned how to balance the two, how to use her knowledge of the celestial arts and combine it with the ferocity of Hell's warriors. She had become something unique, a force that neither the angels nor the demons had seen before.

As the war raged on, Eve had risen through the ranks, proving herself time and again on the battlefield. She had pushed back the angelic invaders, her black wings cutting through the sky like a blade, her magic and combat skills devastating her enemies. With every victory, she had grown stronger, more confident in her role as both a priestess of Asmodeus and a battle priestess of Hell.

Now, as she stood in the midst of the dream, the storm swirling around her, Eve could feel the weight of her past pressing down on her. She had come so far since that first battle, since that first encounter with Vesperion. But the memories still haunted her - the choices she had made, the battles she had fought, the sins she had embraced.

Her heart raced as the storm closed in, the echoes of her past swirling in the wind. She was no longer the angel of chastity, nor was she any longer simply a fallen angel, but the being she had become long after her fall - a demon of lust, a priestess of Asmodeus, and a battle priestess of Hell.

With each passing moment, the lines between dream and memory blurred, forcing Eve to confront the truth she had been avoiding for so long: her past was not something she could outrun. It clung to her like a second skin, as much a part of her as the darkness she now wielded with such ease. The restlessness she felt now was not merely a product of the ceremony, nor was it the consequence of her responsibilities as a priestess. It was the echo of a war that had never truly ended - a war that still raged deep within her, one that had shaped her existence from the moment she had fallen.

Eve twisted beneath the weight of her memories, feeling them flood her consciousness with the intensity of a battle she could not escape. The once-pristine angel of chastity, who had embodied the very virtue she now rebelled against, was gone. In her place stood a demon priestess, bound to the shadows and the will of Asmodeus. Yet, the conflict that had driven her fall still simmered within her soul, a constant reminder that the war between light and dark was not merely external but deeply personal. The ritual had stirred the embers of that inner struggle, pulling her back into a past she had tried to forget but could never truly leave behind.

Her eyes fluttered open, breaking the fragile barrier between dream and reality. She found herself still in her chamber, the soft, flickering glow of the temple's torches casting long, dancing shadows across the stone walls. The familiar scent of incense hung in the air, comforting in its routine presence, but it did little to calm the storm within her. The memories of Celestia, the battles she had fought, and the choices that had led her here - all of it lingered, vivid and unrelenting. Even now, as a priestess of the temple, the weight of her transformation pressed down on her with a heaviness that refused to dissipate.

The feeling of conflict remained, the eternal struggle between light and dark, virtue and sin - a battle she had once believed was over but now knew would continue long after the flames of tonight's ritual had faded. As much as she had embraced her new identity, the remnants of who she had been still clung to her, pulling her back into moments of doubt and reflection. She was no longer the celestial being she had once been, and yet, the echoes of that life still haunted her, reminding her that the past could not simply be erased.

Tomorrow, she would return to her duties as a priestess of Asmodeus, her role as a leader and guide to those who followed the same path of darkness and lust. She would stand before her followers, confident and composed, wielding the shadows with the ease of one who had mastered them. But tonight, in the stillness of her chamber, she allowed herself to remember. To feel the pain of what she had lost, the weight of what she had gained, and the unrelenting pull of both worlds tugging at her soul. For now, she would reflect on the choices that had led her here and the battles yet to come, knowing that her war was far from over.

4

The Will to Power

The Temple of Asmodeus was alive with dark energy, its ancient stones thrumming with the latent power of countless rituals and invocations. Thick plumes of incense hung in the air, carrying with them the scents of sulfur, myrrh, and something unnamable - an infernal essence that seemed to seep into the very walls of the temple itself. The light from braziers and candles flickered, casting long shadows that twisted and swayed with the movement of the followers who filled the temple's great hall. Each of them had come to witness the evening's ritual, a ceremony that promised to draw on the very essence of Asmodeus.

Eve stood at the heart of it all, a vision of dark beauty draped in the ceremonial robes of her station. Black and crimson cloth flowed around her like liquid shadows, hugging her form and accentuating the sharp lines of her wings, which stretched wide behind her. The ethereal red glow that pulsed from the tips of her wings bathed her in an otherworldly light, making her seem both angelic and demonic - an embodiment of the power she represented.

The congregation sat in rows of pews before her, their heads bowed in reverence, though their eyes betrayed their hunger. They were a mix of demons, fallen angels, and mortal souls who had found their way to the temple, all seeking the same thing - power. And it was Eve's responsibility, as both priestess and battle priestess, to guide them. But Eve knew that the true path to power was far more complex than mere ambition or strength.

She raised her hands, calling for silence. The chants of the acolytes that had filled the hall moments before ceased, and a heavy stillness settled over the room. The acolytes and the congregation all looked up at her expectantly, their eyes wide with anticipation. Eve could feel their desire, their longing to understand the deeper mysteries of power and control. But she also knew that most of them were still blinded by their own ambitions, too caught up in their desire for dominance over others to see the broader truth.

Eve stood before the assembled followers of Asmodeus, her presence a beacon of both strength and grace. The torches along the walls flickered, casting long shadows that danced with the rhythm of her breath. The air was thick with anticipation, the followers waiting eagerly to hear the words of their revered priestess.

Today was no ordinary sermon. Today, Eve would speak not just of rituals or traditions but of something far more profound - the very essence of power itself. She would delve into the philosophy of the "Will to Power," a cornerstone of Asmodeus' teachings, and one of the most misunderstood principles in the mortal and celestial realms alike. In this temple, strength and power were not mere tools - they were life itself.

Eve stepped forward, her wings spreading slightly, as though they too prepared to take flight. She looked out at the congregation, her eyes filled with the weight of the truth she was about to unveil. In this moment, there would be no turning back; these words would shake the foundations of their understanding and challenge their very perceptions of good and evil, right and wrong.

"Brothers and sisters of the Temple of Asmodeus," Eve began, her voice steady and rich with authority, "today we gather not to reflect on the past, but to look toward the future - the future you will shape through the power you wield. What does it mean to truly possess power? How can we rise beyond the chains of false morality, of weakness, and become the architects of our own destiny? Today, we will explore these questions together, and in doing so, uncover the heart of Asmodeus' greatest teaching - the Will to Power."

"Power," Eve's voice rang out, commanding the attention of every soul in the hall, "is not given freely. It is not a gift. It is something you must seize, something you must earn."

Her words resonated through the chamber, as all in attendance absorbed the gravity of her message. Eve stepped forward, her wings shifting slightly behind her, the dark energy around her rippling with each movement. She could feel the raw potential of the gathered followers, but she also felt their lack of understanding. Too many of them believed that power was a simple matter of dominance, of crushing those beneath them in a show of strength. But that was not the true lesson of Asmodeus.

Eve allowed the silence to linger for a moment longer, the air heavy with anticipation. She surveyed the congregation, noting the flicker of understanding in some eyes, the confusion in others. This was the crucial point in her sermon - where simple teachings gave way to the harder truths, the ones that few dared to face. But Eve had always believed that it was through challenge, through discomfort, that true growth occurred.

As Eve stood before the temple, her voice strong and clear, she sensed the rising energy among the congregation. Her sermon had already begun to stir their souls, challenging their notions of power, morality, and the very essence of existence. But before she delved deeper into the philosophy of the Will to Power, she knew they needed to come together as one. And what better way to unite them than through a hymn - an anthem that would speak to their hearts and remind them of their purpose. "Please open your hymnals to page 131, 'To Power We Ascend,' and join in," she announced.

Eve raised her hands, signaling to the followers. The temple grew silent, the anticipation thick in the air. She nodded to the demonic choir assembled in the shadows, and their voices rose in perfect harmony, filling the chamber with a haunting melody.

The congregation, swaying with the rhythm, joined in the hymn, their voices echoing throughout the temple. Together, they sang:

From the depths of the abyss we rise,

In shadows born, beneath the crimson skies.
The flames of strength within us burn,
To power we ascend, never to return.

The voices grew louder, a powerful chorus of demonic souls singing in unison, their words an offering to Asmodeus himself. The air around them vibrated with the force of their conviction. Eve could feel the ancient power awakening, as though Asmodeus was listening, watching, and ready to bestow his blessings upon those who would dare to rise.

O mighty Asmodeus, we heed your call,
Through your will, we shall stand tall.
In the darkness, we find our might,
With every step, we conquer the night.

The walls of the temple reverberated with the hymn, as though the very stones sang along. Eve's dark wings shimmered with red energy as she led them, her voice rising above the others, a guiding beacon of strength and power.

No chains can bind, no fear can hold,
In your name, we seek the bold.
The weak shall tremble, the strong will reign,
Through the Will to Power, we break the chain.

As they sang, Eve saw the transformation in their eyes - a fire igniting within, a hunger for the strength that Asmodeus promised. These were no longer mere followers; they were warriors of the dark path, ready to embrace their destiny.

O mighty Asmodeus, we heed your call,
Through your will, we shall stand tall.
In the darkness, we find our might,
With every step, we conquer the night.

The hymn became more than just words - it was a declaration. Each voice carried the weight of their collective resolve, their defiance against the celestial forces, and their commitment to Asmodeus. It was a testament to the power they sought and the destiny they would claim.

In fire and in shadow, we carve our way,
Guided by your teachings, we shall never stray.
The old morality, cast aside with scorn,
In your temple of power, we are reborn.

As they reached the bridge, the atmosphere within the temple shifted. It was as though the very essence of Hell had responded to their call, enveloping them in a palpable energy. Eve stood at the center of it all, the embodiment of the will to power, her presence drawing strength from each word.

O mighty Asmodeus, we heed your call,
Through your will, we shall stand tall.
In the darkness, we find our might,
With every step, we conquer the night.
To power we ascend, in your name we rise,
With Asmodeus before us, we claim the skies.

As the hymn came to its powerful conclusion, the temple fell into a reverent silence. Eve stood at the altar, her wings folded behind her, a satisfied smile tugging at her lips. The hymn had done more than unite them - it had reminded them of their purpose, their potential. They were no longer bound by the false morality of Heaven, nor were they limited by the constraints of their mortal existence. They were beings of power, and through Asmodeus, they would ascend to heights they had never imagined.

Eve allowed the silence to linger for a moment longer, letting the gravity of their shared experience sink in. Then, she spoke once more, her voice softer now, but no less commanding.

"Through this hymn, we have called upon the essence of Asmodeus. We have declared our will to rise beyond what we are, to ascend through the power we wield. Remember this feeling, my brothers and sisters, for it is through this unity, this strength, that we will conquer all who stand in our way."

She paused, her black eyes sweeping across the gathered faces. "Now, let us continue our journey into the Will to Power."

"Power," she began once again, her voice low but commanding, "is not a gift that is handed down from the heavens, nor is it something bestowed upon the weak. Power must be taken. It must be earned. And most importantly, it must be wielded with purpose."

She took a step forward, her black wings unfolding slightly as if to emphasize the weight of her words. "What some among you may fail to grasp - is that power is not simply the ability to command others, to impose your will upon the world. No, the Will to Power is far more than mere domination."

She let her gaze sweep across the room, locking eyes with several acolytes. "It is the force that drives all life, the eternal struggle to overcome, to transcend. It is the force that pushes you to become more than what you were, more than what you are. The Will to Power is not static - it is dynamic, always in motion, always seeking to grow, to expand, to consume."

Eve's words echoed off the cold stone walls of the temple, reverberating like the beating of a dark, cosmic heart. She paused for a moment, letting her words sink in before continuing.

"Many are content to exist in their station, to accept the roles that have been handed to them by fate or circumstance. They believe that their power is limited by the world around them, by the rules of society, by the so-called natural order. They live in fear of disrupting the balance, of overreaching. These people are slaves to the old morality - the morality of weakness, of complacency, of submission."

Eve's voice rose slightly, her tone sharp and cutting. "But we in the Temple of Asmodeus know that such morality is a lie. We do not adhere to the false dichotomy incredibly popular among mortals - good versus evil, light versus dark. These are the chains of those too afraid to embrace their true nature. The Will to Power rejects these distinctions. It is not concerned with right or wrong; it cares only for strength, for vitality, for growth. It is the ultimate expression of life itself."

She raised her hand, palm outstretched, as if she could pull the very energy of the room into her grasp. "The Will to Power demands that you break free from the chains that bind you. It demands that you transcend the limits imposed upon you by others - be they mortal laws, celestial decrees, or even the constraints of your own mind."

Eve could see the tension in the room, feel the unease among some of the younger acolytes. Good. This was not meant to be easy. It was meant to provoke, to unsettle, to ignite the fire of ambition deep within their souls.

"Do not mistake me," she continued, her tone softening but still carrying its sharp edge, "the Will to Power is not cruelty for cruelty's sake. It is not mindless domination or destruction. It is a path of discipline, of understanding, of self-mastery. To wield power effectively, you must first conquer yourself - your fears, your doubts, your desires. True power does not stem from controlling others. It comes from within, from the ability to master your own will."

She turned her gaze to the older members of the temple, those who had already proven their strength, who had already embraced the teachings of Asmodeus. "You know this truth," she said, her voice rich with approval. "You have walked this path, and you understand that power is not an end but a means. The Will to Power is not about the accumulation of authority for its own sake. It is about what you do with it, how you shape the world around you, how you impose your vision upon reality."

Eve took another step forward, her wings shifting slightly as she did. "Those who possess true power," she continued, "do not seek validation from others. They do not need to be seen or acknowledged by the weak. They do not seek the approval of those who cling to their fragile notions of morality. No, the truly powerful are those who recognize that life itself is a constant struggle, a never-ending battle for supremacy. And in this battle, there are no rules, no guarantees - only the relentless drive to rise above."

She extended a hand toward the altar, where the sigil of Asmodeus gleamed with dark, infernal light. "Asmodeus himself is the embodiment of this truth. He rose to his station not because it was given to him, but because he seized it, because he understood that power is not a birthright but a prize to be won. He teaches us that to hesitate is to invite defeat, that to show weakness is to forfeit your claim to power."

Eve's eyes gleamed with a dark intensity as she looked out at the gathered followers. "The Will to Power is a guiding principle of this temple. It is the force that shapes us, that defines us, that drives us forward. But it is not for the faint of heart. It is not for those who seek comfort or security. It is for those who are willing to risk everything, to challenge everything, to question everything."

She let her words hang in the air for a moment before delivering the final blow. "You must be willing to sacrifice everything, even your own sense of self, to become something greater. This is the path that Asmodeus has laid before us. It is the path of power, the path of freedom, the path of true strength."

Eve lowered her hand and took a deep breath, her eyes still locked on the congregation. "So ask yourselves," she said, her voice a whisper that seemed to fill the entire temple, "are you content to remain as you are? To be bound by the old morality, by the constraints of weakness and fear? Or will you embrace the Will to Power and claim your place among the strong?"

She stepped back, her wings folding gracefully behind her as she let the silence return. The room was heavy with the weight of her words, the truth of her message sinking into the minds of the listeners. This was not a sermon for the faint-hearted. It was a challenge - a call to rise above, to transcend, to become more.

"Those who seek power must understand one thing," Eve continued, her tone sharp but measured. "To wield power without understanding is to invite destruction. True power is not about crushing your enemies, it is about mastering yourself. It is about control - over your desires, over your fears, over your very nature."

As she spoke, Eve's eyes swept across the room, taking in the faces of the acolytes before her. Some looked eager, hungry to grasp the power she spoke of. Others appeared more cautious, uncertain of what she was asking them to consider. But all of them were listening, hanging on her every word.

She turned toward the altar at the center of the room, where a flame burned - a physical manifestation of Asmodeus' presence. Its light was harsh and unnatural, casting jagged shadows that flickered across the stone floor. Eve approached the flame with purpose, her hand outstretched, hovering just above the fire. The acolytes watched with bated breath, their gazes fixed on her every movement.

"This flame," Eve said, her voice dropping to a near whisper that still carried throughout the hall, "is a symbol of Asmodeus' power. It is a reminder that power is not something to be feared, but something to be embraced. But it is also a test. Only those who are willing to burn, who are willing to endure, can truly claim it."

Without hesitation, Eve lowered her hand into the flame. The acolytes gasped in unison, their shock palpable, but Eve showed no sign of pain. Her expression remained calm, serene even, as the fire licked at her skin. When she finally withdrew her hand, it was un-scathed - no marks, no burns, only the faintest trace of infernal energy clinging to her fingertips.

"This is the power of Asmodeus," Eve said, holding her hand aloft for all to see. "It is not a power that is easily claimed. It requires sacrifice, endurance, and most importantly, control."

The acolytes were silent, their eyes wide with awe. Eve could feel their desire intensifying, their need to understand how they, too, could harness such power. But she knew that many of them would falter on the path. The hunger for dominance often clouded one's judgment, making it difficult to see that the true challenge was not in conquering others, but in mastering oneself.

As Eve finished speaking, the congregation stood silent, hanging on her every word, their spirits stirred by the hymn and the power it invoked. She could feel the energy of the room - charged, alive, vibrating with the collective will of those who sought to embody the teachings of Asmodeus. It was time to bring the ceremony to a close, but she knew the benediction must leave them with a final reminder of their purpose, their strength, and their devotion.

Raising her arms once more, her wings spreading wide behind her, Eve's voice echoed through the vast temple, a deep resonance filling the air.

"Children of the abyss, warriors of Asmodeus, you have sung a hymn of power, and in doing so, you have called forth the strength that lies within each of you. The path we walk is not one of weakness or submission, but one of dominion, mastery, and the unfettered will to ascend above all who would oppose us." Her dark eyes scanned the crowd, locking with several of the followers, ensuring that her words were felt as much as they were heard.

"Asmodeus, the Dark Lord, grants us his blessing not through charity, but through our own unyielding resolve. We do not kneel as beggars; we rise as conquerors. We are not confined by the limitations of Heaven or the false morals they preach. Here, we thrive, not despite the darkness, but because of it. In this temple, we find the purity of our purpose, the strength of our desires, and the ultimate truth - that power is not given, it is taken."

A low murmur rippled through the assembly, the words striking chords of recognition and affirmation. Eve smiled slightly, knowing that each of them was reflecting on the fire ignited within their own souls.

"Go now, not as mere servants of the dark, but as embodiments of Asmodeus' will. Let no weakness take root in your heart. Let no false virtue chain your soul. You are the masters of your fate, the creators of your destiny. And as long as you stand within the shadow of Asmodeus, you shall never fall."

The light in the room seemed to dim even further, the flickering candles casting long, deep shadows across the walls, as if the darkness itself was listening to her words. Eve lowered her arms, her wings folding neatly behind her as she prepared to leave the altar. But before stepping away, she offered one final invocation:

"May the fire of ambition burn eternally within you. May the darkness of Hell guide your steps. And may the name of Asmodeus be forever carved into the hearts of those who would dare to challenge our power. Ave Asmodeus."

With that, the temple was filled with a deep, resonant hum - a sound that seemed to come from the very foundation of the temple itself. It was a sound of power, of purpose, of unshakable resolve. The congregation stood tall, their eyes burning with the same fierce determination that Eve carried within her.

As the ritual concluded and the acolytes began to disperse, Eve remained by the altar, her thoughts turning inward. She had been in their position once, hungry for power and driven by the need to prove her strength. But her journey had taught her that power was not about winning or losing. It was about becoming more - about transcending the limitations of mortal and demonic understanding. And it was that lesson that she needed to impart to her acolytes, though she knew few of them would truly grasp it.

Her musings were soon interrupted by the arrival of Serak, one of the temple's most senior acolytes. His presence was imposing, his tall, muscular frame casting a long shadow as he approached. He wore the scars of countless battles with pride, each one a testament to his loyalty to the temple and to Asmodeus.

"Priestess," Serak said, bowing his head respectfully. "The sermon was successful, but there are whispers among the acolytes. Some of them believe that power can only be taken through violence, that to seize what they want, they must crush those who stand in their way."

Eve regarded him with a measured gaze, her expression unreadable. This was a common misunderstanding, especially among the younger acolytes. They saw power only in terms of brute strength and domination, failing to grasp the deeper truth that Asmodeus' teachings held.

"Those who believe that violence is the only path to power are misguided," Eve said, her voice firm. "Violence has its place, yes. But power, true power, comes from control. Those who rely solely on violence will burn out long before they achieve anything of lasting value."

Serak nodded, though his expression remained troubled. "Many of them are too blinded by their own ambition to see that, Priestess. They crave power, but they do not understand its true cost."

Eve sighed softly, knowing that Serak spoke the truth. The acolytes' hunger for power was both their greatest strength and their greatest weakness. They wanted so desperately to prove themselves, to rise above their peers, but in their eagerness, they often overlooked the lessons that could lead them to true mastery.

"They will learn," Eve said, her voice cold. "Some of them will learn the easy way, through understanding and discipline. Others will learn the hard way, through failure and pain. But in the end, they will all learn."

Serak bowed his head again, though the weight of his concerns still hung in the air. "I will continue to guide them, as you have instructed. But I fear that some of them may not survive the lessons."

"That is the nature of power," Eve replied, her tone as unyielding as the flame she had touched. "Not everyone is meant to wield it. Those who cannot control themselves will fall, and that is as it should be. Power is a gift, but it is also a burden. Only those strong enough to carry it will endure."

With that, Serak took his leave, his steps echoing softly in the great hall as he disappeared into the shadows. Eve watched him go, her thoughts once again turning to the teachings of Asmodeus and the challenges that lay ahead for her and her acolytes. The will to power was a dangerous path, one that required both strength and wisdom. And as she had learned through her own trials, it was not a path for the weak.

The next morning, Eve stood on the grand balcony of the temple, gazing out over the infernal landscape below. The sky above was a churning mass of dark clouds, tinged with crimson, as if the very air itself was infused with the blood of those who had fallen in battle. The land stretched out before her in a seemingly endless expanse of fire and shadow, the molten rivers winding their way through the blackened earth like veins of molten gold.

Hell was a harsh place, unforgiving and brutal, but to Eve, it was home. She had come to understand its ways, to embrace its challenges, and to rise above them. Here, in this realm of darkness and fire, she had found something that the celestial realm had never offered her - freedom. Freedom from the rigid moral codes of the angels, freedom from the expectations that had once bound her.

Here, in Hell, she had discovered her true self.

Eve's wings twitched slightly as she reflected on her journey. She had once been consumed by rage, driven by a desire for vengeance against those who had wronged her. But over time, she had learned that power was not about crushing her enemies - it was about mastering her own impulses. It was about choosing her path, not out of anger or hatred, but out of purpose.

5

Beyond Good and Evil

The moon hung high in the night sky, casting a silvery glow across the Temple of Asmodeus. The darkened corridors and shadowed chambers of the temple were quiet, save for the occasional whisper of the wind against the stone walls. In one such chamber, Eve sat alone, her thoughts a turbulent sea of introspection and conflict.

The flickering light of a solitary candle on her desk cast long, wavering shadows on the walls, making the room feel both intimate and isolating. The quiet was almost oppressive, the stillness broken only by the soft rustle of Eve's robes as she shifted in her seat. Her gaze was fixed on the intricate patterns of the candle's flame, which seemed to dance in rhythm with the storm within her mind.

The chamber, normally a place of reflection and solitude, now felt like a crucible for her thoughts. The silence around her was heavy with the weight of her desire for newfound understanding, as if the very walls of the temple were listening to her internal struggle.

Eve's fingers traced the edges of a well-worn book of philosophical texts, its leather cover smooth beneath her touch. The book, once a source of comfort and guidance, now seemed to hold the promise of further revelations. She wondered if the answers she sought lay within its pages or if her journey required her to forge new paths of understanding. The moonlight streaming through the window seemed to underscore her resolve, casting a silver path that guided her thoughts toward the unknown future.

As a priestess of the temple, Eve had always been a figure of reverence and authority. Her role was one of wisdom and spiritual guidance, a beacon for those who sought enlightenment and understanding. Yet, beneath the surface of her serene exterior lay another facet of her identity - a fierce battle priestess who fought with unrelenting strength to protect the temple from external threats. The duality of her existence, the tension between her nurturing role and her warrior spirit, had become increasingly apparent. She found herself grappling with the limits of binary thinking and the constraints it imposed on her understanding of herself and the world.

Eve's reflection was abruptly interrupted by the arrival of a prisoner, a captured angel bound and restrained. Her once resplendent wings were now tattered and stained, and her expression conveyed a profound mixture of defiance and despair. The sight of the angel was a stark reminder of the ongoing celestial conflict - a relentless war that had compelled Eve to grapple with her beliefs about morality, power, and her place within the grand scheme of existence.

The angel was led into the chamber, her steps measured and cautious, as if each movement was an echo of her internal struggle. The cold, dim light of the temple seemed to accentuate the gravity of the moment. Eve's thoughts raced as she observed the celestial, now a prisoner in the very realm she had once deemed anathema. Here was a being who had, like Eve herself, occupied a position of high status and privilege. Yet, their worlds had collided in a catastrophic fall from grace, leaving them both to navigate the complexities of their new realities.

As the angel was brought before Eve, their eyes met, and a flicker of recognition passed between them. The angel's gaze was filled with a tumultuous mix of accusation and sorrow, a reflection of the profound inner conflict she was experiencing. Her voice, though trembling with anger and pain, carried an air of authority that spoke of her celestial status.

"You, who once bore the light of Heaven," the angel said, her voice cracking with emotion. "You have chosen to lead others down a path of darkness. How can you justify this? How can you embrace a life of power and dominance when you once stood for purity and virtue?"

Eve's eyes narrowed as she met the angel's challenging gaze. "You speak of darkness and virtue as if they were absolutes," Eve responded, her tone steady and measured. "But what is morality, if not a construct designed to control and manipulate? The very idea of good and evil is shaped by those in power to serve their own ends. My path is not defined by these artificial divisions. It is shaped by a deeper understanding of the nature of existence and power."

The angel's eyes widened in disbelief, and frustration etched deeper lines into her face. "You have betrayed everything you once stood for. How can you not see the danger in embracing such a philosophy?" she demanded, her voice a mix of anguish and accusation.

Eve rose from her seat and walked slowly toward the angel, each step deliberate and purposeful. Her presence was imposing, a reflection of her own internal struggle with the notions of power and morality. She stopped a few feet away from the angel, her gaze unwavering. "I have not betrayed my true self," she said firmly, her voice carrying the weight of her convictions. "I have transcended the limitations of conventional morality. The teachings of Nietzsche, which I have embraced, tell us that morality is a construct meant to subjugate the strong and elevate the weak. To truly understand power, one must see beyond these constructs and embrace a more profound understanding of existence."

The angel's silence was palpable, her struggle evident in the furrow of her brow and the depth of her troubled gaze. She was clearly grappling with the complexity of Eve's argument, the stark dichotomy between her former celestial beliefs and the radical shift in perspective that Eve represented.

Eve took a deep breath, allowing the gravity of the moment to sink in. She knew that the angel's current state was a reflection of her own journey - a journey that had led her to question and ultimately reject the binary notions of morality she had once held dear. "You are not alone in your confusion," Eve continued, her voice softening. "I, too, have wrestled with these ideas. The path I walk now is not one of simple darkness or light but of understanding the deeper currents that shape our existence. True power, as I have come to see it, is not about imposing one's will on others but about mastering oneself and transcending the limitations imposed by conventional morality."

The angel's eyes remained fixed on Eve, searching for some semblance of the light she once knew. "But how can you be certain that this path is not merely another form of manipulation, another way of controlling others under the guise of enlightenment?" she asked, her voice tinged with a mix of skepticism and hope.

Eve paused, considering the angel's question with the seriousness it deserved. "I do not claim to have all the answers," she admitted. "What I have learned is that the pursuit of power and understanding is a personal journey. It is about finding one's own truth within the chaos of existence and rejecting the false binaries that seek to define us. My role here, as both a priestess and a battle priestess, is to guide others towards a greater understanding of their own paths, not to impose my will upon them."

The angel's expression softened slightly, her defiant stance wavering as she absorbed Eve's words. The weight of her former beliefs clashed with the new understanding Eve was offering, creating a turbulent mix of hope and doubt. "Perhaps," she said quietly, "there is some truth in what you say. But it is hard to see beyond the confines of what we have been taught, to envision a reality that defies the very principles we once held sacred."

Eve nodded, recognizing the validity of the angel's struggle. "It is not easy to break free from the confines of deeply ingrained beliefs," she said. "But it is through this struggle that we find our own strength and truth. The path of the individual is not one of easy answers but of continual questioning and growth. If you are willing to explore beyond the limits of your former beliefs, you may discover a new understanding of yourself and your place in this world."

The angel remained silent, her gaze distant as she contemplated Eve's words. The room was filled with a heavy silence, a reflection of the profound internal conflict both beings were experiencing. Eve watched as the angel wrestled with her thoughts, knowing that the journey towards understanding was a deeply personal one, fraught with challenges and revelations.

As the confrontation came to an end and the angel was led from the room, Eve knew that this moment of exchange was more than just a philosophical debate; it was a reflection of her own journey and the ongoing struggle to reconcile her past with her present. The angel's presence was a reminder of the complexities of morality and power, and of the need to continually question and redefine one's understanding of these concepts.

With a final, lingering look at the angel, Eve turned away, her thoughts already turning to the future and the battles yet to come. The path of understanding was fraught with difficulty, but it was a path she was committed to exploring, no matter where it might lead.

Once again now surrounded by the quiet of her chamber, Eve sank into a deep, contemplative silence. The room was dimly lit by flickering candles, casting elongated shadows on the walls. She sat on a low, ornate cushion, her back straight and her posture calm, but her mind was anything but peaceful. The recent confrontation with the angel and the weight of Nietzsche's teachings pressed heavily upon her.

Eve's gaze fell upon an old, worn volume of Nietzsche's works lying open on a nearby table, its pages filled with her notes and annotations. The words on those pages had sparked a profound shift in her understanding of morality and power, challenging the very foundations of her beliefs. She began to immerse herself in recollections of the numerous discussions she had engaged in with fellow followers of Asmodeus. These debates had often centered around the nature of power and morality, but Nietzsche's ideas had introduced a radical perspective that resonated deeply with Eve.

She recalled a particularly heated discussion with one of her peers, Varaak, a staunch traditionalist within the temple. Varaak had argued passionately that the will to power was a means to achieve dominance over others, to impose one's will and control the weaker. Eve had countered this argument by suggesting that true power was not merely about subjugation but about transcending the constraints imposed by conventional morality. Nietzsche's assertion that morality was a construct designed by the weak to control the strong had unsettled many within the temple, but Eve found it illuminating.

In her mind's eye, Eve replayed the moment of realization she had experienced during that conversation. As she had argued, "Morality, as traditionally understood, is a tool wielded by the weak to curb the strength of the powerful. It is a set of constraints designed to create order and control, to enforce a uniformity that suppresses individual will and strength." She had seen Varaak's face flush with frustration, her eyes narrowing as she struggled to counter Eve's perspective. The debate had ended inconclusively, but the seeds of doubt had been planted in Eve's mind.

As Eve delved deeper into her reflection, she considered Nietzsche's concept of the "Übermensch," the ideal individual who rises above the limitations of conventional morality to create their own values and live authentically. The idea of the Übermensch had captivated Eve's imagination, presenting a vision of a being who transcends the dichotomies of good and evil to forge a new path of self-determination and strength.

In her inner dialogue, Eve pondered the possibility of transcending societal moral frameworks entirely. She imagined what it might be like to exist beyond the constraints of traditional morality, to achieve a higher state of being where one's values were self-created and self-affirmed. "Is it truly possible," she mused, "to step beyond the binary of good and evil, to redefine one's existence free from the judgments and constraints imposed by others?"

Her reflections naturally extended to her role in the ongoing celestial vs. Hell war. This conflict, she recognized, was a direct manifestation of the binary thinking that plagued conventional morality. Both Heaven and Hell, in their struggle for dominance, were locked in a clash of opposing forces, each side imposing its vision of order upon the other. To Eve, this struggle seemed emblematic of the very limitations she sought to transcend.

She recalled a recent strategic discussion that involved several of the priests and priestesses of the temple along with the high priest and priestess, where the focus had been on consolidating power and asserting dominance over Heaven's forces. In the heat of the discussion, Eve had found herself questioning the very purpose of this struggle. "Are we not," she had asked, "simply perpetuating the same binary conflict that confines us, rather than seeking a higher path that transcends these limitations?"

The room had fallen silent, the weight of Eve's question hanging heavily in the air. Some had been uncomfortable with the challenge to their established views, while others had been intrigued, prompting a shift in the nature of the debate. Eve's thoughts had since crystallized: the key to understanding power was not to simply align oneself with one side or the other but to rise above the conflict, to forge a new path that was not bound by traditional moral divisions.

As Eve considered this perspective, she began to believe that true power lay not in the mere exercise of force but in the ability to transcend artificial divisions and create a new understanding of existence. The struggle was not just about asserting dominance but about overcoming the constraints imposed by conventional morality and the limitations of binary thinking.

Her thoughts wandered to her own dual identity as both a revered priestess and a battle priestess. The tension between these roles had always been a source of internal conflict, but now Eve saw it in a new light. The duality of her identity, she realized, was a reflection of the broader struggle to reconcile conventional morality with her evolving understanding of power and existence.

In her quiet chamber, Eve grappled with the implications of her insights. The path ahead was fraught with challenges and uncertainties, but she was resolute in her commitment to explore these new ideas. She understood that the journey was not about finding definitive answers but about continually questioning and redefining her understanding of power, morality, and existence.

As the night wore on, Eve's mind remained restless, but there was a sense of clarity emerging from the turmoil. She was on a path of exploration and self-discovery, driven by a desire to transcend traditional boundaries and forge a new understanding of herself and her place in the world. The journey was far from over, but Eve was prepared to face the challenges ahead with determination and an open mind, ready to continue her quest for a deeper understanding of true power and existence.

The heavy oak door to Eve's chamber creaked open, and the high priestess entered, her presence commanding the room with an air of authority. The dim light from the sconces cast long shadows across the ornate tapestries that adorned the walls, creating a setting ripe for the philosophical debate that was about to unfold. The high priestess, known for her unwavering adherence to the traditional doctrines of the temple, had come to discuss a matter of deep concern.

Eve, seated at her mahogany desk, looked up from her writings and musings, her face a mask of serene curiosity. She motioned for the high priestess to take a seat, and the two women faced each other, a palpable tension hanging in the air. The high priestess was clad in rich, ceremonial robes, her demeanor as rigid as her beliefs.

The high priestess wasted no time, her voice cutting through the silence with a sharp edge. "Eve, I have been hearing troubling reports about your teachings and the direction you seem to be taking. Your ideas about power and morality are at odds with the core principles that have guided our temple for centuries. Are you truly suggesting that we abandon the very foundations upon which our understanding of power is built?"

Eve met the high priestess's gaze with calm determination. "I believe we must explore beyond the conventional understanding of power. The traditional doctrine emphasizes dominance and submission as the highest forms of existence, but I question whether this is the full extent of what power can be."

The high priestess's eyes narrowed, her expression a mix of confusion and frustration. "And what would you propose instead? That we disregard the importance of dominance and submission in defining power? That we reject the very principles that have shaped our existence?"

Eve leaned back in her chair, her fingers steepled as she considered her response. "Not at all. I propose that we expand our understanding of power. The principles of dominance and submission are indeed aspects of power, but they are not the entirety of it. True power involves more than just asserting control over others; it is also about embracing one's own path and shaping one's own existence."

The high priestess crossed her arms, clearly agitated. "So, you are suggesting that power should be defined solely by one's personal vision, disregarding the role of dominance and submission? This sounds like a dangerous deviation from our teachings."

Eve's tone remained steady, her voice a soft contrast to the high priestess's sharpness. "I am suggesting that we reconsider how we define power. The binary of dominance and submission is one way to understand it, but it does not capture the full complexity of existence. Nietzsche's concept of the Übermensch - an individual who creates their own values and lives beyond conventional morality - offers a broader perspective. It challenges us to see power not just as control over others but as a means to transcend limitations and create something new."

The high priestess's brow furrowed as she processed Eve's words. "But does not the concept of the Übermensch risk undermining the very structure that holds our society together? If everyone were to create their own values and reject traditional notions of power, what would become of our order and discipline?"

Eve's expression was thoughtful, her eyes reflecting the weight of her contemplation. "The challenge is not to undermine order but to redefine it. By expanding our understanding of power, we are not discarding our principles but evolving them. True power lies in the ability to transcend the constraints of conventional morality and to forge a new path that reflects our individual and collective growth."

The high priestess leaned forward, her voice tinged with a mix of urgency and concern. "And what of the struggle for dominance? Is it not through the assertion of power that we achieve our goals and maintain our place within the hierarchy? How can you justify moving beyond these principles without undermining the very foundation of our authority?"

Eve took a deep breath, her mind racing through the implications of the high priestess's arguments. "The struggle for dominance is indeed a part of the power dynamic, but it is not the whole story.

True power is not merely about asserting control; it is about understanding the broader context in which we operate. By transcending traditional notions of power, we can create a more nuanced understanding that allows us to navigate our roles within the hierarchy while also embracing our individual growth."

The high priestess's gaze remained skeptical, but there was a flicker of contemplation in her eyes. "You speak of transcending limitations and creating new frameworks, but how do we ensure that this does not lead to chaos or a loss of structure?"

Eve's response was measured, her voice steady as she addressed the concern. "The goal is not to create chaos but to foster growth and evolution. By redefining our understanding of power, we can adapt our structures to reflect the complexities of our existence. The challenge is to find a balance between maintaining order and embracing the potential for transformation. It is through this balance that we can achieve a more profound understanding of power and existence."

The high priestess sat back, her arms still crossed as she absorbed Eve's words. The room was thick with the weight of the debate, both women reflecting on the implications of their perspectives. Eve could see the internal struggle in the high priestess's eyes, a sign of the deep conflict between traditional beliefs and new ideas.

After a moment of silence, the high priestess spoke again, her voice softer but still firm. "You have presented a compelling argument, Eve. I will need time to reflect on these ideas and consider their implications for our temple and its teachings."

Eve nodded, a sense of satisfaction mingled with the uncertainty of their discussion. "I appreciate your willingness to engage in this dialogue. It is through such discussions that we can challenge our understanding and grow. I look forward to continuing this exploration of power and morality together."

As the high priestess rose to leave, Eve watched her with a mixture of hope and anticipation. The debate had been intense, but it had also been an opportunity for both women to confront their beliefs and consider new possibilities. With the high priestess's departure, Eve was left alone with her thoughts, her mind still buzzing with the implications of their conversation.

In the quiet of her chamber, Eve continued to reflect on the teachings of Nietzsche and their impact on her understanding of power and morality. The path ahead was uncertain, but she was resolute in her commitment to exploring new perspectives and forging her own path. The debate with the high priestess had only deepened her resolve to transcend traditional limitations and embrace a more nuanced understanding of existence.

As she prepared for the challenges that lay ahead, Eve felt a renewed sense of purpose. The journey to redefine power and morality was fraught with difficulty, but it was a journey she was ready to undertake. With the vision of the Übermensch guiding her, Eve was determined to navigate the complexities of her role and find her own path in the ever-evolving landscape of the temple and beyond.

As the evening deepened, Eve sat alone in her chamber, her thoughts swirling with the weight of recent revelations. The debate with the high priestess had illuminated new facets of her journey, reshaping her understanding of power and morality. Her reflections had crystallized her path forward - a path of transcendence that moved beyond the binary constraints of good and evil.

Eve gazed out of the window, where the dim glow of Hell's fiery landscape illuminated the darkening sky. The flames flickered, casting dancing shadows that seemed to echo the duality she had long grappled with. She realized that her journey was not merely about navigating the traditional doctrines of the temple but about redefining them through her own philosophical lens.

The struggle with the high priestess had been intense, yet it had provided her with profound insights into the nature of power. The traditional emphasis on dominance and submission, while foundational, was not the sole determinant of strength or authority. True power, Eve had come to understand, involved embracing and transcending these conventional boundaries, shaping her own values and understanding the broader context of existence.

With a renewed sense of purpose, Eve turned her attention to the tasks ahead. Her role within the temple had evolved; she was no longer confined by the rigid expectations of her previous position. Instead, she was poised to guide her followers with the wisdom she had gained from her philosophical exploration. The teachings of Nietzsche and her own experiences had equipped her with a deeper comprehension of power, one that integrated both strength and self-awareness.

As she prepared for the challenges that lay before her, Eve felt a blend of anticipation and resolve. The path she was forging was fraught with uncertainties, but it was a path she was ready to embrace. The journey of self-discovery and philosophical exploration had not only deepened her understanding but also reshaped her role within the temple.

Eve's thoughts turned to the future with a sense of optimism. She was prepared to navigate the complexities of her role, guided by the insights she had gained. The road ahead might be unpredictable, but Eve was confident that it would lead her to a deeper understanding of herself and the forces that shaped her world. With this confidence, she faced the future, ready to continue her journey of transformation and transcendence.

6

The Path of the Individual

Some weeks later, the flickering torchlight cast dancing shadows on the cold stone walls of Eve's private chamber, a sanctuary amidst the chaos of the temple. As she sat in contemplative silence, Eve's mind wrestled with the profound implications of Nietzsche's philosophy as she occasionally scribbled some notes in the margins of her leather bound tome. Her growing realization that individual strength transcended mere domination over others brought a new depth to her understanding of power. She had begun to see that true strength lay not in controlling others but in mastering oneself and forging one's own path.

Eve's thoughts drifted to the concept of the "Übermensch" - the idea of transcending human limitations to become an individual who creates their own values. This idea resonated with her on a deeply personal level. It was not just about rising above others but about rising above the limitations imposed by conventional morality and societal norms. The path to becoming such an individual required a deep understanding of oneself and an unwavering commitment to one's own principles.

The moon hung high in the night sky, casting a silver glow through the temple windows and bathing the chamber in a serene light. Eve was lost in her thoughts, the quietude of the room offering little solace as her mind wrestled with the philosophical implications of her recent debates. The candle flickered softly, its light dancing with shadows on the walls, creating a visual representation of the tumult within her.

Her philosophical musings were interrupted by the arrival of a young demon acolyte, their face a mixture of uncertainty and frustration. The acolyte's presence was like a sudden gust of wind that disrupted the calm, bringing with it a fresh wave of emotion and urgency.

Eve looked up, her gaze shifting from the candle to the acolyte. "You seem troubled," she said gently, her voice a soft balm against the sharp edge of the young demon's anxiety. "What weighs on your mind?"

The acolyte hesitated, their eyes darting around the room as if searching for the right words. "I feel as though I'm constantly being judged by my position within the hierarchy," they said, their voice tinged with frustration and a touch of desperation. "I'm told that to be strong, I must seize power from others, climb the ranks, and prove my worth. But I'm not sure if that's the path I truly want to follow."

Eve nodded, her expression thoughtful. She recognized the struggle in the young acolyte's words - the same struggle she had faced in reconciling her own path with the expectations of the temple. "True strength," she said slowly, "is not solely about dominating others or rising through the ranks. It's about mastering your inner self and forging your own path. The path of the individual is about creating your own values and finding strength in who you are, not just in what you achieve in relation to others."

The acolyte's eyes widened, a flicker of hope mingling with their confusion. "But how do I find that strength? How do I navigate the expectations of the temple while staying true to myself?" Their voice trembled slightly, betraying the depth of their inner conflict.

Eve leaned forward, her gaze steady and encouraging. "Finding your path requires courage and self-reflection. It means understanding what truly matters to you and staying true to those values, even when it goes against the grain of traditional expectations. The path you forge for yourself will be uniquely yours, and that is where true power lies."

The young demon's shoulders relaxed slightly, as if a burden had been lifted. "But isn't it risky to go against the grain? What if I fail or am seen as weak?" they asked, their concern evident in their voice.

Eve smiled gently, understanding the fear that came with stepping away from the familiar. "Risk is an inherent part of any journey, especially one that seeks to transcend conventional boundaries. But it is through facing these risks and confronting our fears that we truly grow. Strength is not about avoiding failure or criticism but about embracing the process of self-discovery and remaining true to your own values."

The acolyte took a deep breath, absorbing Eve's words. "So you're saying that the path to true power is about more than just achieving dominance?" they asked, their voice now tinged with curiosity.

"Yes," Eve replied, her voice firm but kind. "True power is about understanding and embracing who you are, beyond the limitations of traditional roles and expectations. It's about creating your own values and defining your own path. The journey may be difficult, and you may face opposition, but it is a path worth taking because it leads to a deeper understanding of yourself and your place in the world."

The conversation marked a significant shift in Eve's approach. She was no longer merely advocating for traditional Asmodean dominance but was beginning to emphasize a more nuanced philosophy that valued personal freedom and self-discovery. Her guidance was not about imposing her views on others but about helping them find their own way.

As the young acolyte absorbed Eve's counsel, their expression transformed from one of confusion to one of contemplation. "Thank you," they said quietly, their voice filled with gratitude. "I think I understand now. It's not just about climbing the ranks but about finding my own path and staying true to myself."

Eve nodded, a sense of fulfillment washing over her. "You're welcome," she said softly. "Remember, the path you choose is yours to define. Embrace it with courage, and you will find your way."

With a final nod, the acolyte rose and left the chamber, their steps more assured than before. Eve watched them go, a sense of satisfaction and hope stirring within her. The conversation had not only provided guidance to the young demon but had also reaffirmed her own beliefs about the nature of power and self-discovery.

As the moonlight continued to cast its silvery glow through the chamber, Eve's thoughts turned once more to her own journey. The path of the individual was a challenging one, fraught with uncertainties and opposition, but it was a path she was committed to exploring. She knew that the road ahead would be filled with more debates, challenges, and moments of introspection, but she felt a renewed sense of purpose.

Eve's gaze returned to the flickering candle, its light now symbolizing her own inner journey - a journey of self-discovery, transcendence, and the forging of a new path. With a deep breath, she prepared to continue her exploration, knowing that each step she took would bring her closer to a deeper understanding of herself and the forces that shaped her world.

However, Eve's evolving philosophy did not go unnoticed. Tensions began to rise within the temple as her teachings had in recent weeks started to clash with the traditional interpretations of Asmodeus' will. Other priestesses, bound by their adherence to strict doctrines, began to question Eve's new approach. The temple's hierarchy grew concerned with her increasing emphasis on personal freedom and her apparent rejection of rigid morality.

The moon hung high in the night sky, casting a silvery glow across the Temple of Asmodeus. The darkened corridors and shadowed chambers were tranquil, save for the occasional whisper of the wind against the stone walls. In one such chamber, Eve sat alone, deep in philosophical contemplation. The soft flicker of candlelight danced across the room, providing a gentle illumination that contrasted sharply with the turmoil she felt within.

The silence was abruptly shattered by the sound of hurried footsteps and the creaking of heavy wooden doors being flung open. Lysandra, Eve's mentor, and archpriestess known for her staunch adherence to traditional doctrines, stormed into the room. Her face was set in a hard, determined expression, and flanking her were two templar knights, their armor gleaming ominously in the dim light.

Eve looked up, her serene demeanor interrupted by the unexpected intrusion. "Lysandra," she said with measured calm. "To what do I owe the pleasure of this visit?"

Lysandra's gaze was cold and unyielding. "Eve," she began, her voice laced with authority, "you have been summoned to stand before Judge Arion. Your recent teachings and philosophical explorations have been deemed blasphemous to the will of Lord Asmodeus."

Eve's brow furrowed in confusion and concern. "Blasphemous? I have only sought to expand our understanding of power and morality. How can seeking a deeper truth be considered a betrayal?"

The high-ranking priestess stepped closer, her eyes narrowing. "You speak of transcending boundaries and creating your own values," she said, her voice rising with intensity. "But what of our duty to uphold the will of Asmodeus? Is it not our role to enforce his teachings, to ensure that his power remains unchallenged? Your ideas threaten to undermine the very foundation of our beliefs."

Eve stood, her expression resolute. "The will of Asmodeus is not a static doctrine but a living principle that evolves with us. True power lies not in rigid adherence to old ways but in the ability to grow and adapt. My teachings do not seek to undermine our beliefs but to expand our understanding of power and morality."

Lysandra's face flushed with anger. "The teachings of Asmodeus are clear and unchanging. Your attempts to redefine them are not only dangerous but also heretical. You are challenging the very core of our faith."

The tension in the room was palpable as the templar knights shifted uneasily. Eve took a deep breath, her mind racing as she sought to respond to the gravity of the accusation. "If my teachings are a threat, then let us address them openly and with reason. I am ready to defend my beliefs before the judge."

Lysandra's expression softened slightly, though her resolve remained firm. "Very well. We will proceed to the tribunal. The judge will hear both sides, and the truth will be determined."

The procession to the tribunal was solemn and heavy with anticipation. Eve walked with Lysandra and the templar knights, her mind a whirlwind of thoughts and emotions. The temple's grand hall, where the tribunal was held, was a stark contrast to the chamber she had left behind. It was vast and austere, adorned with dark tapestries and flickering torches that cast ominous shadows.

As Eve entered the hall, she was met by Judge Arion - a figure of stern authority draped in ceremonial robes. The judge's gaze was piercing as he took in the scene. "We are gathered here to address the charges against Eve," Arion's voice boomed, echoing through the hall. "Lysandra, you may present your case."

Lysandra stepped forward, her demeanor unyielding. "Your Honor, Eve's teachings advocate for a departure from the established doctrines of Asmodeus. She has publicly stated that true power lies in transcending traditional boundaries and creating one's own values. This directly contradicts the principles of our faith, which emphasize the importance of dominance and submission in maintaining the will of our Lord."

Lysandra's words were met with murmurs of agreement from some of the gathered priests and priestesses. Eve stood calmly, her gaze unwavering. "If I may," she said, raising her hand, "I wish to address the charges."

Judge Arion nodded, granting her permission. "Proceed."

Eve took a step forward, her voice steady and clear. "The teachings of Asmodeus are indeed foundational to our faith, but they are not meant to be a cage that limits our growth. My exploration of power and morality is not a rejection of Asmodeus but an attempt to understand His will in a deeper and more nuanced way. I believe that true power is about evolving and adapting, not merely adhering to rigid doctrines."

Lysandra's eyes narrowed, her frustration evident. "You speak of evolution and adaptation, but these are merely excuses for abandoning the core tenets of our faith. The teachings of Asmodeus are clear, and your departure from them threatens the stability of our order."

Eve responded calmly, her voice carrying an air of conviction. "The core tenets of our faith are indeed important, but they are not immutable. As we grow and learn, our understanding of these tenets must also evolve. To limit ourselves to a static interpretation of doctrine is to deny the dynamic nature of our existence and our relationship with Asmodeus. My teachings seek to broaden our understanding, not to undermine it."

Judge Arion listened intently, his expression unreadable. After a moment of silence, they addressed Lysandra. "Do you have any further evidence or arguments to support your claims against Eve?"

Lysandra shook her head. "No further evidence, Your Honor. My arguments are based on the interpretation of our doctrines and the perceived threat to our order."

The judge turned to Eve. "And do you have any final statements before we deliberate?"

Eve nodded, her expression resolute. "I urge the tribunal to consider the possibility that our understanding of Asmodeus' will can grow and evolve. True strength lies not in resisting change but in embracing it and using it to enhance our power and our faith."

The judge's gaze was contemplative as he looked between Eve and Lysandra. The chamber was silent, the weight of the decision heavy on everyone present. After a few moments of deliberation, Arion spoke.

"Having heard the arguments from both sides, it is clear that Eve's teachings, while unconventional, do not constitute blasphemy against the will of Asmodeus. Her approach represents a different perspective on understanding power and morality but does not inherently contradict the principles of our faith. The tribunal finds Eve not guilty of the charges of blasphemy."

A wave of relief washed over Eve, and she felt the tension in her shoulders ease. Lysandra's face was a mask of frustration, but she said nothing more. The tribunal was dismissed, and the crowd began to disperse.

As Eve made her way out of the hall, she was met with a mix of reactions - some of respect, others of skepticism. The path ahead would be fraught with challenges, but Eve was prepared to continue her journey of exploration and understanding.

In the quiet of her chamber later that night, Eve reflected on the events of the day. The confrontation with Lysandra had been intense and revealing, but it had also reaffirmed her belief in the importance of questioning and evolving. The path of understanding was not an easy one, but it was one she was committed to following, no matter where it might lead.

Eve's gaze settled on the flickering candlelight, its steady flame symbolizing her own inner journey - a journey of growth, discovery, and the relentless pursuit of a deeper truth.

The atmosphere in the war room was tense and filled with the muted clamor of preparation. The chamber, lined with dark stone walls and illuminated by the flickering light of torches, was dominated by a large, ornate table covered with maps, diagrams, and strategic plans. High-ranking officials and seasoned commanders of the Temple of Asmodeus had gathered, their expressions grave and focused. At the head of the table stood Lord Vesperion, his formidable presence commanding attention as he surveyed the gathered assembly.

Eve entered the room, her demeanor a blend of resolve and introspection. As the battle priestess, she was expected to lead and strategize, yet her evolving philosophy created an internal conflict that shadowed her every decision. Her dual role as both priestess and battle priestess now stood at a crossroads, as she grappled with the tension between her growing belief in internal strength and the external demands of the impending conflict.

Lord Vesperion, his eyes gleaming with an inscrutable intensity, greeted Eve with a nod. "Battle Priestess Eve," he said, his voice resonating with authority, "we are about to finalize our strategy for the coming battle. Your insight and leadership will be crucial."

Eve nodded, taking her place at the table. "Lord Vesperion, I am prepared to contribute. But I must admit, I am wrestling with a conflict. My evolving understanding of power and morality is at odds with the role I am expected to fulfill in this battle."

The other officials exchanged glances, their curiosity piqued by Eve's admission. Lord Vesperion, however, remained focused. "We all face conflicts within ourselves," he said. "But now is not the time for doubt. The forces of Heaven and Hell are converging, and our strategy must be precise. We need to address both the practical aspects of the battle and your philosophical concerns."

A high-ranking official, Archpriestess Lysandra, who had long been known for her tactical acumen, stepped forward. "We face an enemy that is relentless and powerful. Our strategy must account for their strengths while exploiting their weaknesses. Your role, Eve, will involve both direct engagement and strategic oversight."

Eve met Lysandra's gaze, her expression thoughtful. "Direct engagement and strategic oversight - these are familiar roles. Yet, my recent reflections suggest that power is not merely about control and dominance but about understanding and evolving. How do we reconcile this perspective with the demands of our military engagements?"

Lord Vesperion's gaze was piercing. "Power in its truest form involves more than just control. It involves adaptability, foresight, and the ability to inspire others. Your understanding of power as an evolving force can be a strength in this battle, allowing you to anticipate and respond to the enemy's moves with greater flexibility."

Eve nodded, taking in his words. "Very well. Let us review the strategy."

The room fell silent as Liora and other officials began to outline the battle plans. Maps were spread across the table, highlighting key locations and potential points of conflict. The forces of Heaven were expected to launch a series of coordinated attacks aimed at overwhelming their defenses, while Hell's forces would need to maneuver strategically to counter these assaults.

Lysandra pointed to a location on the map. "Here is where we anticipate the enemy will focus their initial assault. We will need to fortify our defenses and position our forces to counter their advance. Eve, your role will involve leading a contingent to secure this area and then launching a counteroffensive."

Eve studied the map, her mind racing with possibilities. "What about our approach to the enemy's secondary forces? Should we anticipate a diversionary tactic or a direct assault?"

Another high-ranking official, Lord Kieran, known for his strategic brilliance, spoke up. "The enemy has been known to employ diversionary tactics to confuse and divide our forces. We should prepare for this by establishing reserve units that can respond swiftly to changing conditions."

Eve's thoughts turned to her philosophical reflections. "If we are to anticipate and counter their tactics, it is essential that we remain adaptable and open to unconventional strategies. Our strength lies not just in our numbers or firepower, but in our ability to think beyond traditional approaches."

Lord Vesperion's expression softened slightly. "Your insight is valuable, Eve. The ability to adapt and think creatively will indeed enhance our chances of success. We must integrate your perspective into our overall strategy."

As the discussion continued, the room was filled with an intense focus as Eve shared her detailed tactical insights. The officials gathered around the table, maps spread out before them, listened intently as she began to outline her strategy for leveraging both the environment and psychological warfare to their advantage.

"First," Eve began, her finger tracing a route on the map, "we need to consider the terrain and how it can work to our advantage. The enemy will likely use the mountainous region here"-she indicated a rugged area on the map-"as a natural barrier and defensive position. However, we can use this to our benefit by setting up concealed traps and ambushes."

Lord Kieran, known for his strategic acumen, nodded thoughtfully. "How do you propose we deploy these traps effectively?"

Eve's eyes gleamed with determination. "We'll use the mountainous terrain to create chokepoints where the enemy will be forced to funnel through narrow passes. At these chokepoints, we can set up hidden pits and barriers, rigged with magical wards that will trigger upon enemy approach. Additionally, we should place elite strike teams in concealed positions to launch surprise attacks when the enemy is most vulnerable."

Archpriestess Lysandra leaned in, intrigued. "What about the psychological aspect? How can we use this to further demoralize the enemy?"

Eve took a deep breath, her mind shifting to the psychological tactics she had been contemplating. "Psychological warfare can be as effective as physical attacks. Our goal should be to create an atmosphere of fear and uncertainty among the enemy forces. Here's how we can achieve this:

1. **Deception Operations** - We can create false intelligence and misleading signals to confuse the enemy. For example, by sending out decoy signals indicating a larger force than we actually have, we can make the enemy believe that they are facing a much greater threat. This can cause them to hesitate or make strategic errors.

2. **Psychological Warfare Units** - Deploy units specifically trained in psychological operations. These units can use sound-based tactics, such as creating loud, eerie noises and dissonant chants from hidden locations. This will disrupt the enemy's concentration and create an atmosphere of dread.

Additionally, we can employ illusionary magic to make our forces appear more numerous and fearsome.

3. **Propaganda and Misinformation** - Spread rumors and false information among the enemy's ranks. We can infiltrate their communication channels and plant stories of our supposed invincibility or of betrayals within their ranks. By undermining their morale and creating distrust among their troops, we can weaken their resolve.

4. **Psychic Assaults** - Utilize our own forces with psychic abilities to project fear and doubt directly into the minds of key enemy leaders. This can create confusion and paranoia, leading to poor decision-making and a breakdown in their command structure.

5. **Symbolic Displays** - Demonstrate our power through dramatic displays. For example, we could stage mock rituals or perform powerful magic at key locations, showcasing our dominance. This will serve to intimidate the enemy and reinforce the perception of our superiority."

The room fell silent as the officials absorbed the weight of Eve's suggestions. Lord Vesperion broke the silence with a nod of approval. "These tactics are comprehensive and reflect a deep understanding of both strategic and psychological warfare. Integrating these approaches will enhance our chances of achieving a decisive victory."

Archpriestess Lysandra's expression was one of admiration. "Your insights are impressive, Eve. The combination of environmental leverage and psychological tactics could indeed shift the balance of power in our favor."

Eve's gaze remained steady. "It's essential that we maintain flexibility in our tactics. The enemy will likely adapt to our strategies, so we must be prepared to adjust our plans as needed. We should also ensure that our forces are well-coordinated and informed about the psychological tactics we'll be using, so they can execute these plans effectively."

Lord Vesperion's demeanor softened as he addressed Eve. "Your contributions are invaluable, Eve. This battle will be a testament to our ability to innovate and adapt. Your approach will be incorporated into our final strategy."

As the meeting continued, the details of the strategy were fleshed out with Eve's insights. The officials and commanders worked together to integrate her recommendations, creating a multifaceted plan that combined traditional military tactics with psychological and environmental strategies.

The strategy session stretched into the night, with the team working diligently to finalize their plans. As the hours passed, Eve's internal conflict began to subside, replaced by a renewed sense of purpose. The battle ahead would test not only her tactical skills but also her evolving philosophy. She realized that her understanding of power could serve as a guiding principle in both her role as a battle priestess and her broader journey of self-discovery.

When the final plans were set and the meeting came to a close, Lord Vesperion addressed the group once more. "We have a solid strategy in place, one that integrates our traditional strengths with Eve's innovative insights. Let us proceed with confidence and determination. The fate of our forces - and perhaps the future of our understanding of power - rests on the outcome of this battle. Ave Asmodeus."

Eve left the war room with a renewed sense of purpose. The strategy was robust, and her philosophical reflections had found a place within the practical demands of the upcoming battle. The path ahead was still likely to be fraught with challenges, but she felt prepared to face them with a clear vision and a comprehensive plan. The storm clouds on the horizon were no longer just a symbol of conflict; they were a challenge to be met with determination and strategic brilliance.

As she gazed out at the darkened landscape, Eve knew that the coming battle would test not only her tactical skills but also her evolving understanding of power. The integration of her philosophical insights into the strategy marked a significant step in her journey, demonstrating that her evolving beliefs could coexist with her role as a battle priestess. The future was uncertain, but with her strategy and insights in place, Eve felt ready to confront whatever lay ahead.

7

Fire and Ash

The sky above Hell darkened with ominous clouds, roiling and swirling with unnatural intensity. An eerie light pierced through the churning mass, casting an otherworldly glow over the infernal landscape. The usually oppressive heat of the realm seemed to retreat in the face of the celestial invasion, replaced by a chilling crackle of energy that filled the air with palpable tension.

The angels descended from their radiant realm with a thunderous chorus of celestial hymns and the blinding brilliance of their divine forms. Their coordinated attack began at the fringes of Hell's territory, where the first explosions of light and sound shattered the stillness of the infernal expanse. The precision of their assault was evident as they targeted key strategic points - ancient fortresses, magical nexuses, and strategic supply routes - each location crucial to maintaining the realm's fragile defenses.

As the celestial forces advanced, the ground trembled under the weight of their divine onslaught. Brilliant rays of energy seared through the air, clashing with the dark, molten streams that erupted from Hell's core. The normally oppressive heat of the infernal landscape now became a battleground of contrasts: the searing heat of demonic fire met the cold, blinding light of angelic power, creating an environment of extreme chaos and destruction.

The defenders of Hell, caught off guard by the sudden intensity of the attack, scrambled to respond. The once orderly and structured defenses of the realm were thrown into disarray. Demonic warlords and their legions, caught between the infernal fires and the heavenly light, struggled to mount a cohesive resistance.

Angels, their forms aglow with a resplendent divine light, moved with a grace and precision that defied the chaotic environment. Their wings, vast and majestic, created sweeping gusts of wind that stirred up clouds of ash and debris as they descended upon the battlefield. Each angel's appearance was a blinding spectacle, their armor gleaming with an ethereal radiance that contrasted starkly with the dark, molten landscape of Hell.

The celestial forces unleashed torrents of heavenly fire, streams of brilliant, purifying, light that scorched the ground and seared through Hell's defenses with blistering heat. The precision of their attacks was astonishing; they targeted critical points with unerring accuracy, striking at the weak spots in the infernal fortifications. Each burst of divine energy was accompanied by a thunderous roar that reverberated across the plains, shaking the very air and creating shockwaves that toppled structures and sent demonic forces scrambling.

Their tactics were the epitome of flawless coordination. Groups of angels moved in perfect formation, their actions synchronized to perfection. Some angels engaged directly with Hell's defenders, wielding their swords with divine precision, while others took to the skies, launching aerial strikes that rained down destruction upon the infernal forces below. The air was filled with the clash of steel, the roar of infernal flames, and the piercing cries of both combatants and the anguished terrain.

The rocky landscape, once a symbol of Hell's rugged strength, now bore the scars of the celestial onslaught. Boulders and jagged outcroppings were shattered by the force of the angelic fire, and molten fissures erupted in the wake of the divine assault. The ground itself seemed to quake under the relentless pressure, as if the very land was being torn apart by the conflict.

Hell's defenders, taken aback by the sheer ferocity and precision of the angels' assault, struggled to mount an effective resistance. The infernal forces, though fierce and determined, were caught in a desperate scramble to respond to the celestial invaders. The once orderly lines of defense were disrupted, and the demonic legions fought valiantly but found themselves pushed back by the relentless advance of the angelic host.

As the celestial forces pressed their assault on the second circle, the infernal command deployed its own specialized units trained in psychological operations, a crucial aspect of their defensive strategy. These units, masters of psychological warfare, were tasked with undermining the morale and concentration of the angelic invaders, leveraging fear and confusion to their advantage.

Hidden within the rocky outcroppings and labyrinthine tunnels that crisscrossed the infernal plains, these units began their operations. From concealed positions, they unleashed a barrage of sound-based tactics designed to disorient and terrify the celestial forces. The air was soon filled with a cacophony of eerie, dissonant noises that pierced through the din of battle. Low, guttural growls and high-pitched wails reverberated across the battlefield, creating an unsettling atmosphere that gnawed at the nerves of the angels. These sounds, amplified through infernal enchantments, seemed to come from nowhere and everywhere at once, sowing seeds of doubt and fear among the celestial troops.

The psychological units also employed an array of haunting chants and sinister melodies, sung in an ancient, guttural tongue that seemed to echo from the very depths of Hell. These chants were not merely auditory; they were infused with dark magic, designed to unsettle and bewilder. The dissonant harmonies created an overwhelming sense of dread, their rhythms erratic and unpredictable, further fracturing the angels' sense of order and discipline.

In addition to these auditory tactics, the units deployed powerful illusionary magic to manipulate the battlefield's appearance. Through a series of complex spells and enchantments, they conjured illusions that made the infernal forces appear more numerous and formidable than they truly were. Massive, spectral phantoms of demonic beasts and towering, shadowy figures emerged from the shadows, their forms flickering and shifting as if they were real. These illusions, enhanced by the dark magic of the psychological units, created a disorienting effect that amplified the sense of an overwhelming infernal force.

The angels, accustomed to facing tangible threats, were momentarily thrown off balance by the sudden onslaught of psychological tactics. Their once unshakable confidence was challenged as they struggled to differentiate reality from illusion. The eerie noises and haunting chants combined with the terrifying illusions created a sense of encroaching darkness and doom, making the celestial forces question their previous certainty of victory.

Eve stood at the forefront of the temple ground's defensive line, her presence commanding and formidable. The sky above, darkened with ominous clouds and streaked with flashes of celestial light, set a dramatic backdrop to the conflict. Her battle armor, adorned with infernal runes, gleamed with an unsettling glow that pulsed rhythmically, echoing the very heartbeat of Hell. The armor's dark, intricate designs seemed to writhe and shift in response to the energy of the battlefield, amplifying her already formidable aura.

As the celestial forces descended upon the temple, the ground beneath Eve's feet trembled with the weight of the impending clash. The once-stable terrain now quaked under the relentless assault of angelic forces, their forms radiant with divine light, contrasting starkly with the infernal darkness that enveloped the land. The air was thick with the acrid scent of sulfur and the sharp tang of divine fire, mingling into a heady concoction of destruction and chaos.

Eve's dual role as a priestess and a battle priestess was evident in her every movement. Her strategic acumen, honed through countless hours in the war room, now manifested in the battlefield's chaos.

With every command, her voice cut through the cacophony of clashing forces and roaring infernos, clear and resolute.

"Hold the line!" Eve's voice rang out, piercing the tumult like a beacon. The din of battle was a constant roar, but her authoritative tone commanded attention. Her eyes, burning with a fierce determination, scanned the battlefield as she directed her contingent of templar knights and demons. Her orders were sharp and decisive, each command calculated to bolster their defenses and counter the angelic onslaught.

The clash between celestial light and infernal fire was a breathtaking spectacle, a vivid contrast of energies that danced violently across the battlefield. The angels, their wings unfurled and shimmering with divine brilliance, launched pinpoint strikes aimed at the heart of Hell's defenses. Their movements were synchronized, a testament to their flawless tactical training. Each angelic unit seemed to move as one, their divine fire lancing through the air with precision and purpose.

In response, Eve's inherent demonic power flared to life. Dark flames erupted from her outstretched hands, their eerie glow casting long, flickering shadows on the scorched ground. She summoned shadowy barriers that rose from the very depths of the infernal realm, darkened walls coalescing into formidable defenses that absorbed and repelled the celestial onslaught. The dark flames and shadowy barriers contrasted sharply with the blinding radiance of the angels' attacks, creating a chaotic interplay of light and shadow.

Despite the overwhelming energy of the battlefield, Eve's focus remained unwavering. Her eyes, sharp and calculating, tracked the movements of the angels as their strategy unfolded. She could see the pattern emerging - a calculated assault designed to disrupt and weaken, aiming to dismantle Hell's defensive infrastructure. Each angelic strike was precise, targeting key strategic points with ruthless efficiency. It was a methodical effort to break through the defenses, and Eve understood that every second was crucial.

Her mind raced as she analyzed the unfolding battle, the weight of her responsibilities pressing heavily upon her shoulders. She could see how the angels were exploiting weaknesses in their defenses, their coordinated strikes threatening to breach the line and create chaos within the temple grounds. She knew that to counter this, she had to act quickly and decisively, employing both her strategic insights and her formidable demonic abilities.

With a commanding gesture, Eve directed a group of templar knights to reinforce a vulnerable flank, their heavy armor gleaming as they moved into position. The knights, their faces set in grim determination, formed a protective line, their weapons at the ready. Beside them, demons from the lower ranks rallied, their infernal forms merging seamlessly with the defensive line.

As the battle raged on, Eve's tactical brilliance became apparent. She directed her forces with a keen understanding of the ebb and flow of battle, her orders orchestrating a symphony of defense and counterattack. She integrated new insights into her strategies, adapting to the evolving tactics of the celestial forces with an innovative approach. Her decisions were informed by a deep understanding of both demonic power and celestial tactics, a blend of insights that proved invaluable in the heat of conflict.

The clash of holy light and infernal fire created a surreal, almost hypnotic spectacle. The air was filled with the roar of battle, the shriek of celestial fire, and the growl of demonic wrath. As the battlefield continued to shift, Eve remained a steadfast presence, her command unwavering as she guided her forces through the maelstrom of combat.

In the midst of the chaos, Eve's mind remained clear and focused. She could see the broader picture of the conflict, the interplay of strategy and power, and the critical role her leadership played in shaping the outcome. Her dual nature, the blend of priestess and battle priestess, was both a strength and a burden, but it was also a source of unparalleled power and insight.

The clash of holy light and infernal darkness continued to rage, the outcome of the battle uncertain and hanging in the balance. Yet, as Eve stood at the forefront, her commanding presence and unwavering focus offered a glimmer of hope in the midst of the infernal chaos.

The invasion's impact reverberated beyond the battlefield, shaking the very foundation of the Temple of Asmodeus. The sacred halls, once vibrant with the rhythmic cadence of demonic rituals and the subtle hum of dark magic, were now steeped in a palpable sense of urgency and confusion. The clash between celestial and infernal forces had disrupted the temple's daily operations, leaving the air thick with the scent of burning incense mixed with the acrid tang of fear and uncertainty.

Rituals that were crucial to maintaining the temple's arcane defenses and spiritual equilibrium were abruptly halted. The intricate, meticulously performed ceremonies that had once ensured the stability of the realm's defenses were abandoned mid-incantation, their uncompleted spells dissipating into the ether as the ritualists scrambled to address the immediate threat. The usual reverent silence of the temple's inner sanctum was replaced by the discordant murmurs of temple inhabitants, their voices a chaotic blend of anxiety and determination as they struggled to maintain their composure.

Archpriestess Lysandra, the head of the temple, was a figure of intense authority amid the upheaval. Her regal robes, adorned with the sigils of her office, flowed around her as she moved with a sense of urgency that was almost palpable. Her steps echoed through the marble corridors, a staccato rhythm of command and control. Lysandra's face was set in a determined scowl, her eyes narrowing as she barked orders to the scattered officials who had been pulled from their usual duties to respond to the crisis. The normally organized hierarchy of the temple was in disarray, its members scrambling to manage the internal chaos while also coordinating with the defensive efforts on the front lines. Lysandra's leadership was crucial, her every command aimed at restoring order and ensuring that the temple could contribute effectively to the defense against the celestial invasion.

Erephia, the high priestess, found herself at the heart of the temple's upheaval. Her usually calm and composed demeanor was shadowed by the gravity of the situation, the weight of responsibility pressing heavily upon her. In this crisis, Erephia's role had shifted dramatically from her usual duties of guidance and mentorship to a vital focus on healing and triage.

Amidst the chaos, Erephia's expertise in healing was indispensable. She moved with determined efficiency through the temple's corridors, her hands steady as she attended to the injured soldiers being brought in from the battlefield. Each soldier was a testament to the fierce combat outside, their injuries ranging from severe burns to deep, debilitating wounds. Erephia's touch was both gentle and skilled, as she worked to stabilize the wounded with a combination of divine magic and medical knowledge.

Her role extended beyond merely treating physical injuries; she was also a source of emotional support. Erephia offered words of comfort and encouragement to the soldiers, her soothing presence a balm for their fears and pain. Despite the overwhelming pressure, she maintained a sense of calm that helped to bolster the morale of those around her. Her tireless efforts to keep the wounded stable and reassured were crucial in preventing panic and maintaining order.

As she managed the influx of casualties, Erephia coordinated with other temple healers, ensuring that each patient received the appropriate care while prioritizing the most critical cases. Her leadership in this role was a cornerstone in maintaining the temple's internal operations during the invasion. By keeping the healing process efficient and organized, Erephia played a crucial role in stabilizing not just the injured but the temple's overall sense of unity and resolve.

In the temple's war room, the atmosphere was one of focused intensity. Lord Vesperion, with his characteristic air of authority, was organizing meetings and briefing his subordinates. His tactical acumen, honed through years of experience, was essential in keeping the response to the invasion efficient and coordinated. Despite the chaotic environment, Vesperion's presence was a beacon of stability. He methodically reviewed strategies, issued commands, and assessed the ongoing situation with a calm that belied the strain he was under. The toll of managing both the battlefield and the temple's internal strife was evident in his eyes, the exhaustion etched into the lines of his face. Yet, his unwavering dedication to his role provided a crucial anchor for the temple's response efforts.

The juxtaposition of chaos and control within the temple was a stark reminder of the high stakes of the celestial invasion. The temple, a bastion of demonic power and ritualistic precision, was being tested as never before. The response to the invasion required not only military prowess but also the ability to adapt and maintain internal cohesion under unprecedented pressure. As the battle raged outside, the true measure of the temple's strength was being demonstrated within its sacred halls, where leaders like Lysandra, Erephia, and Vesperion fought to keep their realm from descending into disarray.

As the battle's tumultuous symphony raged across Hell's scorched landscape, the very heart of the infernal realm trembled under the celestial onslaught. A group of angels, their forms radiant with an unearthly brilliance, surged closer to the sacred precincts of the Temple of Asmodeus. Their divine light pierced through the encroaching darkness, casting an otherworldly glow that starkly contrasted with the surrounding chaos.

Their approach was marked by a palpable sense of righteous authority, as if their very presence was a proclamation of their holy mission. The air around them crackled with celestial energy, a beacon of their divine purpose. As they drew nearer, the sacred boundaries of the temple - usually a bastion of power and darkness - became vulnerable to their encroachment.

Eve, sensing the imminent threat to the temple's sanctum, moved swiftly to intercept the celestial intruders. Her path converged with theirs in a dramatic standoff at the temple's entrance, where the dim glow of her infernal armor met the blinding radiance of the angels. With a fierce determination, she stood resolute, her form a dark silhouette against the backdrop of the celestial luminescence.

The angels' advance faltered as they encountered Eve, their serene expressions tinged with surprise and curiosity. She faced them with a fierce intensity, her demonic power crackling around her like a tempestuous storm. The celestial beings, accustomed to imposing their divine will without opposition, were met with a force that embodied both the unyielding might and philosophical depth of Hell's defenders.

Eve's stance was both a physical and ideological barrier, a testament to her role as the guardian of the temple. As the angels pressed forward with their righteous determination, they found their path obstructed by Eve's unwavering resolve. Her presence was a declaration of defiance, a refusal to let the sanctity of the temple be compromised by the encroaching divine forces.

One angel, his armor shimmering with a spectral luminescence, stepped forward with an air of disdain mingled with pity. His gaze was piercing, his voice echoing with a scornful resonance. "Eve, Priestess of Asmodeus," he declared, his tone both commanding and contemptuous, "you stand against the forces of righteousness. How do you reconcile your role in this battle with the nature of your existence?"

The question struck Eve like a lightning bolt, slicing through the fog of her internal struggle. The clash of divine and infernal energies around her seemed to mirror the clash within her own heart. As the angels' words resonated in the air, they pried open the depths of her philosophical turmoil, forcing her to confront the very essence of her dual role.

Eve's heart raced, her breath coming in short, sharp bursts as she faced the angels. Their presence was a stark reminder of her existential conflict, their challenge a catalyst for her deep-seated doubts. The devastation wrought by their divine fire, the relentless pursuit of their celestial agenda, intensified the dissonance within her. Was her role merely one of opposition, a mere defiance against a higher purpose, or did it hold deeper, more profound implications?

Amid the clamor of clashing forces and the roar of infernal flames, Eve felt a growing sense of turmoil within herself. The angels' fervent righteousness seemed almost tangible, a force as palpable as the holy light they wielded. Their challenge was not just physical but philosophical, forcing her to confront the nature of power, morality, and her own existence. The celestial beings, in their divine wisdom, questioned her very purpose and duty, pushing her to scrutinize her alignment and the meaning of her actions.

In the heart of the battlefield, Eve's resolve hardened. She knew she could not afford to be consumed by doubt, not when the fate of Hell was at stake. With a deep breath, she centered herself, her eyes locking onto the angelic leader. Her voice cut through the din of battle, steady and resolute. "Your righteousness is a blade with two edges," she declared, her tone firm. "You speak of virtue and divine will, but you fail to recognize the complexity of existence. It is not merely about light versus darkness, but about balance, power, and the nature of choice."

The angel's eyes narrowed, his wings flaring with a radiant intensity. "And what is the nature of your choice, Eve?" he demanded. "To oppose the divine, to stand against the greater good?"

Eve's response was both a declaration and an exploration of her evolving understanding. "I do not stand against good or light," she explained, her voice gaining strength. "I stand for balance, for the acknowledgment that power and morality are not defined by simplistic binaries. My role is not just to combat the divine but to challenge the notion that righteousness must always prevail at the expense of diversity and complexity. The nature of existence is not a battlefield where good and evil are merely opposing forces; it is a spectrum where power, choice, and purpose intertwine."

As Eve spoke, her voice carried the heavy burden of her internal struggle, resonating with a profound intensity that cut through the tumultuous noise of the battlefield. Her words, filled with defiant resolve, echoed with a rallying cry that drew the attention of both her demonic allies and the encroaching celestial forces. The very air around her seemed to vibrate with the weight of her convictions.

Her demonic power flared in response, dark flames leaping and swirling around her like a living aura of shadows. The fiery contrast created an almost tangible divide between her and the blinding light of the angels. The battlefield became a spectacle of opposing energies

- a visual and metaphysical clash that transcended mere physical confrontation.

The angels, momentarily disoriented by the intensity of Eve's display, faltered in their advance. The blinding radiance of their divine forms clashed violently with the dark infernal flames, each side struggling to assert its dominance. Eve's movements were deliberate and charged with purpose, reflecting her deep understanding of the balance between opposing forces.

With a fierce determination, Eve gathered the swirling dark flames around her, shaping them into a concentrated orb of destructive energy. Her eyes narrowed as she focused on her target - the towering angel leading the group, whose aura of sanctity seemed to challenge the very essence of Hell. The angel's expression shifted from confident disdain to a mix of surprise and alarm as Eve prepared her attack.

She thrust her hand forward, sending the orb of dark flames hurtling towards the angel. The energy surged through the air with a roar, a whirlwind of shadows and fire that seemed to bend the very fabric of reality. The orb crashed into the angel with a thunderous impact, the collision sending a shockwave through the surrounding area. The angel was momentarily engulfed in the dark flames, his divine light flickering and wavering under the intense pressure of Eve's assault.

The explosion of dark energy illuminated the battlefield with a harsh, flickering light, creating an unsettling contrast against the celestial glow. The angel staggered back, struggling to maintain his composure as the infernal flames licked at his radiant form. Eve watched with a mixture of grim satisfaction and deep contemplation, her attack a manifestation of her struggle to reconcile her role in the conflict with her own philosophical beliefs.

As the angel recovered from the assault, his expression shifted from shock to fierce resolve. The clash of energies continued, a dynamic interplay of divine righteousness and infernal defiance. Eve, fully aware of the symbolic nature of the battle, prepared for the next phase of the confrontation, determined to defend the sanctity of the temple and navigate the complex interplay of power and morality that defined her role.

The angels, caught in the crossfire of their divine mission and Eve's resolute stance, found themselves grappling with the complexities of her arguments. Their once unyielding belief in their divine purpose was challenged by Eve's profound insights, causing a momentary hesitation in their advance.

Despite the intensity of the conflict, Eve's focus remained unwavering. She maneuvered through the battle with a newfound clarity, her actions reflecting her philosophical revelations. The celestial beings' challenge had ignited a deeper understanding within her, a realization that the nature of power was not simply about opposing or subduing but about recognizing and respecting the intricate balance of existence.

In the midst of the clash, Eve faced the angelic leader once more, her voice steady and her resolve unshaken. "Your vision of righteousness is constrained by its own limitations," she said. "True power lies in acknowledging the complexity of existence and embracing the balance between light and darkness. My role in this battle is not to oppose righteousness but to redefine it in the context of our shared reality."

The confrontation reached a crescendo as Eve's words and actions culminated in a decisive moment. Her powers, fueled by her philosophical insights, surged with an intensity that pushed back against the angels' divine onslaught. The battle continued to rage around them, but Eve's newfound understanding guided her every move, shaping her approach to the conflict.

As the celestial beings retreated, their forms flickering with uncertainty, Eve felt a profound shift within herself. The clash of ideologies had illuminated her path forward, clarifying her role and purpose in the ongoing struggle. The turmoil within her had given way to a renewed sense of resolve, a determination to navigate the complexities of power and morality with both clarity and strength.

In the aftermath of the confrontation, Eve stood amidst the smoldering remains of the battlefield, her breath steady and deliberate as she took in the scene before her. The once-pristine temple grounds were now a tableau of devastation - scorched earth, shattered statues, and remnants of the celestial and infernal clash strewn across the landscape. The air was thick with the acrid scent of burnt ozone and the metallic tang of spilled blood, mingling with the fading echoes of battle cries.

Eve's eyes scanned the area, taking in the destruction wrought by the celestial assault. The temple's outer walls bore the marks of fierce impact, with cracks spreading like spiderwebs across their ancient surfaces. The once-flourishing gardens were now a wasteland of charred foliage and broken statues, their beauty marred by the ravages of war. The once-vibrant banners of the temple fluttered tattered and torn in the smoky wind.

Despite the chaos, Eve felt a renewed sense of resolve stirring within her. The battle had tested her in ways she had not anticipated, but it had also provided clarity. Her philosophical insights, born from the heat of conflict and the weight of her internal struggle, now served as a guiding light. The confrontation with the angels had sharpened her understanding of her role and the nature of power, revealing the path she needed to take.

As she prepared to face the remaining challenges, her focus was unwavering. She surveyed the damage with a strategic eye, noting the areas that required immediate attention and the weaknesses that needed to be addressed. The temple's defenders, though battered, were regrouping and tending to the wounded, their spirits lifted by Eve's display of strength and conviction.

Eve moved among them, offering a reassuring presence and coordinating the efforts to restore some semblance of order. Her actions were guided by a deepened understanding of the balance between light and darkness, her newfound clarity shaping her approach to the rebuilding efforts and the ongoing defense of the temple.

The battle was far from over, and the threat of further celestial incursions loomed large. Yet, with the clarity of her philosophical insights and the strength of her convictions, Eve felt prepared to confront the challenges ahead. The aftermath of the confrontation had forged a new direction for her - one that would shape the fate of the temple and the outcome of the conflict.

8

Shadows of Doubt

The war room buzzed with a sense of urgency, the air thick with anticipation as the temple's leadership gathered to reassess their strategies. Torches flickered against the stone walls, casting long shadows across the maps and charts that lined the room, each one detailing the outcomes of the recent battle. The room was a blend of ancient infernal tradition and the raw reality of the ongoing celestial invasion. High-ranking officials stood around the large, ornate table that held the center of the room, their eyes scanning over reports and maps marked with the positions of both the forces of Hell and Heaven.

Eve stood at the head of the table, her expression pensive yet determined. The initial battle had been grueling, the clash between the forces of Hell and the angels far more fierce than anticipated. Hell had held its ground, but it had not been without significant cost. The angels' tactics had proven to be more sophisticated, their strikes precise and well-coordinated. They were not the mindless holy zealots that some within the temple had expected - they were formidable strategists.

Lord Vesperion, his expression still marked by the heat of battle, raised his voice, cutting through the low murmurs of the room. "We need to adapt our strategies," he said, his tone firm yet contemplative. His sharp eyes swept across the officials gathered before him. "The angels' ability to coordinate and strike with such precision has shown us the need for a more flexible and responsive approach. They strike fast, break through our lines, and disappear before we can retaliate properly. This isn't a fight where we can simply meet force with force."

Eve nodded in agreement, her mind already working through potential adjustments. She had spent the hours after the battle reflecting on the implications of the angels' tactics, blending her philosophical insights with the practical needs of warfare. "Many of our initial strategies leaned too heavily on traditional methods of defense," Eve began, her voice steady and thoughtful. "While they've served us well in the past, the angels have shown that they are not bound by the same rigid strategies. Their adaptability has proven to be a significant advantage, and we must respond in kind."

She pointed to the maps spread before them, where key locations had been marked - territories that were under threat and others where Hell's forces had managed to hold their ground. "We cannot continue to rely solely on brute force. The angels' precision and discipline have created weaknesses in our standard defenses. We need to outmaneuver them, not just in the physical sense but in the psychological as well."

The room quieted as she outlined her proposal. Eve had always been known for her ability to think beyond the conventional, and her recent reflections on power and morality had only deepened that capacity. Her time spent grappling with the nature of dominance and strength had led her to question the conventional wisdom of warfare that Hell had relied upon for centuries.

"We should leverage our strengths in ways that we haven't yet explored fully," Eve continued, her voice gaining momentum. "We've seen how effective psychological warfare can be. Where we've employed deception and psychological tactics, we've made significant strides in disrupting the angels' morale. We need to expand on this. Instead of engaging them directly at every opportunity, we can use misdirection and fear to weaken them before we strike."

Lord Kieran, another high-ranking official known for his strategic acumen, leaned forward, his eyes narrowing in thought. "Psychological warfare," he repeated. "You believe this could turn the tide?"

Eve nodded, her gaze intense as she spoke. "Their tactics are precise, yes. But they are also rigid in their sense of righteousness. The angels believe they are invincible because they are on what they perceive to be the side of good. If we can exploit that arrogance, if we can make them doubt themselves, we can create openings that brute force alone won't achieve."

She gestured toward one of the key strategic points on the map, a location where Hell's forces had held off an angelic assault but had suffered heavy casualties. "For example, we know that they rely on these fast, coordinated strikes. We could set traps, make it seem as though our defenses are weaker than they are, luring them into a false sense of security. Once they've overcommitted, we can strike with our full force."

Lord Vesperion listened closely, his piercing gaze fixed on Eve. He respected her insights, particularly when it came to unconventional thinking. "Deception will be key," he agreed. "But how do we ensure that they fall into the trap without realizing it?"

Eve's eyes gleamed with determination as she elaborated. "We need to manipulate the battlefield in ways they aren't expecting. We can create false weaknesses, planting misleading information that makes it appear as though certain strongholds are under-defended. Additionally, we should lean into our magical strengths - illusionary magic can make our forces appear larger, more overwhelming. If we can convince them that they are outnumbered or outmatched, even when they are not, their morale will falter."

Another priestess, Varaak, spoke up from across the room, her voice cautious. "You're suggesting we play with their perceptions of reality, essentially turning their own beliefs against them."

"Exactly," Eve responded. "Their sense of righteousness, their belief that they are the chosen ones, is both their greatest strength and their greatest vulnerability. If we can make them question that, even for a moment, we gain the upper hand."

The room hummed with agreement as the officials considered the implications of Eve's strategy. It was risky, but then again, they were facing an enemy that was far more adept than they had originally thought. To simply meet the angels head-on, without any shift in tactics, would be a mistake.

Lord Vesperion glanced around the room, his expression serious. "Eve is right. We must evolve if we are to win this war. It is not just a battle of blades and fire but one of minds and morale. We will integrate these psychological tactics into our broader strategy."

Eve's heart swelled with a mixture of anticipation and resolve. Her philosophical reflections had not just influenced her personal journey but had begun to shape the very nature of Hell's defense. The angels had come seeking to impose their will, but Eve was determined to show them that Hell's power was not something to be underestimated - nor was its ability to adapt.

Eve felt the weight of the coming days settle on her shoulders. The battle had only just begun, and there would be many more challenges ahead. But with each step, she grew more certain that the path she was forging - one that balanced strength, cunning, and philosophy - was the key to not just surviving the celestial invasion but prevailing against it.

As Eve concluded her presentation, a murmur of dissent rippled through the room, with a few warlords at the back exchanging disapproving whispers. Noticing the unrest, Vesperion stepped forward, his voice commanding, "If you have something to say, speak it." This invitation unleashed a torrent of heated debate, as what had once been a unified front now splintered into sharp disagreements. Strained voices filled the war room, revealing the deep ideological divides that were beginning to fracture the leadership against the Temple of Asmodeus.

Tensions had been simmering since the first wave of the angelic forces. While the temple had managed to hold its ground, the cost had been great, and the angels' relentless attacks had shown no signs of slowing. Now, as the leadership team debated how to proceed, the cracks in their unity became more apparent with each passing moment.

Lord Vesperion stood at the head of the table, his commanding presence a reminder of the need for strong leadership. "We've held our own so far, but that won't last forever," he said, his voice firm but measured. "The angels are adapting faster than we anticipated. If we don't shift our tactics soon, we risk losing key strategic points."

Archpriestess Lysandra, seated beside him, nodded in agreement. "Their precision is unlike anything we've faced before. We need to adjust, and fast. A traditional defense won't suffice."

At the other end of the table, Varaak, a staunch traditionalist and high-ranking official, crossed her arms over her chest and leaned forward, her expression hardening. "Adjust? What we need is to strengthen our defenses, not abandon them. These angels are arrogant, thinking they can waltz into Hell and defeat us. What we need is overwhelming force to push them back."

Her voice dripped with disdain as she glanced toward Eve, who had been quietly observing the debate from her position at the table. Eve knew that Varaak's gaze was more than just a look - it was a challenge. Varaak had always been resistant to change, and Eve's recent suggestions of integrating psychological warfare and adaptability into their tactics had not been well-received by the traditionalists.

Eve met Varaak's gaze with calm resolve. "Overwhelming force is one aspect of our strategy," Eve began, her voice steady. "But the angels have shown that they are not easily defeated by brute strength alone. They adapt quickly, and their precision is key to their success. If we don't counter that with something more than raw power, we risk playing into their hands."

Lord Kieran, another progressive voice in the room, nodded in agreement with Eve. "We've already seen how effective psychological tactics can be," he said, his voice thoughtful. "The fear and confusion we've sown in their ranks have given us some key victories. We need to expand on that, create more opportunities to exploit their weaknesses."

Varaak's eyes flashed with irritation. "Psychological tactics," she scoffed. "Deception and mind games? Those are tools of the weak. What we need is strength, power. Anything less will be seen as weakness by the angels, and they'll exploit it."

The tension in the room thickened as the two sides dug in their heels. Eve could feel the weight of the conflict pressing down on her. As a battle priestess and a leader in the temple, she was expected to navigate the competing factions and keep them united. But as the arguments continued, she realized just how difficult that task would be.

Eve took a deep breath, stepping forward into the debate. "The angels are not infallible, but they are disciplined. They believe in their righteousness, and that makes them both predictable and dangerous. Yes, we need strength, but we also need adaptability. If we continue to fight them on their terms, we'll lose ground. We need to make them question their own resolve. We need to turn their sense of superiority against them."

Varaak's jaw tightened. "And how do you propose we do that? By tricking them? By making them doubt their cause?"

"Precisely," Eve replied, her eyes steady. "Their greatest strength is their belief that they are fighting for good, that their cause is just. But if we can make them doubt that - even for a moment - we create an opening. Psychological warfare isn't just about deception. It's about exploiting their weaknesses. And their arrogance is a weakness."

Varaak shook her head, clearly unconvinced. "I still say that our defenses need to be strengthened. We can't risk letting them get any closer to the temple."

Lord Vesperion, who had been listening quietly to the debate, raised a hand to silence the room. "Both of you make valid points," he said, his tone authoritative but measured. "We cannot afford to rely on just one strategy. Varaak, your concerns are valid - we do need to bolster our defenses. But Eve is also right. We need to be adaptable, and we need to use every tool at our disposal, including psychological tactics."

The room fell silent for a moment as Vesperion's words sank in. Eve could feel the eyes of the other leaders on her, some filled with curiosity, others with skepticism.

Archpriestess Lysandra, who had remained quiet during the debate, spoke up. "Eve's strategies have already proven effective in several key engagements. We've seen how demoralizing the use of psychological warfare can be for the angels. But we need to strike a balance. Strength and adaptability. Force and strategy. That's how we'll win this war."

Varaak's expression softened slightly, though she remained unconvinced. "I'll concede that there's merit in what Eve is suggesting. But I still believe that relying too heavily on deception is dangerous. The angels are no fools. They'll catch on."

"They may," Eve agreed, "but by the time they do, it will be too late. If we combine psychological warfare with our traditional strengths, we can outmaneuver them. We can break their lines without breaking ourselves in the process."

Lord Kieran leaned forward, his eyes gleaming with interest. "I think Eve is onto something. We've been thinking too narrowly. We need to be as unpredictable as the angels are precise. That's how we'll win."

The tension in the room began to dissipate, though the underlying ideological divide remained. Eve knew that the traditionalists like Varaak would not easily be swayed from their belief in brute force and direct confrontation. But for now, there was enough agreement to move forward.

Vesperion nodded. "Very well. We'll incorporate both strategies. Varaak, you'll oversee the strengthening of our defenses. Eve, you'll continue to develop your psychological warfare tactics. We'll need both to survive the next wave."

As the meeting adjourned, Eve felt a mixture of relief and trepidation. The battle with the angels was far from over, and now, more than ever, she felt the weight of both the external conflict and the internal struggles within the temple. She had managed to secure support for her ideas, but the divisions within the leadership were growing, and the path forward was uncertain.

As the debate continued, the atmosphere in the war room remained thick with tension, yet no one made a move to leave. Eve lingered near the maps and battle plans, her gaze fixed but her thoughts racing. This war was no longer just about brute strength or flawless strategy - it had become a battlefield for ideals. She understood that the divisions within the temple ran deeper than tactics; they were rooted in differing beliefs about the nature of power and morality. As she stared at the spread of maps before her, Eve wondered how much longer she could walk the tightrope between the traditionalists and the progressives, all while grappling with her own evolving philosophy of what it truly meant to wield power.

Amid the simmering disagreements, Eve turned inward, seeking moments of clarity through philosophical debates with the temple's leaders. These conversations - often with figures like Lord Vesperion and Archpriestess Lysandra - were not mere intellectual sparring but vital reflections that guided her next steps. In the heat of these dialogues, Eve found not only insight into the temple's strategic adjustments but also a deeper understanding of herself. She could feel the weight of her dual role as priestess and battle priestess pressing down on her, and it was in these debates that she sought to balance power, morality, and her evolving sense of identity in the face of the ever-growing conflict.

In the dimly lit quiet of a secluded chamber within the temple, Eve sat across from Lord Vesperion, the flickering light of a single torch casting long shadows on the walls. Their voices were low, their words measured as they delved into a conversation that transcended the immediate concerns of war. The subject was power, and as always, it was a topic that both fascinated and troubled Eve.

"Power," Lord Vesperion mused, his voice calm but filled with the weight of centuries of experience, "is often viewed as a tool for control, a way to dominate others and shape the world to one's will. But it can also be a means of understanding - of evolving beyond the constraints that bind us."

Eve nodded, absorbing his words. Her own journey had led her to question the simplistic view of power as mere dominance. "If power is more than just control," she began, "then how do we reconcile it with the moral choices we are forced to make? The angels believe their cause is righteous, that they fight for good. But what if their vision of good is flawed? What if their path isn't the only one?"

Vesperion's gaze was steady as he replied, "The angels are bound by their own moral code, one that has been shaped by millennia of rigid adherence to a single idea of righteousness. But morality is not so simple. It is fluid, shaped by perspective and circumstance. What is righteous to them may not be righteous to us, and vice versa."

Eve considered this, her mind turning over the implications. "Then does that mean morality itself is a construct, something we create to justify our actions? And if so, how do we decide what is truly right?"

"Perhaps there is no 'right' in the way we've been taught to believe," Vesperion suggested, his voice thoughtful. "Perhaps the only truth is power - power to shape the world as we see fit, and to create our own morality in the process."

Eve's thoughts were a whirlwind. She had long struggled with the idea that good and evil were not the absolutes she had once believed. Her encounters with the angels had only deepened that struggle, forcing her to confront the reality that the lines between light and dark, between good and evil, were far more blurred than she had ever imagined.

Later, Eve's eyes met with Archpriestess Lysandra, whose wisdom had guided her through many difficult moments. Their conversation, though different in tone, was no less profound. Lysandra posed a question that cut to the heart of Eve's dilemma.

"Is righteousness a static ideal," Lysandra asked, her eyes reflecting the flickering light, "or does it evolve with our understanding of power and morality?"

Eve leaned back in her chair, her gaze distant as she pondered the question. "I once believed that righteousness was absolute, that there was a clear path to follow. But now... I'm not so sure. The angels believe they fight for righteousness, yet their actions bring destruction. Can righteousness truly exist in such a rigid, unyielding form?"

Lysandra smiled faintly. "Perhaps righteousness is not about adherence to a set of rules or principles, but about the choices we make in the pursuit of power. If we choose to wield power with understanding, with a willingness to evolve, perhaps that is the truest form of righteousness."

Eve nodded slowly, feeling the truth in Lysandra's words. It was not an easy truth, but it was one that resonated with the philosophical journey she had been on since the start of the conflict. Power, morality, righteousness - all of these concepts were intertwined, and none of them were as simple as she had once believed.

The insights gained from her conversations with Lord Vesperion and Archpriestess Lysandra fueled Eve's strategic thinking. Eve now proposed a series of innovative adjustments to their battle tactics. Standing before the gathered leaders, she outlined her plan, her voice calm but filled with conviction.

"We can no longer rely solely on traditional methods," she restated once again, her eyes scanning the room. "The angels have shown us that they are willing to adapt, and so must we. We must blend our strengths - both physical and psychological - and use every tool at our disposal to disrupt their strategies."

Eve's voice was calm yet charged with the authority of her position, as her eyes scanned the faces around the war room. She could feel the weight of their attention, and the intensity of their doubts. She let her words settle into the silence before continuing, allowing the gravity of what she was about to say to build.

"Our strength must come not only from the sheer force of our armies," Eve said, her voice gaining momentum. "But from the very essence of who we are. We are not merely demons bound by our nature to fight - we are the rightful keepers of this realm, protectors of the Second Circle, and enforcers of Asmodeus' will. The angels, for all their self-righteousness, are the invaders here. They dare to impose their will on a realm that has existed in balance long before their intrusion."

The room was silent, the weight of her words felt by all. Eve's mind turned toward the deeper purpose that drove Hell's existence. The Second Circle was not just a prison for mortal souls, but a necessary realm of consequence. The mortals who found themselves here had sinned, and the demons of Hell - like Eve and her allies - were fulfilling their purpose by delivering the punishment those souls had earned. "The work we do here, the suffering we inflict on the damned, is not cruelty - it is justice. We are bound by a higher imperative, one that transcends the simplistic notions of good and evil. This realm is not a place of arbitrary torment, but of balance. For every mortal who walks the path of sin, there must be consequence, and we are that consequence. For those mortals that seek a higher path, and turn from their sin, then we teach them the way to salvation, we allow them to grow as we change their very belief systems."

She paused again, her gaze hardening. "The angels seek to disrupt that balance. They believe their cause is righteous, but their righteousness is misplaced. By imposing their vision of order upon our realm, they are the ones who are committing a grave sin. They seek to undo the justice we carry out, to erase the suffering of those who have earned their fate. And that, my brothers and sisters, is why they must be stopped."

Eve's voice softened slightly, but her resolve remained unshaken. "We are not the aggressors. We exist in this realm by right, doing the work that has been ordained to us. The angels are the ones who trespass, the ones who seek to impose their flawed vision of good upon a world where it does not belong."

She shifted her weight, drawing the room's attention back to the tactical discussion. "That is why our presence on the battlefield must carry more than just physical power. We must remind the angels, and ourselves, of the righteousness of our cause. We will stage displays of our strength, not just to overwhelm their forces, but to unsettle their minds. We will break their conviction, show them that they do not belong here, that their mission is futile. Every strike we make, every movement we take, will remind them that Hell is not theirs to claim."

Her eyes gleamed as she laid out her plan further. "Symbolic displays of power can be more than mere intimidation - they can seed doubt, and doubt is a weapon that lingers long after the battle is done. We will perform rituals that reflect our mastery over this realm, and let the very ground beneath their feet remind them they are trespassing."

Eve's conviction was palpable. "At the same time, we must remain adaptable. The angels will try to use their light against us, their rigid adherence to their 'higher law.' But we will show them that their law has no place here. As they evolve, so must we, shifting tactics as the battle requires, proving that Hell is not a static place but a living, breathing realm capable of far more than they expect."

She looked at her fellow leaders. "Our strength lies in our ability to uphold the natural order of this realm. We must fight not just with force, but with purpose. With every attack, we reaffirm our right to exist, to carry out the justice that has been entrusted to us. The angels are the intruders. We, in contrast, stand as the rightful guardians of the Second Circle, protectors of the balance that has endured since the dawn of time. Let them come," she finished, her voice low and resolute, "and let us remind them why they can never claim this place as their own."

Her final words hung in the air, charged with the certainty of a leader who believed not just in victory, but in the righteousness of the fight. Eve knew this battle was not only a fight for survival but for the preservation of Hell's natural order. In her heart, she could feel the power of that truth settling deeply, galvanizing her, and strengthening her resolve for the battles ahead.

The room buzzed with discussion as the other leaders weighed in on the new strategy. Eve's innovations had breathed new life into their efforts, giving them hope that they could turn the tide of the battle. Yet, for Eve, this was about more than just winning a war. It was about understanding the nature of power and morality, and about finding her place in a world where the lines between good and evil were no longer clear.

As the meeting drew to a close, Eve felt the weight of the decisions she had made, but also a sense of clarity. Her path was no longer defined by rigid moral codes or simple dichotomies. Instead, she walked a more complex, nuanced path - one where power was not just about control, but about understanding, growth, and evolution.

The chapter of her life as a mere follower of tradition was closing, and a new one was beginning - one that would shape not only the outcome of the war but the future of the temple itself. Eve was ready to embrace it, with all its uncertainty, and with the strength of her newfound convictions.

9

The Battle for Balance

The air around the temple grounds buzzed with anticipation as Hell's forces prepared for their counteroffensive. Eve stood at the command center's edge, her dark gaze fixed on the battlefield below. The strategic adjustments she had proposed - feints, psychological warfare, and symbolic displays of power - had been meticulously integrated into the battle plan. Now, it was time to see those strategies in action.

Her mind whirred with possibilities. The forces of Hell were not just relying on brute strength today; they were armed with a more nuanced understanding of their enemy, a willingness to manipulate perception, and a deep-rooted belief in their own right to defend the Second Circle. The angels had come thinking themselves righteous, but Eve knew their overconfidence would be their downfall.

As the signal was given, Hell's army surged forward. From her vantage point, Eve could see the dark mass of demons advancing like a wave, while overhead, angels glided in tight, calculated formations, their bright wings shimmering in stark contrast to the crimson and black of Hell's forces. But the angels would soon learn that today, light alone would not save them.

Eve's strategy hinged on an initial series of feints and diversions designed to throw the angelic forces into disarray. In the first stage of the counteroffensive, small units of demons charged forward, only to pull back at the last second. These feints forced the angels to commit to unnecessary defenses, spreading their formations thin and exposing vulnerabilities. As the angels adjusted, anticipating another direct charge, Hell's forces attacked from unexpected angles - skirmishers and elite strike teams emerging from the shadows, tearing through their ranks with brutal precision.

Illusionary magic, one of Eve's key strategic additions, played a vital role. Conjured shadows of false demon armies appeared to rush the angels from multiple directions, creating confusion among their ranks. The angels, used to facing straightforward physical opponents, struggled to adapt to the psychological tricks. Their attempts to organize were further disrupted by eerie, dissonant chants that echoed through the air, causing their concentration to falter. The sound-based tactics disoriented the angelic commanders, their orders drowned in a cacophony of demonic voices.

Eve's forces knew these tactics well, using the environment to their advantage. Hidden pits and barriers had been set in the rocky terrain, turning Hell's own harsh landscape into a weapon. Several angels, their focus on countering the feints, fell victim to the traps. Others, attempting to rally their forces, were ambushed by strike teams lurking in concealed positions, their attacks swift and lethal.

Watching from her post, Eve saw the battlefield light up with the clash of infernal fire and heavenly radiance. The air sizzled as hellfire collided with divine energy, creating shockwaves that rippled through the sky. Flames leaped from the ground, and the bright arcs of angelic swords cut through the air like streaks of light, only to be extinguished by the shadowy counterattacks of Hell's soldiers.

But it wasn't just the physical destruction that turned the tide - it was the psychological effect of Eve's strategy. The angels, for all their divine might, were unused to fighting an enemy that didn't follow predictable patterns. As their carefully calculated strikes were met with overwhelming unpredictability, their morale began to falter. Eve had been right: fear and doubt were weapons just as effective as any blade.

"Send in the psychic assault teams," Eve commanded, her voice cutting through the clamor around her. These specially trained demons had the ability to project fear directly into the minds of their enemies, causing disarray and making them question their own righteousness. As the psychic waves hit, Eve could sense the tremors in the angelic ranks. Some faltered mid-flight, clutching their heads, while others hesitated in their movements, their previously synchronized strikes becoming erratic.

One angel, a commander with wings of gleaming gold, tried to rally his troops, shouting orders to regroup. But Eve had anticipated such resistance. A squadron of Hell's elite, led by a demon known for his mastery of tactical deception, swooped in from behind, their movements so swift and precise that the commander didn't have time to react. With a single, coordinated strike, the demon squadron overwhelmed the angelic commander, bringing his resistance to a swift and brutal end.

On the ground, Eve led by example. Her armor, etched with the infernal runes of protection and strength, seemed to pulse with dark energy. Flames crackled in her hands as she directed blasts of hellfire toward the advancing angels. She darted through the chaos, her movements graceful yet lethal. With every attack, she infused her strikes with both physical force and her philosophical understanding of power. The angels, who had once fought with unwavering conviction, now hesitated, unsure of themselves in the face of this overwhelming assault.

A group of angels tried to flank her, descending from above with their swords gleaming. Eve saw them coming and didn't falter. Summoning her demonic power, she conjured a wall of black flame that surged upward, cutting off their approach. The angels faltered, their wings singed by the intense heat, and Eve took the opportunity to strike. She lunged forward, dispatching them with a series of well-placed blows, each movement deliberate, each strike carrying the weight of her dual role as a battle priestess, her claws now dripping with divine blood as she gave out an intense war cry.

Heroic moments punctuated the battlefield as Eve's troops, energized by her leadership, fought with renewed fervor. Hell's forces, once faltering, surged forward with fierce determination. Demonic battalions advanced with precision, their weapons slicing through the celestial ranks. Elite knights, clad in blackened armor, engaged angelic warriors with relentless force, breaking their formations with each strike. Nearby, warlocks unleashed devastating spells, their dark magic crackling through the air and searing through angelic defenses.

One particular moment of valor unfolded as a squadron of Hell's elite knights engaged a group of angelic warriors who had been attempting to regroup. The knights, clad in blackened armor adorned with infernal runes, moved as a single entity, their formation flawless despite the chaos around them. With each strike, they shattered the once-imposing ranks of the angels, their blows resonating with a force that seemed to defy the very nature of the celestial beings.

Nearby, a unit of warlocks, their robes flowing like shadows, unleashed a barrage of dark magic upon the retreating angels. The air crackled with arcane energy as spell after spell erupted from their outstretched hands. Bolts of shadowy lightning arced through the battlefield, searing through angelic armor and sending their adversaries reeling. The warlocks' coordinated spellcasting was a testament to their unwavering focus and their commitment to Eve's vision.

The celestial invaders, previously unyielding, began to falter as their formations fragmented. Attempts to regroup were met with swift counterattacks. Hell's forces had anticipated the retreat and strategically cut off escape routes, trapping the angels in pockets where they could be overwhelmed.

The battlefield, now scarred and chaotic, stood as a testament to the courage and resilience of Hell's defenders. With the celestial invaders driven back, the forces of Hell celebrated a significant victory, reshaping the course of the conflict.

As the battle raged on, Eve's strategic brilliance became evident. The feints had worked perfectly, drawing the angels into positions where they could be surrounded and picked off. The psychological tactics had sowed doubt and fear, and the symbolic displays of power - demon banners raised high, ancient runes glowing ominously - had shaken the angels' confidence in their cause.

From her vantage point, Eve could see the tide turning. What had begun as an uncertain counteroffensive was now a decisive assault. The angels, caught off-guard and disoriented, were no longer the indomitable force they had appeared to be. Hell's forces pressed their advantage, driving the invaders back, claiming victory one skirmish at a time.

By the time the sunless sky began to darken further, Eve's forces had pushed the angels into full retreat. The battle had been fierce, but the tactical brilliance of Hell's counteroffensive - combined with the integration of Eve's philosophical insights - had proven too much for the invaders.

Breathing heavily, Eve stood at the edge of the battlefield, surveying the aftermath. The once-bright wings of the angels now littered the ground, their celestial light dimming in the face of Hell's dark fire. Though the war was far from over, the first major victory belonged to Hell. Eve knew there would be more battles ahead, but for now, her strategy had succeeded.

As dawn broke over the scarred landscape of Hell, the ceaseless turmoil of battle persisted. The day's light did little to soothe the infernal heat or to quell the relentless combat. The last pockets of resistance from the angelic forces were being methodically dismantled by Hell's defenders. Amidst the chaotic clash of holy and infernal forces, Eve's path converged with a crucial confrontation - one that would not only define the immediate outcome of the conflict but also challenge her deepest convictions.

The confrontation was inevitable, and Eve knew it would be as much an ideological battle as a physical one. The angelic leaders, resplendent and imposing, emerged from the haze of battle, their forms radiating a celestial brilliance that starkly contrasted with the infernal surroundings. Their presence was both a beacon and a threat, embodying the apex of their vision of righteousness. As Eve approached, the air thickened with a palpable tension, a clash of purpose and principle that crackled with every step.

The angelic leaders wasted no time in revealing their grand design. Their leader, a figure of both majesty and menace, stepped forward, his voice carrying the weight of divine authority. "Eve," he began, his tone a mix of disdain and revelation, "you stand against the forces of divine justice. This strike against Hell was not merely ordained by God, but a decision made by us, the angels. We have taken it upon ourselves to prove to our Father that the time to end the battle between good and evil is now, not at the end of days."

The declaration was startling. Eve's mind raced as she processed the revelation. The angels' mission was not a celestial command but a self-imposed crusade, an assertion of their own authority and vision of righteousness. The implications were profound and unsettling, challenging the very framework of the conflict she had been fighting within.

Eve faced the angelic leaders with a mixture of determination and inner turmoil. The conviction in their eyes was unyielding, their belief in their cause absolute. They questioned her right to challenge their vision, their questions probing the depths of her beliefs and the nature of her role in the conflict. "How can you, a mere servant of darkness, dare to oppose us?" the leader demanded, his voice echoing with both scorn and superiority. "Your very existence defies the divine order we strive to uphold."

The exchange was intense, a verbal and ideological duel that mirrored the physical battle unfolding around them. The angelic leaders personified the rigid dichotomy of good versus evil that Eve had been grappling with. Their arguments were not just against her but against the entire nature of her being, challenging her to justify her stance in a world that seemed increasingly divided along stark lines of righteousness and damnation.

The battle raged with an intensity that was almost palpable, a fierce struggle that transcended mere physical confrontation. On one side stood the angelic forces, their divine power wielded with both precision and fervor. Their attacks were imbued with a sense of righteousness that made each strike seem almost holy, a testament to their unwavering conviction in their celestial mission.

The angels moved with a coordinated grace, their movements synchronized in a deadly ballet of light and fury. One angel, cloaked in an aura of searing brilliance, launched a radiant spear of energy toward Eve. The spear cut through the air with a blinding light, its divine essence aimed directly at her heart. Eve, anticipating the attack, conjured a barrier of shadowy flames that erupted from her hands. The radiant spear collided with the dark barrier, creating a violent explosion of light and shadow that rippled through the air. The force of the impact sent shockwaves across the battlefield, a stark reminder of the clash of ideologies that was being waged with each blow.

Eve countered with a sweeping arc of crimson fire, her hands tracing a path through the air as if sculpting the flames themselves. The infernal fire surged forward, crashing into the ranks of the angels with a roaring inferno. The heat was almost unbearable, a stark contrast to the cool, divine light of the angelic forms. An angel with wings of shimmering gold attempted to deflect the flames with a shield of celestial light, but the sheer intensity of the infernal fire forced him back, his shield barely holding against the onslaught. The angel staggered, his resolve momentarily faltering as the flames licked at his armor.

Not to be outdone, another angel, towering and clad in resplendent armor, swung a massive sword imbued with divine power. The sword cut through the air with a swift arc, aimed directly at Eve's side. Eve barely had time to react, her instincts kicking in as she summoned a swirling vortex of shadows to intercept the attack. The clash of metal against shadow was deafening, sparks flying as the sword bit into the dark barrier. Eve gritted her teeth, pushing back with all her might, her hands trembling as she fought to maintain the barrier's integrity.

In response, Eve thrust her palm forward, unleashing a concentrated burst of scarlet energy that surged toward the angelic leader. The energy blast struck the angel squarely in the chest, sending him sprawling backward. He struggled to regain his footing, his divine light flickering as he tried to counter the infernal assault. The impact of the carmine colored energy left a deep scorch mark on his armor, a testament to the force of Eve's strike.

The angels' attacks came with relentless precision, their divine light cutting through the shadows with an almost surgical accuracy. One angel, encased in a shimmering cloak, darted toward Eve with a series of rapid strikes, her hands blazing with holy fire. Each strike was a precision attack, aimed to exploit any weakness in Eve's defenses. Eve twisted and turned, her movements a fluid dance of evasion and counterattack. She parried the strikes with a dark blade of shadow, each clash resonating with the ideological struggle between her and the angels.

The angels' light was nearly blinding, a radiant force that sought to overwhelm her with its purity. Yet, Eve's infernal power matched their divine light with an intensity of its own. She wove a tapestry of dark flames and shadowy barriers, each spell and incantation a manifestation of her complex understanding of power and morality. The battlefield was a chaotic canvas of light and dark, each clash of energies a vivid reminder of the internal conflict that raged within Eve.

As the battle intensified, Eve's internal struggle became more pronounced. The rigidity of the angels' vision - an unwavering belief in the binary division of good and evil - seemed to mock her own nuanced views on power and morality. Their insistence on a clear-cut dichotomy clashed sharply with her evolving understanding of the nature of conflict and balance. Each attack, each parry, was not just a physical contest but a reflection of the deeper ideological clash that was taking place.

Eve grappled with the realization that the angels' perspective was both a challenge and a catalyst for her own growth. Their absolute righteousness and clear delineation of morality stood in stark contrast to her own beliefs, pushing her to confront and refine her understanding of power. The battle, fierce and unrelenting, became a crucible in which Eve's convictions were tested and ultimately reshaped.

In the midst of the chaotic battlefield, a moment of intense clarity struck Eve with an almost overwhelming force. As she grappled with the physical and emotional toll of the conflict, a profound realization began to reshape her understanding of herself and her role in the war. At that pivotal moment, the raw surge of her Infernal Titan power erupted with a stunning display of godlike might.

Eve's form began to shift, revealing an imposing figure towering at twelve feet tall. Her skin, previously concealed beneath her battle armor, now glistened with intricate tattoos resembling the stars and nebulae of the galaxy. These celestial patterns seemed to pulsate with a life of their own, casting an ethereal glow that contrasted starkly with the surrounding darkness. The transformation was both awe-inspiring and disorienting - a dramatic manifestation of her true nature.

Her once-familiar fallen angel features had transformed dramatically. She bore elongated vampire fangs that glinted menacingly as they caught the flickering light of the battle. Her entire body was enveloped in swirling black smoke, an ever-shifting cloak of shadows that obscured her form and seemed to writhe and twist with a life of its own. The black smoke danced around her, blending with the fiery red aura that radiated from her core. A third eye blinked open in her chest, its gaze deep and unsettling, as if peering into the very essence of existence. This fiery energy surged outward, a manifestation of her immense power and the depth of her demonic essence.

The celestial leaders, who had been so assured in their righteousness, were momentarily taken aback by the sight before them. Their eyes widened in astonishment as they witnessed the sheer force of Eve's emerging power. The black flames and shadows, combined with her fierce, glowing aura, created a spectacle that was both terrifying and mesmerizing. The contrast between the divine radiance of the angels and the dark, otherworldly energy of Eve's true form highlighted the ideological clash at the heart of their conflict.

In this moment, Eve's wings, which had always been a subtle hint of her fallen celestial nature, were now fully revealed. They stretched out in a display of raw, powerful grace, matching the grandeur of her transformed figure. The sheer magnitude of her presence, combined with the intricate cosmic patterns on her skin and the enveloping cloak of shadow, conveyed a sense of ancient, unfathomable power that transcended the simplistic dichotomies of good and evil.

As the battlefield raged around her, Eve's newly revealed form was both a stunning display of raw power and a profound shift in her understanding of the conflict. The manifestation of her Infernal

Titan form, a towering figure with a galaxy of stars etched into her skin and enveloped in swirling shadows, had transformed the battle's dynamic. Yet, as the raw energy of her Titan form began to wane, she knew that she needed to act decisively.

With a deep, resonant growl that seemed to echo from the very depths of her being, Eve prepared to unleash the full extent of her Titan power. The celestial leaders, still reeling from the sight of her transformation, braced themselves as she summoned the formidable energy that pulsed through her veins. Her fiery red aura flared, intensifying as she focused her will and harnessed the dark forces around her.

In an awe-inspiring display of raw power, Eve raised her arms, and a swirling crimson wave began to coalesce around her. The wave was a spectacular fusion of black flames and red energy, crackling with a fierce intensity. The ground beneath her trembled as the wave grew, its energy pulling in the surrounding shadows and creating a vortex of destructive force.

With a decisive thrust, Eve unleashed the crimson wave, sending it cascading toward the remaining angelic forces. The wave surged forward with a blistering speed, its path marked by a trail of fiery destruction. As it advanced, the wave consumed everything in its path, obliterating the battlefield with its overwhelming power.

The celestial leaders, their radiant forms now dimmed by the encroaching darkness, were caught off guard by the sheer force of the attack. The crimson wave engulfed them in an inferno of black and red energy, the divine light of their forms flickering and fading as they were swept away by the unstoppable tide. The force of the wave was so immense that it tore through the very fabric of the battlefield, leaving nothing but smoldering remnants and a profound silence in its wake.

The remaining angels, who had been holding their ground with unwavering conviction, were similarly consumed by the wave. Their attempts to resist were futile against the overwhelming power of Eve's attack. The crimson wave surged over them, reducing their forms to ash and dissipating their divine essence into the ether.

As the last remnants of the angelic forces were annihilated, the crimson wave began to recede, its energy waning as it completed its course. The fiery red aura surrounding Eve slowly dimmed, and the swirling black smoke that had enveloped her form dissipated. The towering Titan form shrank, reverting back to Eve's usual appearance, now once again grounded in her fallen guise.

Breathing heavily, Eve surveyed the aftermath of her devastating attack. The battlefield was littered with the remains of the celestial forces, the air still charged with the residual heat of the crimson wave. The clash of energies and the intensity of the confrontation had left her exhausted but resolute. Her perspective on power and morality had shifted dramatically, and the revelation of her true form had given her a renewed sense of purpose.

As she returned to her usual form, the profound clarity of her experience remained with her. Eve understood that her role in the conflict was not merely one of opposition but a deeper exploration of balance and duality. Her actions on the battlefield were a testament to her evolving understanding, and she was now prepared to navigate the complexities of the struggle with a renewed sense of determination and insight.

The aftermath of the revelation was both empowering and sobering. Eve had faced the angelic leaders with a renewed determination, her understanding of her role in the conflict transformed by the experience. The battle continued, but her approach was now shaped by a deeper insight into her own nature and the nature of the struggle she was part of. The confrontation with the angelic leaders had not only tested her physically and ideologically but had also illuminated her path forward in a conflict that was as much about inner resolution as it was about external victory.

The aftermath of the battle laid bare the cost of the conflict. Hell's forces had claimed a decisive victory, but the price of triumph was starkly apparent. The once-grand defense walls of the Temple of Asmodeus stood in ruins, its sacred halls also somewhat scarred by the celestial assault. The defenders, weary but unbroken, began the arduous process of rebuilding and reassessing their position.

The temple's leadership faced the daunting task of restoring order amidst the wreckage. The invasion had not only caused physical devastation but had also exposed and intensified internal divisions. As the remnants of the angelic forces were cleared away and the survivors regrouped, it became clear that the conflict had revealed both the strengths and vulnerabilities of Hell's forces. New strategies had proven effective, but the path to recovery and unity was fraught with challenges.

Amidst the rubble and the reconstruction, Eve found herself at a critical juncture. The intense battles and personal revelations had profoundly altered her understanding of her role in the eternal struggle. The raw power of her newly revealed form, and the philosophical conflicts it embodied, had reshaped her perspective on power and morality. As she surveyed the damage and the slow resurgence of the temple's vitality, Eve grappled with the magnitude of her journey.

In quiet moments of reflection, Eve contemplated the revelations she had experienced. The fierce confrontations with the celestial leaders had forced her to confront the dichotomies she had once grappled with, and her emergence as a formidable force had solidified her resolve. The journey had not only tested her physical limits but had also deepened her insight into her own nature and the complexities of the cosmic struggle.

Standing at the crossroads of her destiny, Eve prepared herself for the next phase of the conflict. The path ahead promised both external battles and internal growth. The journey towards balance and understanding was far from over. The lessons learned from the battle and the newfound clarity about her true form provided Eve with a renewed sense of purpose. As she embraced the role of a leader and a warrior, she knew that navigating the evolving landscape of power, morality, and destiny would require both strength and wisdom.

With the temple's recovery underway and the echoes of the recent conflict still resonating, Eve faced the future with a blend of determination and anticipation. The trials she had endured and the truths she had uncovered had prepared her for the challenges yet to come. As the forces of Hell regrouped and the fires of war smoldered, Eve was ready to forge ahead, guided by her profound insights and a resolute commitment to the complex balance of power and destiny that lay before her.

Act 2: The Struggle of Duality

10

Unveiling the Hidden Truths

As the crimson glow of the infernal torches flickered along the temple walls, Eve moved quietly through the empty corridors, her steps barely making a sound. It was late, the hour when most of the acolytes were lost in their dreams or nightmares, but Eve's mind was ablaze. An unease had settled over her in recent days, an incessant whisper that pulled her from her chambers and guided her deeper into the heart of the temple. Something - no, someone - was calling to her.

She had spent years within these stone walls, yet tonight felt different. The air was thicker, heavier, and the shadows seemed to twist and curl around her, almost as if they were sentient. Her fingers grazed the smooth surface of the ancient stone, feeling the cold, rough texture against her skin as she traced the inscriptions etched along the corridor's spine. The familiar carvings depicted the great deeds of Asmodeus, the rituals of power and devotion, all worn smooth by centuries of worship and touch. But tonight, she wasn't drawn to the known; she was seeking the unknown.

After what felt like hours of wandering, Eve came upon a door at the end of a narrow passageway, hidden behind a thick curtain of crimson velvet. She paused, her heartbeat quickening as she reached out to touch the door's cool, ornate handle, which was carved in the shape of entwined serpents. She had walked these halls many times, but she had never seen this door before. It was as though it had simply appeared, drawn into existence by the will that urged her forward.

Taking a breath, she pushed it open, and it creaked as though waking from a long slumber. Beyond the door was a spiral staircase, descending into the depths of the temple, into a darkness that seemed to swallow the light. The pull grew stronger, and without a moment's hesitation, she began to descend.

As Eve stepped onto the cold, obsidian floor at the bottom of the staircase, she felt an unsettling chill crawl up her spine, as if the shadows themselves were whispering forgotten secrets. Her eyes fell upon an ancient, circular chamber, its walls carved with strange symbols that pulsed faintly with a life of their own. In the center, an imposing pedestal stood, bathed in an eerie, ethereal light that seemed to have no discernible source, as if it emerged from the very air itself. The light flickered, casting strange patterns across the floor, creating the illusion that the chamber was alive, breathing, watching.

Surrounding the pedestal were piles of scrolls and aged tomes, bound in cracked leather and tarnished gold, each cover bearing intricate, faded runes. Dust and cobwebs coated them, relics of a time long past, untouched by mortal hands. These were not the teachings of Asmodeus she had devoted herself to all her life. No, these were far older, their very presence resonating with an aura of mystery and power, as if they held the truths of the universe itself. They had been forgotten, abandoned by those who sought only the immediate gratification of power without the deeper understanding that came with true knowledge.

Eve moved forward, her breath quickening as she approached the pedestal, her eyes inexorably drawn to the largest tome resting at its center. Its cover bore the faint, ghostly image of a great serpent devouring its own tail - the ouroboros, the eternal cycle of life and death, creation and destruction. With trembling hands, she lifted the cover, and the pages responded with a faint, otherworldly glow. As she read the first words, written in an ancient, forgotten tongue, a shiver ran through her:

"That which is done is eternal. The will to power is the force that drives all existence."

These words struck her like a blow, and her mind began to race. She had heard whispers of such philosophy before but had dismissed them as heretical nonsense. Now, faced with the raw, undeniable truth etched into these pages, she felt the world around her begin to shift. Each line she read was a revelation, peeling back the layers of her understanding, revealing a deeper, more complex reality that lay beyond the teachings of the temple.

The words spoke of the **eternal recurrence**, a concept that sent shivers down her spine, reverberating through the core of her very being. It was an idea as ancient as the cosmos itself: that all existence, every fragment of life, was caught in an endless cycle of repetition. Every thought, every action, every triumph and defeat - everything that had ever happened or would happen was destined to repeat itself infinitely. Each moment would not only occur once but would resurface again, with the same intensity and passion, in an endless loop that transcended time and space.

Eve's hand trembled as she traced the words, feeling an ache within her chest as the full weight of this revelation settled over her. The implications were staggering. If this concept were true, then every choice she had made, every tear she had shed, every burst of laughter, every battle fought, and every act of love would not only be a single brushstroke in the vast painting of existence but a stroke that would be drawn and redrawn countless times. This wasn't just about her; it was the essence of all life, all consciousness, caught in the throes of an eternal dance.

At first, the idea seemed suffocating, a cosmic prison with no hope of escape. How could one endure such an existence, knowing that every pain, every failure, every wound would be inflicted again and again? It seemed to strip life of its meaning, reducing existence to an endless cycle of suffering, joy, and fleeting moments of clarity. If all her struggles, all her growth, and all her battles against destiny were destined to be repeated without end, what was the point? Why strive for something different when the outcome would forever loop back upon itself?

Yet, as she stood there, tracing the words etched in ancient script, a realization began to take hold. This was not a condemnation but an opportunity. The eternal recurrence did not demand that one be bound by despair or futility; instead, it offered a chance to affirm life in all its forms, to embrace existence fully, knowing that every moment - whether of bliss or anguish - held its intrinsic worth. It was an invitation to live each moment as if one would choose to live it again, to ask oneself, "Would I do this again? Would I face this trial, this love, this pain, this joy, knowing that it would echo throughout eternity?"

The thought sent shivers down her spine, but this time, they were not of fear. There was an unexpected beauty in this repetition - a beauty she had never allowed herself to see. It was as if the universe was saying, "You are not defined by a single moment, but by the countless times you choose to rise, to fight, to love, to lose, and to rise again." In this infinite cycle, there was a freedom unlike any other. It meant that every experience, no matter how fleeting, was eternal. Every kiss, every wound, every tear shed in sorrow or joy, would be etched into the fabric of time, repeated endlessly, not as a curse but as a testament to the courage it took to live.

Eve's mind expanded with this realization, and she felt herself slipping beyond the constraints of mortal thought, touching the divine essence of existence itself. She saw her life stretched out before her, not as a single thread but as a tapestry woven from countless threads, each one representing a moment she had lived, would live, and would live again. And in that tapestry, there was no beginning or end, no sense of finality, only the beautiful, chaotic, and infinite dance of existence.

She understood now that to accept the eternal recurrence was to embrace life in all its messy, painful, and wondrous glory. It meant rejecting the notion of linearity, of a singular path to follow, and instead acknowledging that every choice, every action, reverberated throughout eternity. It wasn't about finding the right path, but about walking the path that felt true to oneself, over and over again, refining, reshaping, and reimagining it with each iteration.

The words were not a burden, but a challenge - a challenge to live as if every moment mattered, as if every breath was a sacred act that would echo across the universe for all time. In that realization, Eve felt a profound sense of peace. She was no longer bound by fear of failure or regret because, in the grand scheme of the eternal recurrence, every failure was a step toward understanding, every sorrow a brushstroke in the grand painting of existence.

"Yes," she whispered to herself, her voice carrying through the wind, "I would live this life again. And again. And again." Because to live, truly live, was to accept the eternal recurrence with open arms - to find joy not in the certainty of an end, but in the endlessness of the journey.

And in that acceptance, Eve felt herself transcend, rising beyond the chains of mortal understanding, embracing her role as both Eve and Nyx, mortal and titan, boundless and free.

"Do you accept this truth?" The voice was soft, echoing from the shadows around her.

Eve's head snapped up, her eyes darting around the chamber, but she saw no one. Her heart raced, her senses sharpening. "Who's there?" she demanded, trying to keep her voice steady.

The voice didn't answer directly. Instead, she felt a presence, an energy that seeped into her very bones, coiling around her like a serpent. It was a dark, intoxicating force that made her blood sing, and she knew, with a certainty that came from somewhere deep and primal, that this was Nyx.

"Why do you resist?" Nyx's voice was like velvet, both gentle and dangerous, threading itself through Eve's thoughts. "You stand on the precipice of true understanding, yet you cling to the chains that bind you. Why?"

Eve swallowed, her mouth dry, her mind whirling. "I serve Asmodeus," she replied, but the words felt hollow, even as they left her lips. She had said them so many times before, believed them without question, but now, faced with this presence, they seemed like little more than a lie.

"Do you?" Nyx's tone was mocking, yet there was no malice in it. "Or do you serve yourself? Have you not felt it, Eve? The pull toward something greater, something beyond the petty squabbles of demons and angels?"

Eve clenched her fists, her nails biting into her palms as she tried to focus. "Why should I listen to you?" she hissed, more out of fear than defiance. "You're just another voice, another force trying to bend me to your will."

Nyx laughed, a sound that echoed through the chamber like the chiming of distant bells, a melody both haunting and beautiful. It was a laugh that carried the weight of ages, of battles fought and lost, of truths whispered in the dark corners of existence. Eve's eyes gleamed with an ethereal light, her presence radiating an aura that seemed to bend reality itself. "I do not wish to bend you, child. I wish to **free** you," she continued, her voice rich with an ancient, almost maternal warmth. "The path of power is not found in servitude, but in embracing the chaos, the uncertainty, and the truth that lies beyond the doctrines you've been fed."

The words hung heavy in the air, like smoke curling around Eve, weaving into the fabric of her thoughts. Nyx's voice was a beacon in the darkness, challenging every belief that had been ingrained in her soul, every whisper that had told her she was meant to serve, to submit, to be less than what she was. "You see," Nyx continued, "true power is not a gift to be bestowed upon you by another. It is not something you earn by kneeling or by proving yourself worthy to a higher force. It is a fire that you kindle within your own heart, a flame that refuses to be extinguished by the winds of fate or the chains of expectation. It is the courage to face the void and say, 'I am here. I am more than what you have made me.'"

Eve's gaze fell back to the tome resting in her hands, its pages glowing faintly with a light that seemed to pulse in time with her heartbeat. Her eyes traced the lines about the will to power, each word etched with an intensity that burned into her mind. There, in those ancient texts, she found a reflection of herself - the struggle, the desire, the yearning for something more than just obedience. It was as if the words were alive, speaking directly to the depths of her soul, urging her to question, to challenge, to break free from the shackles that had bound her for so long.

She thought back to the countless rituals, the blood spilled, the prayers chanted, all in service to a being who demanded power and submission. She could feel the weight of those moments pressing down upon her shoulders, the countless hours spent in supplication, the nights spent whispering incantations in the dark, hoping for a glimpse of approval, a sign that she was enough. But now, under Nyx's gaze, those moments felt hollow, like echoes of a life that wasn't truly hers. She saw herself kneeling, offering up her strength, her essence, to something that would never be satisfied, no matter how much she gave. It had always been about taking, always about bending her will to something greater.

But what if power was not meant to be taken or given, but rather **created**? What if power was an act of rebellion, a declaration of one's existence against the void, against the endless forces that sought to crush individuality and desire? What if power was not about conquest or domination, but about the unyielding flame that burned within, the light that refused to be extinguished no matter how dark the world became? What if power was the act of looking into the abyss and daring to say, "I will not be defined by you"?

Eve could feel something stir within her, a flicker of defiance, a spark of the divine that had always been there, buried beneath layers of fear and obedience. It was a voice that whispered of possibility, of the freedom that lay beyond the walls she had built around herself. "What if," she thought, "I am more than just a vessel for another's power? What if I am meant to be the creator of my own destiny, to carve my path with my own hands, to find strength in the chaos rather than fear it?"

And for the first time, the doctrines she had clung to for so long began to truly crumble, falling away like dust caught in the wind. She realized that power was not about finding the right master to serve, nor was it about bending others to her will. It was about standing in her truth, embracing the uncertainty of existence, and finding beauty in the struggle itself. It was about daring to be, in all her flawed, glorious, chaotic entirety.

Nyx watched her from within, the light in her eyes growing ever brighter. "Yes," she whispered, her voice soft but powerful, "You are beginning to understand. Power is not found in the certainty of doctrines, nor in the promises of gods. It is found in the courage to walk your own path, even when that path leads into the darkness. It is in the willingness to face the unknown, to embrace the chaos, and to know that you are the only one who can define your worth."

Eve nodded slowly, the truth of Nyx's words settling into her bones. For the first time in her life, she felt something more than mere obedience, more than duty or obligation. She felt the stirrings of her own power, a power that was hers alone, untamed and unyielding. And in that moment, she realized that she was not a pawn, not a servant, not a tool to be used. She was a creator, a force of nature, a being of endless potential.

She was not meant to be bent or broken. She was meant to rise, to burn, to become.

"What do you want from me?" Eve asked, her voice barely more than a whisper.

"Nothing," Nyx replied, her voice a velvet whisper that seemed to reverberate through the chamber, carrying with it an ageless wisdom. "And everything. I am you, and you are me. You have always been Nyx. I am the darkness that lies within, the truth you've kept buried, the whispers that you've silenced for so long. All I ask is that you listen, that you truly **see**."

Eve's heart pounded in her chest, a wild rhythm that matched the energy fluttering in the air around her. She could feel the weight of those words, the way they wrapped around her like a lover's embrace, both comforting and suffocating. Her fingers brushed against the pages of the ancient tome once more, and in that touch, she felt something awaken within her - an energy that thrummed through her veins, coursing with a power she had never known. It was as if the ink on the pages had seeped into her skin, filling her with the knowledge, the strength, the raw essence of everything that Nyx represented.

In that moment, Eve understood. Nyx was not an external force, not some shadow that sought to consume her or bend her will. Nyx was her - her doubts, her fears, her strength, and her desires. Nyx was the embodiment of every suppressed thought, every forbidden longing, every moment of defiance that she had buried beneath layers of obedience and duty. And now, that part of her was rising, demanding to be seen, to be acknowledged.

Eve's breath hitched as she felt memories surge to the forefront of her mind: the countless nights spent on her knees in prayer, begging for guidance; the pain of loss, the sting of betrayal, the unfulfilled yearning for something more. She had always been told that to be strong meant to suppress, to deny, to follow the path laid out for her. But now, as she stood on the precipice of something greater, she felt the truth unraveling before her.

For the first time, Eve allowed herself to let go. She closed her eyes and let the words of the tome sink into her mind, letting the voice of Nyx wash over her like the tide, ebbing and flowing, pulling her deeper into the darkness. And as she did, she felt something begin to break free within her. The chains that had bound her heart and mind for so long began to shatter, falling away like dust, leaving her bare, exposed, and utterly vulnerable.

The lines between Eve and Nyx began to blur, their distinctions fading into the shadows. It was as if the very fabric of her being was unraveling, weaving itself anew into a tapestry that was both terrifying and beautiful. She felt herself being drawn into the darkness, not with fear, but with a profound sense of liberation. The darkness was not her enemy; it was her ally, her companion, her truest self.

In this space between realities, Eve stood face-to-face with Nyx, no longer as a separate entity but as a reflection, a mirror that showed her everything she had ever been and everything she could become. "Why have you hidden from me for so long?" Eve asked, her voice trembling, but there was strength there too, a determination that had been forged in the fires of her trials.

Nyx smiled, a soft, enigmatic expression that spoke of countless lifetimes. "Because you were not ready to see me," she replied. "You clung to the light because you believed it would save you, that it would give you the answers you sought. But light without darkness is blinding, child. It leaves you vulnerable, unable to see the shadows that lurk just beyond its reach. It is only when you embrace the darkness that you can truly see."

Tears welled in Eve's eyes, but they were not tears of sorrow. They were tears of acceptance, of understanding. She had spent so much of her life trying to be something she wasn't, trying to fit into a mold that others had crafted for her. But here, in the darkness, she was free. Free to be raw, to be flawed, to be powerful.

"What does it mean to be you?" Eve whispered, her voice barely more than a breath, as if she were afraid to disturb the fragile truth that hung between them.

"It means to embrace the chaos within," Nyx answered, her voice like the rustling of leaves in a midnight breeze. "To know that you are both the storm and the calm that follows. It means to reject the idea that you must be one thing or the other - that you must be good or evil, light or dark, weak or strong. You are all of these things and more. You are limitless, bound only by the walls you build around yourself."

Eve's fingers tightened around the tome, her knuckles white from the pressure. Every word, every syllable, resonated within her, striking chords that had long lain dormant. She felt a pulse, a heartbeat that echoed in time with her own, and she realized it was the rhythm of the universe itself - the endless cycle of creation and destruction, of life and death, of power and surrender.

"Can I truly be both?" Eve asked, her voice wavering, as if she were standing at the edge of a great chasm, ready to leap but not quite able to take that final step.

"You already are," Nyx replied, her tone gentle but firm. "You are the one who stands between worlds, the one who walks the line between what is and what could be. You are Eve, and you are Nyx. You are immortal, and you are eternal. The moment you stop trying to separate these parts of yourself, you will understand what it means to be truly free."

Eve closed her eyes, and in that darkness, she saw it - the infinite expanse of the cosmos, stretching out before her, vast and unending. She saw stars born and die, watched galaxies spiral into oblivion, witnessed the dance of creation and destruction that had played out since the beginning of time. And in that moment, she knew. She knew that she was not bound by the laws of this world, by the expectations of others, or by the fears that had held her captive for so long.

"I am ready," she whispered, her voice echoing through the chamber, stronger now, resonating with a power that had always been hers but had remained hidden, waiting for this moment to be unleashed.

And in the silence that followed, Eve felt something stir deep within her soul - a spark, a flame, a will to power that could not be denied. It burned with the intensity of a thousand suns, searing away the doubts and fears that had clouded her vision. It was a power that came not from domination, not from submission, but from the simple, unyielding truth of her existence.

Eve opened her eyes, and for the first time, she saw. She saw the world not as it was but as it could be. She saw herself standing amidst the darkness, not as a frightened child, but as a warrior, a queen, a force of nature. And as she looked into the eyes of Nyx, she did not see a stranger, an enemy, or a monster.

She saw herself.

A slow smile spread across her lips, and in that smile, there was a promise - a promise to never again be bound, to never again be silent. She would walk her path, not as Eve or Nyx, but as both. She would embrace the chaos, the uncertainty, and the power that lay within her, and she would become something more.

In that moment, Nyx was born anew, and the universe trembled in anticipation of what she would become.

"I am ready," she whispered, her voice echoing through the chamber.

And in the silence that followed, Eve felt something stir deep within her soul - a spark, a flame, a will to power that could not be denied.

11

The Struggle Within

E ve stood in the center of the bathhouse, her form partially submerged in the steaming water that filled the vast, stone-hewn pool. The dim lighting from the glowing embers nestled in iron braziers cast soft, flickering shadows that danced along the mosaic-tiled walls, depicting scenes of Asmodeus's conquests and the eternal struggle between desire and power. The air was thick with steam, mingling with the scent of lavender and crushed myrrh that clung to her skin, enveloping her in a fragrant, almost otherworldly warmth.

She let the water lap gently against her body, its heat seeping into her muscles and easing the tension that had built over hours spent hunched over the ancient texts. Her fingers traced the surface of the water, and as she did, the ripples formed concentric circles that expanded outwards, echoing the chaos swirling in her mind. She had immersed herself in the words of the old scriptures, allowing them to flow through her like water cascading over stones, but now they surged within her, reverberating with a power she struggled to contain.

Eve tilted her head back, her hair cascading like an ink-black waterfall over her shoulders, and stared up at the vaulted ceiling of the bathhouse. Tendrils of steam drifted upward, and she watched them with half-lidded eyes, her mind still reeling from the revelations she had unearthed. The words of eternal recurrence and the will to power wound themselves around her thoughts like a serpent coiling around its prey, and the heat of the bath did little to soothe the storm brewing within her.

Slowly, Eve reached for a nearby jar of scented oils, her fingers brushing against the cool surface of the glass. She poured a small amount into her palm, the rich, amber liquid catching the light of the braziers, and began to anoint her arms, her movements deliberate and slow, as if each stroke would somehow ease the burden of the knowledge she now carried. The scent of sandalwood and rose mingled with the steam, enveloping her in a fragrant cocoon that felt both comforting and stifling.

As her hands moved across her skin, Eve's gaze fell upon her reflection in the water. The flickering light cast strange patterns across her face, and for a moment, she scarcely recognized the woman staring back at her. It was as if the darkness of Nyx lingered just beneath the surface, shifting and swirling with every movement, every breath. It reminded her of the shadows that now seemed to cling to her soul, refusing to let go, whispering truths she had long tried to deny.

With a sigh, she sank deeper into the water, allowing it to rise over her shoulders, feeling its warmth cradle her as she closed her eyes. For a brief moment, the chaos in her mind quieted, replaced by the rhythmic dripping of water from the edges of the pool, the soft crackling of embers, and the faint echoes of her own heartbeat. The ancient texts' teachings drifted through her consciousness, intertwining with the whispers of Nyx, blending into a single, haunting melody that sent shivers down her spine.

As she rubbed the oil along her arms, Eve couldn't help but trace the faint scars that marked her skin, each one a reminder of the battles fought, of the choices made, of the price paid for power. And yet, in this dimly lit sanctuary, amidst the soothing embrace of the bath, she felt something stir within her - something ancient, something powerful. It was as though the water itself carried the knowledge of those who had come before her, those who had walked the path of power, who had faced their fears, and emerged stronger.

Eve dipped her hands back into the water, watching as the oil spread in iridescent patterns, shimmering like liquid gold. She whispered to herself, repeating the lines she had read only hours before: "The will to power is not merely an ascent but a descent into oneself, a journey through darkness to find the light within." The words echoed off the stone walls, mingling with the steam and fading into the silence, but their weight remained, heavy and undeniable.

She let her head rest against the edge of the pool, feeling the cool stone press against her damp skin, her eyes drifting shut once more. In the darkness behind her eyelids, she saw visions of Nyx, her movements fluid and graceful, a dance that blended shadow and light, strength and vulnerability. She saw herself within that dance, each step a choice, each motion a reflection of her own desires and fears.

A faint smile tugged at the corners of Eve's lips, and she let herself sink deeper into the warmth, allowing it to wash away the remnants of doubt, of uncertainty. Here, in this sanctuary of steam and water, she felt the boundaries between herself and Nyx blur, felt the power droning through her veins, a steady, unyielding rhythm that matched the beat of her own heart.

She whispered to the darkness, to herself, to Nyx, "If power is a journey, then I will walk it. If it is a dance, then I will lead." And as her words faded into the silence, Eve felt something shift within her, a sense of clarity that cut through the fog of her thoughts like a blade. She opened her eyes, and for a moment, she saw not the reflection of a priestess, but of a goddess - a being who stood poised on the edge of eternity, unafraid, unyielding, ready to face whatever lay ahead.

The steam rose around her, enveloping her in a veil of warmth and mystery, and as Eve submerged herself fully, letting the water cover her, she felt a calm wash over her, a stillness that belied the storm within. When she resurfaced, she was not merely Eve, the priestess, nor Nyx, the Titan. She was both and more - a force that would not be denied, a will that could not be broken.

"Embrace it, Eve," Nyx's voice whispered, smooth and alluring, wrapping around her thoughts like silk. "You know what lies beyond the chains of light and shadow. You must learn to harness it."

Eve pressed her palms to her temples, trying to block out the persistent echo of Nyx's presence. It was becoming harder to distinguish her own thoughts from the Titan's, and each passing moment felt like a battle waged within her mind. She could feel the darkness stirring, the primordial force that had lain dormant for so long, now pushing against the boundaries of her consciousness.

"Stop it!" she hissed, her breath coming in quick bursts. "I need to think clearly."

"Clear thinking is an illusion," Nyx replied, an undercurrent of amusement lacing the words. "What is clarity but a tool to keep you shackled? It is in the chaos that you will find your truth."

Eve shivered at the challenge in Nyx's tone. She closed her eyes, letting the shadows envelop her as she tried to focus on the tangible - her training as a priestess, the sacred teachings of Asmodeus, the established dogma that had shaped her existence. But with each breath, the weight of those teachings grew heavier, suffocating her spirit and igniting the flames of rebellion deep within.

As visions began to swirl before her, they unfolded like ancient scrolls unraveling in her mind, each one revealing fragments of Nyx's past, moments etched into the very fabric of existence. Eve felt herself pulled into the heart of the darkness, where the beginning of time seemed to blur and dissolve, leaving only the infinite canvas of the cosmos. Her surroundings shifted, and she stood upon an unseen precipice, staring into the vast expanse of a starless void. In that silence, the visions took shape, painting themselves across the darkness with colors that defied description, hues that seemed to change as if alive.

The first vision took her to a place before time began, to a cosmic battlefield where Nyx stood against an army of radiant beings. Angels, their wings shimmering with a light so pure it burned to look upon, clashed with titanic shadows that seemed to flow like ink across the sky. The ground beneath was not solid but instead rippled like liquid silver, reflecting the chaos above in a distorted, shimmering mirror. Nyx moved with an elegance that was both brutal and beautiful, a warrior clothed in darkness, her form shifting and blurring with every step as if she were made of the void itself.

Eve watched as the Titan unleashed her power, and the stars trembled at her command. With a sweep of her hand, Nyx conjured a tempest of black flame that consumed her foes, their screams echoing through the emptiness, swallowed by the vastness of the abyss. Every movement she made was precise, every strike a dance that spoke of mastery over both life and death. The angels tried to respond, their weapons flashing with light, but against Nyx's onslaught, they seemed like mere fireflies, flickering before the eternal night.

In one moment, an angel of immense power stepped forward, his wings outstretched, glowing with the radiance of a thousand suns. He raised a blade forged from the heart of a star, its edge cutting through reality itself. As he lunged, Nyx did not retreat. Instead, she met his attack with open arms, allowing the blade to pierce her form. Eve gasped, feeling the pain resonate in her own chest, but Nyx's smile only widened. She grasped the blade with her bare hands, darkness swirling around her wrists, and in an instant, the weapon shattered into shards of light that dissolved into nothingness. The angel fell to his knees, his light fading, and Nyx whispered something into his ear, a truth that made him weep before he too was consumed by the shadows.

The vision shifted, and Eve was drawn into the next fragment of Nyx's past. This time, she stood atop a mountain, staring out over an ocean of molten gold. Waves of liquid fire crashed against jagged cliffs of obsidian, and the air shimmered with heat, distorting the world into something otherworldly. In the distance, colossal serpents, their scales glittering like diamonds, coiled around massive pillars of stone, their eyes glowing with an ancient, predatory hunger. Nyx stood alone upon the peak, her hair billowing behind her like a veil of midnight, as one of the serpents rose from the sea, towering over her like a god.

It struck with lightning speed, its jaws snapping shut with the force of a thunderclap, but Nyx did not flinch. Instead, she raised her hand, and from her fingertips, tendrils of darkness erupted, intertwining with the serpent's body, binding it in place. The creature thrashed, its golden blood spilling across the rocks, each droplet forming miniature suns that flared and died in an instant. Nyx's eyes glowed with an inner light, and she whispered words of power that echoed through the realm, ancient incantations that shook the foundations of reality itself. The serpent began to change, its body unraveling into threads of light that spiraled around Nyx, weaving themselves into her flesh, merging with her, until she stood alone once more, a being that was part darkness, part light, and something far greater than both.

As the vision dissolved, Eve found herself in a new place, standing upon a field of shattered glass that stretched out to infinity. Above her, the sky was a swirling maelstrom of colors, a kaleidoscope of shifting patterns that made her head spin. She looked down and saw countless reflections of herself staring back, each one wearing a different expression - fear, anger, joy, sorrow, love, and hatred. And in each reflection, she saw Nyx, the Titan's eyes gazing back at her, challenging her to look deeper.

Suddenly, the ground cracked open, and out of the fissures, figures began to emerge - warriors clad in armor of bone and steel, their eyes burning with a cold, malevolent light. They charged toward Nyx, swords drawn, voices raised in a war cry that made the air tremble. Eve watched as Nyx stood her ground, unyielding, her eyes gleaming with a ferocity that sent shivers down her spine.

In an instant, Nyx moved, faster than thought, her form blurring as she weaved between her attackers. Her hands became claws, talons of shadow that tore through flesh and bone as if they were paper. Blood sprayed across the field, each droplet catching the light and transforming into tiny galaxies that swirled and spun before dissolving into the air. One by one, the warriors fell, their bodies collapsing into dust, and as the last one fell, Nyx stood triumphant, her chest heaving, her eyes glowing with an intensity that seemed to pierce through the fabric of reality.

Eve felt the vision pulling her deeper still, and now she stood in a place that defied all logic, all understanding. She was surrounded by darkness, but within that darkness, countless stars blinked into existence, each one a memory, a moment in time that had been forgotten. She saw herself as a young demon once more, staring up at the night sky, wondering if there was more to life than what she had been told. She saw herself kneeling before the altar of Asmodeus, praying for power, for purpose, for something to fill the void inside her. She saw herself standing at the temple, her hands stained with blood, her heart heavy with the weight of all she had done.

And then, she saw Nyx. Not as a Titan, not as a goddess, but as a reflection of herself. A woman with eyes as dark as the void, filled with the same doubts, the same fears, the same longing for something more. In that moment, Eve understood. The battles Nyx had fought were not just against angels, or serpents, or warriors - they were against herself. Against the fear of being forgotten, of being powerless, of being alone. Every strike, every spell, every whispered incantation was a declaration, a defiance against the universe that sought to contain her.

Eve felt tears streaming down her face, and she reached out, her hand passing through the vision, touching the heart of the darkness. And for the first time, she felt a warmth, a pulse of life that spread through her veins, filling her with a sense of belonging, of purpose. She was not just Eve. She was Nyx. She was every battle fought, every scar earned, every tear shed. She was the chaos and the order, the shadow and the light, the beginning and the end.

As the vision began to fade, Eve stood in the silence, her heart still echoing with the beat of Nyx's power. And as she looked into the darkness, she saw not an enemy, but a reflection of herself - whole, unbroken, and free.

"Why do you resist the truth?" Nyx taunted, her voice a siren's call. "You are more than a mere servant of Asmodeus. You are destined for greatness, but only if you stop clinging to the frail constructs of morality."

"I can't just abandon everything I've been taught," Eve muttered to herself, her voice barely above a whisper. "Can I?"

The walls of her sanctuary felt like they were closing in around her, the weight of her responsibilities pressing heavily on her chest. With Nyx's consciousness awakening within her, she felt the rift widening between who she had been and who she was becoming. Doubt gnawed at her, but the allure of power and the promise of freedom from dogma beckoned her closer.

Eve made a decision. She needed to talk to someone, to confide in a fellow acolyte, to seek guidance. Perhaps they could help her find clarity, help her understand the growing conflict within. But as she crossed the threshold of the bathhouse, she couldn't shake the feeling that she was stepping into hostile territory.

The corridors of the temple felt foreign, the shadows stretching longer, deeper. The air sputtered with tension, and as she approached the common room, she could hear the hushed voices of her fellow acolytes engaged in fervent discussion. Gathering her courage, she pushed the heavy door open.

Inside, she was met with wary glances and muted conversations that ceased abruptly. The room, usually filled with warmth and camaraderie, felt cold and unwelcoming. A knot of anxiety twisted in her stomach as she stepped further into the space, feeling the weight of their scrutiny.

"Eve," one of the acolytes, Malen, spoke up, his tone cautious. "What brings you here? We thought you were lost in meditation."

"I... I need to talk," Eve stammered, her voice trembling slightly. "I've been reading some ancient texts, and I feel like there's more to our teachings than we've been led to believe."

The silence that followed was deafening. Eyes exchanged glances, and Eve could sense the rising tension as her fellow acolytes shifted uncomfortably. Finally, another acolyte, Rhea, spoke up. "What do you mean, Eve? The teachings of Asmodeus are absolute. We cannot question them."

"Why not?" Eve challenged, her heart racing. "What if there's truth beyond what we've been taught? What if the conflict we're facing is more complicated than just good versus evil?"

Malen's expression hardened, his brow furrowing. "You've been reading too much. The ancient texts can lead you astray. They are not our path."

"No, they can show us a different path," Eve insisted, her voice rising with passion. "They speak of power, of freedom, of embracing the chaos that exists within us all. Can't you see? We're trapped in our own beliefs!"

The room erupted into chaos, voices overlapping as the acolytes expressed their doubts and fears. Eve felt a swell of frustration and isolation wash over her. This was not the acceptance she had hoped for; it was rejection. Each word spoken against her felt like a dagger, slicing through her resolve.

"What has gotten into you, Eve?" Rhea snapped. "You sound like a heretic. Are you turning your back on Asmodeus?"

Eve's heart sank. "I'm not turning my back. I'm trying to understand!"

"Understanding? Or sedition?" Malen's voice was cold, and Eve recoiled as if struck. "You're playing with fire, Eve. The temple doesn't tolerate such thoughts."

The group's hostility enveloped her, and she felt as if she were standing alone in a storm, battered by the winds of their disbelief. The walls that had once felt comforting now felt like they were closing in, suffocating her.

Eve turned on her heel, the weight of their suspicion heavy on her shoulders. She stumbled back into the corridor, the laughter and chatter of her fellow acolytes fading behind her. Each step away from the common room echoed in her mind like a relentless drumbeat, and as she walked, Nyx's voice whispered in her ear.

"They do not understand you, Eve. They cling to their chains, while you seek to break free. You must embrace your true self."

"Shut up!" she snapped, shaking her head. "I can't keep doing this."

"Doing what? Hiding from your power?" Nyx countered, the seductive allure returning to her voice. "You are destined for greatness, yet you let them keep you small."

Eve leaned against the cold stone wall, her breath quickening as the conflict within her surged once more. The darkness of Nyx clawed at her, and she felt the Titan's presence swell, a reminder of the freedom that lay just beyond her reach. But the memories of her fellow acolytes, their distrust, and their fear were fresh in her mind.

The fight between the light of her teachings and the shadow of Nyx raged on within her, leaving her feeling more fractured than ever.

"Do you wish to remain a prisoner of their beliefs?" Nyx pressed. "Or will you take your place among the stars?"

Eve closed her eyes, grappling with the weight of the choices before her. She wanted to believe in the teachings of Asmodeus, to find solace in their structure, but the allure of the unknown was intoxicating. Nyx's call was a siren's song, echoing through the caverns of her soul, urging her to embrace the chaos that awaited her.

"Show me," she whispered, surrendering to the pull of the darkness, letting it wash over her like a tide.

And in that moment, as the shadows coiled around her, Eve felt a flicker of hope amidst the turmoil. The struggle within would not end tonight, but perhaps it would guide her toward the truth she sought - the truth that lay waiting in the depths of her very being.

Eve closed her eyes and let out a slow, shuddering breath. Her fingers trailed absently over the surface of stone along the wall as she walked, tracing spirals mingling with the soft crackle of distant torches. Each droplet of water that rolled from her hair down her body felt like a whisper, a silent plea for clarity, but clarity remained elusive, hidden in the depths of the darkness that swirled within her.

The marble pillars were carved with images of demons and angels locked in an eternal struggle, their expressions frozen in rage and agony. Eve's gaze moved from one figure to the next as she walked, searching for answers in their stony faces, but finding only echoes of the conflict raging inside her. The soft glow of lanterns flickered against the floor, casting a thousand tiny ripples of light, like stars trapped in a night sky that she could reach out and touch.

Eve's mind drifted to the teachings of Asmodeus, the countless hours she had spent in devotion, the blood spilled in his name, the prayers whispered into the darkness. They had always brought her comfort, a sense of purpose, a path to follow when all else seemed uncertain. The teachings felt distant, hollow - a relic of a life that no longer fit the person she was becoming.

"Show me," she whispered into the stillness, her voice barely audible over the gentle murmur of the acolytes in the distance, and the flames of the torches whispering through the shadows of the hallway. The words felt like a plea, a prayer not to Asmodeus but to something deeper, something that had been lurking within her for as long as she could remember. The darkness within responded, coiling and uncoiling like a serpent, its presence both comforting and terrifying. It spoke to her, not with words but with sensations - the rush of wind through her hair, the warmth of blood on her hands, the electric thrill of power pumping within her veins.

The air grew colder, and the shadows that had once danced along the walls now seemed to inch closer, their edges softening, blurring, until they no longer felt separate from her. Nyx's voice, that familiar, sultry whisper, echoed in her ears, wrapping around her like a velvet ribbon. "You've always known there is more, haven't you? That there is something beyond the words, beyond the rituals... something greater, something truer?"

Eve's heart raced, her pulse a steady drumbeat. "I wanted to believe," she admitted, her voice trembling. "I wanted to find peace in the teachings, to find comfort in the certainty they offered... but it feels like a lie."

A chuckle reverberated through the temple, low and rich, and Eve felt it in her bones, in the very core of her being. "It is a lie, my darling. All that they have taught you is a cage, gilded and adorned to make you feel safe. But what lies outside that cage? Freedom. Power. Truth."

The words sent a shiver down Eve's spine, and she felt herself leaning into them, her body relaxing against the embrace of the amber light.

"Show me," Eve repeated, and this time, her voice was stronger, filled with a determination she hadn't realized she possessed. She could feel the change, the shift deep within her, as if a door had opened, allowing the darkness to flood in. It wasn't the suffocating, terrifying darkness she had always feared - it was warm, inviting, a promise of something more.

She saw herself standing on a precipice, gazing out at a sea of stars that shimmered like diamonds against the velvet of the night. Nyx stood beside her, no longer a mere whisper, but a presence, palpable and real. She was cloaked in shadow, her form shifting and changing like smoke, but her eyes... her eyes were Eve's eyes, glowing with an inner light that felt like a reflection of everything Eve had ever longed to be.

"Do you see?" Nyx murmured, her hand reaching out to rest against Eve's chest, right over her heart. "This is who you are. Not a servant. Not a slave to dogma or doctrine. You are the darkness, the chaos, the force that cannot be tamed. You are the storm that brings the rain and the night that swallows the day."

Eve's breath hitched, and she felt tears prickling at the corners of her eyes. "But what if I'm not ready?" she whispered. "What if I lose myself?"

Nyx's smile was gentle, but there was an edge to it, sharp as a blade. "You've already lost yourself, child. You gave yourself away the moment you believed their lies, the moment you let them tell you who you were. Now, all I ask is that you take yourself back. That you become who you were always meant to be."

Eve felt her heart pounding, felt the surge of power rising within her, and she knew that there was no turning back. She reached up, took Nyx's hand in her own, and brought it to her lips, pressing a kiss against the cool, shadowy skin. "I'm ready," she whispered, her voice barely more than a breath. "I'm ready to be free."

The vision faded, and Eve found herself back in the hallway. But something had changed. The air felt lighter, the shadows less oppressive, and within her chest, she felt the flicker of something new - something fierce and unyielding. She was no longer just Eve, the priestess bound by chains of tradition. She was Nyx, the embodiment of chaos and night, and she would no longer be silenced. She felt the weight of her uncertainty slip away, left behind in the waters that had once held her captive. This was her path now, her journey to take, and she would walk it with the strength and power that had always been hers, waiting in the depths of her soul.

For the first time in her life, Eve felt whole.

12

Embracing the Abyss

The air in the temple was thick with the scent of incense, a heady mixture that curled around Eve like a lover's embrace, drawing her deeper into the ritual's hypnotic rhythm. Flickering flames illuminated the dark stone walls, casting shadows that danced like phantoms, and for the first time, Eve felt their chaotic energy resonate within her. She had often viewed darkness as something to be feared, a shroud that threatened to consume her, but now, with Nyx stirring restlessly in her core, it felt different - inviting, intoxicating.

As she stood before the altar, her heart raced with anticipation and trepidation. The usual chants of devotion filled the chamber, echoing off the obsidian pillars, but they felt hollow today. Eve closed her eyes and took a deep breath, focusing inward. "Let go," Nyx's voice whispered in the recesses of her mind, a sultry caress urging her to surrender. "Embrace me."

As Eve relinquished her hold on herself, the transformation began, rippling through her body like lightning arcing across a stormy sky. Her bones stretched and reshaped, lengthening her limbs until she towered, her frame expanding to a towering twelve feet. The air sparked with energy, and the temple's walls seemed to bend and warp around her, as if they, too, were bowing before the immense power that surged within her.

Her skin shifted, taking on the colors and patterns of an endless night sky, as if the very cosmos had merged with her flesh. Nebulas swirled across her body, vibrant purples, blues, and crimson hues dancing and shifting with every breath. Stars twinkled and flickered, pulsing with light that seemed to whisper the secrets of the universe. It was as if she had become a living tapestry of the cosmos, each movement stirring the celestial expanse that cloaked her.

In the center of her chest, a third eye slowly blinked open, glowing with a soft, radiant light. It moved as though sentient, scanning the chamber with an ancient wisdom, its gaze penetrating through the darkness, seeing into realms far beyond the material world. The eye exuded an aura of profound knowledge, its iris swirling with colors that defied comprehension, containing within it the mysteries of existence itself.

Two mighty horns curled outward from either side of her head, jet-black and gleaming in the dim firelight. They twisted elegantly, rising high above her head like the regal crown of a dark queen, ancient and fierce. Their smooth, polished surface reflected the flickering flames, casting ominous shadows that danced across the walls of the temple. They seemed to throb with energy, humming with the vibrations of the abyss, as if channeling the raw, chaotic power of the universe itself.

From her back, a pair of immense wings unfurled, their feathers blacker than the void, darker than the absence of light itself. They spread wide, covering nearly the entire expanse of the chamber, their tips brushing against the walls, sending tiny embers scattering in the air. These wings were not made of flesh and bone but of feather and shadow, constantly shifting and rippling, their edges blending seamlessly into the darkness that surrounded her. They moved with a grace that belied their size, and when they flapped, they didn't merely stir the air - they commanded it, bending the wind to her will.

Black smoke curled around her form, thick and ethereal, obscuring the details of her body and making her seem as if she were both there and not there, as if she existed somewhere between reality and a dream. The smoke swirled and coiled, concealing her movements, lending her an air of mystery and danger, as though she could vanish into the night at any moment. It drifted around her feet, coiling upward like tendrils, whispering forgotten secrets, as though it carried with it the voices of all who had ever walked in darkness.

Her eyes, now entirely black with pinpoints of light that shimmered like distant stars, stared forward with an intensity that could pierce through souls. They were deep, endless, an eternal abyss that held within them the promise of destruction and rebirth. When she blinked, it was as though a curtain of night was drawn and then lifted again, revealing glimpses of something ancient, something primordial that lay hidden within her depths.

Her fangs elongated, glimmering in the light of the flames that danced around her. Sharp and pointed, they protruded from her mouth, giving her a predatory, feral appearance. They caught the firelight, reflecting it with a dull, metallic sheen, as if forged from the darkest metals of Hell itself. Each time she opened her mouth, it was as though the darkness around her grew deeper, the shadows more pronounced, as if the very act of baring her fangs drew the light out of the room.

As Nyx stood there, fully transformed, she was a sight to behold - a being that was both terrifying and magnificent, a perfect blend of power, chaos, and beauty. She was Eve and yet so much more, an embodiment of the night, of all that lay hidden in the shadows. She did not merely wear the darkness; she **was** the darkness, a living, breathing force of nature that transcended the mundane boundaries of existence.

And as she raised her hand, the celestial patterns on her skin shifted, the stars moving in tandem, as though guided by her will. The third eye in her chest blinked, and a low hum resonated through the chamber, vibrating the very air around her. The temple itself seemed to shudder, the ancient stone walls quivering in response to her power, acknowledging the presence of something far greater than anything they had ever contained before.

The shadows at her feet grew darker, deeper, coalescing into a pool of ink that spread out across the floor, swallowing the light around her. And in that moment, Nyx stood as a queen, not of Hell, not of Heaven, but of the void that stretched between the stars - the infinite expanse where all things began and all things would one day return. She was the embodiment of night, a figure of myth and legend made flesh, and she was magnificent.

"Who are you to dictate the terms of existence?" she thundered, her voice layered with an echo that resonated throughout the chamber. "You cling to your binary beliefs while the true nature of reality lies in chaos, in freedom!"

The acolytes present faltered, exchanging uneasy glances. Malen, standing at the forefront, his expression a mix of confusion and fear, opened his mouth to speak but found no words. Rhea, ever the champion of tradition, stepped forward, defiance flashing in her eyes. "This isn't you, Eve! You've allowed the darkness to twist your mind. Asmodeus teaches us the balance of power, not this reckless abandon!"

Eve, channeling Nyx's essence, felt an exhilarating rush as she embraced the challenge. "What balance?" she retorted, her voice rich with authority. "You serve a system that binds you, that shackles you to a simplistic view of good and evil! The truth is more complex - it's about the will to power, the eternal struggle to shape one's own destiny!"

As her words spilled forth, Eve felt a current of change ripple through the crowd. The more she spoke, the more the followers began to lean in, captivated by her fervor. She pushed further, challenging the dogma they had all accepted without question, urging them to reconsider their positions and the nature of existence itself.

"Is it not possible," she continued, her tone now softer yet imbued with an undeniable strength, "that what you perceive as righteousness is merely a cage? What if true enlightenment comes not from submission to divine rule but from understanding the depths of our own desires, our own darkness?"

"Is it not possible," Nyx continued, her tone now softer yet imbued with an undeniable strength, "that what you perceive as righteousness is merely a cage? What if true enlightenment comes not from submission to divine rule but from understanding the depths of our own desires, our own darkness?" Her words lingered in the air, and her followers, who had grown accustomed to the rigid doctrines of Asmodeus, shifted uneasily. But Nyx pressed on, her eyes gleaming with a light that was equal parts compassion and ferocity.

"Desire is not our enemy," she declared, letting her voice carry the weight of her conviction. "Lust, passion, yearning - these are not mere distractions or sins to be purged, but the very forces that drive us forward. They are the currents that shape our paths, the winds that lift our wings. For too long, we have been taught that lust is a vice to be tamed, that to desire is to be weak. But I ask you - how can one claim power if they deny the very fire that burns within them?"

She stepped forward, her movements fluid, almost hypnotic, as she began to weave through the chamber, drawing her followers' eyes to her every motion. "When we deny our desires, we surrender our power to those who would seek to control us. They would have us believe that our lust, our hunger, our longing for more is something to be ashamed of, something to suppress. But this is a lie. A lie perpetuated to keep us docile, to keep us obedient."

She gestured toward a nearby statue of Asmodeus, a figure of dominance and authority, cast in stone. "Even the great Lord of the Second Circle," she continued, "demands obedience, demands that we bow to his will, that we offer ourselves to him without question. And yet, in his teachings, there is an undeniable truth: desire is power. But it is not power to be given away; it is power to be harnessed, nurtured, and allowed to bloom."

The air in the chamber seemed to thicken, charged with an electric energy, as Nyx's words began to sink in. She could see the flickers of understanding in the eyes of her followers, the first sparks of a fire that would consume the old ways and make way for something new. "To embrace lust," she continued, "is not to be enslaved by it. It is to recognize it as a force that moves us, that drives us to explore, to reach out, to create. Lust is not merely the act of seeking pleasure, but the embodiment of our will to power. It is the desire to connect, to consume, to be consumed in return. It is the yearning to break free from the shackles of what we've been told to be, to revel in the freedom of our own truth."

Nyx's gaze swept over the assembly, her eyes piercing through the shadows, as if daring each soul before her to confront their own fears and doubts. "Think on this," she urged, her voice now a whisper that resonated with the power of a storm. "What if our desires are not chains, but the keys to our liberation? What if, by embracing our lust, our longing, we strip away the illusions that bind us and see ourselves as we truly are?"

She paused, allowing the silence to stretch, to let her words take root in the minds of those who listened. "Lust, my children, is not just a physical act. It is a state of being. It is the hunger to know oneself, to experience life in all its forms, to taste every sensation, to feel every emotion without shame or hesitation. It is the will to break free from the chains of dogma and step into the unknown, unafraid and unbound. It is the courage to say, 'I want, I desire, and I will take what is mine.'"

A murmur rippled through the chamber, the sound of minds awakening, of hearts beating faster with a newfound sense of purpose. Nyx could feel the energy shifting, as if a veil had been lifted, revealing the truth that had been hidden for so long. "So, I ask you," she concluded, her voice echoing like a song, "Will you continue to let others dictate your desires? Or will you claim your power, your lust, your right to live as you see fit?"

In that moment, the chamber felt alive, pulsing with the heartbeat of every soul present. And Nyx, standing at its center, radiated a strength that was neither demonic nor divine, but something greater, something that transcended the binaries that had defined their existence for so long. She had planted the seed of a new way of thinking, one that embraced the chaos, the uncertainty, and the truth of desire. The path she offered was not easy, but it was real, raw, and dripping with the promise of freedom.

A murmur swept through the gathering, and Eve noticed a few heads nodding slowly, their convictions shaken. She felt the energy shift - a small, tentative seed of doubt beginning to take root in their minds. "Question everything," she urged, her voice resonating with the promise of liberation. "Only through embracing the abyss can we truly know ourselves."

As she descended from the altar, the temple began to feel less like a sanctuary of rigid doctrine and more like a crucible for transformation. Her heart soared with the realization that this journey was no longer solely hers; she was forging a path for others to follow, guiding them through the shadows and toward the light of understanding.

But with every moment of triumph came a lingering doubt. As she embraced Nyx's power, was she not also flirting with madness? The voice of Nyx grew louder, more insistent, urging her to dive deeper into the darkness. The internal struggle waged within her - a tension between Eve's lingering humanity and the primal chaos that Nyx represented.

Days turned into weeks as Eve continued to gather her followers, those few brave enough to question their beliefs. They met in secret, hidden from the prying eyes of the temple's more devout members. Under the veil of darkness, they explored Nietzschean ideas, dissecting the concepts of the Übermensch, the will to power, and the rejection of pity, urging one another to embrace their true desires without fear.

Eve became a beacon of hope for those disillusioned by the temple's rigid teachings. She encouraged them to find strength in their individuality, to reject the idea that power was something to be imposed upon others. Instead, they should cultivate it from within, understanding that their existence was a tapestry woven from both light and shadow.

One evening, as they gathered in a secluded alcove of the temple, Eve spoke of the nature of suffering, a recurring theme in their discussions. Eve's gaze swept over her followers, and she continued, her tone deepening with conviction. "Suffering is not an enemy," she proclaimed, allowing the words to linger, "but a teacher, an essential crucible in which we are forged. Nietzsche spoke of the idea that to live is to suffer, and to survive is to find meaning in that suffering. It is not something to be feared or avoided, but rather embraced as the path to our true selves. Through suffering, we shed the illusions we've been taught – the comforts, the lies, the beliefs that have kept us shackled."

She paused, letting her followers absorb her words before continuing. "In suffering, we confront the raw reality of our existence, stripped of all pretense. It forces us to face the darkest corners of our souls, the parts we wish to hide, and in doing so, it offers us a chance to transform. It is only through this confrontation, this unflinching gaze into our own abyss, that we can begin to understand who we truly are. This is the 'will to power' – the ability to look upon our suffering not as victims but as creators, to take what has broken us and shape it into something stronger."

Eve's eyes narrowed, her voice gaining a fervent edge. "Most flee from suffering because it challenges the very foundation of who they believe they are. It shatters the illusions of comfort, of certainty, of righteousness, and lays bare the chaos beneath. But that chaos is not our enemy – it is the source of our power. It is through suffering that we gain the courage to question, to doubt, to break free from the chains of servitude and to redefine ourselves. It is the crucible in which our spirit is tested, where we confront the limits of our endurance, our beliefs, and our desires."

She gestured toward the darkness that filled the alcove, a living, breathing reminder of the unknown. "This path is not easy," she said, her tone now softer, almost tender. "To embrace suffering is to acknowledge that life is not a series of comforts or guarantees but an endless struggle, an eternal recurrence of challenges. And yet, it is through this struggle that we find the strength to rise, to overcome, and to become something more than we ever imagined. In the depths of our pain, we discover the fire that burns within us, a fire that cannot be extinguished."

Her gaze hardened, eyes gleaming with an inner light. "So do not run from your suffering. Face it. Embrace it. Allow it to break you, for only then can you rebuild yourself, stronger, wiser, and free from the lies that have held you captive. This is how we rise above the mundane, how we transcend the boundaries imposed upon us. This is how we become more than human, more than demon – this is how we become gods in our own right."

Eve leaned forward, her voice a fervent whisper that hung in the air like a spell. "By conquering this suffering, by mastering it rather than allowing it to master you, you will not only survive - you will ascend. You will transcend your current existence, breaking through the limitations of your past and emerging as something greater. This journey of self-overcoming is the path to true ascension. When you rise above your pain, you gain the insight and strength needed to claim your own destiny. You become the architect of your fate, the ruler of your existence."

As she spoke, her followers felt the weight of her words, a resonance within their very souls. They understood that this ascent was not merely a goal but a profound transformation, an evolution that would elevate them beyond the confines of their previous lives. In facing their suffering, they would not only find their truth but also unlock the potential for greatness that lay dormant within them. And in that moment, they grasped the power of Eve's teachings - the promise that from the ashes of suffering, they could rise, reborn and empowered, into a new existence that they would define on their own terms.

The group listened intently, their faces illuminated by the soft glow of candlelight. As she shared her insights, Eve could see the transformation taking place within them - eyes that once reflected doubt now glimmered with the light of newfound understanding. They were no longer simply followers; they were becoming thinkers, questioners, and seekers of truth.

But even as the seeds of change began to take root, Eve couldn't shake the feeling that the storm was only just beginning. The temple was not a sanctuary for open thought but a bastion of dogma that would not take kindly to dissent. As she delved deeper into her role as a teacher, she felt Nyx's presence looming ever closer, a constant reminder of the darkness that awaited her should she lose her way.

One night, after a particularly intense gathering, Eve found herself standing alone before the altar, feeling the weight of her decisions pressing down on her like a heavy shroud. The air seemed alive with energy, crackling with the remnants of the fervent discussions and the passionate declarations made by her followers. Shadows flickered in the candlelight, elongating and twisting in the corners of the chamber, and she sensed Nyx watching her, a silent presence just beyond her awareness, waiting for the moment she would fully surrender to the darkness within.

Eve's heart raced, a blend of anticipation and trepidation swirling in her chest. She took a deep breath, allowing the intoxicating scent of incense to fill her lungs. "Am I ready for this?" she whispered into the stillness, her voice trembling slightly, the uncertainty hanging in the air like a fragile thread. "Can I truly embrace the abyss without losing myself?"

As she stood before the altar, memories flooded her mind - moments of doubt, of fear, and of the struggle to define her identity amidst the chaos. She thought of the countless rituals she had performed, the teachings she had adhered to, the dogmas that once provided her solace but now felt suffocating. With each passing day, the tug of Nyx grew stronger, a siren's call beckoning her to step into the shadows where true power lay.

Nyx's voice resonated in her mind, seductive and compelling, like a melody that wrapped around her consciousness. "You are already lost, Eve. Embrace it, and you will find your true self waiting in the shadows." The words echoed within her, reverberating off the walls of her soul, as if inviting her to unravel the layers she had painstakingly built.

Eve closed her eyes, surrendering to the feelings that coursed through her. The uncertainty, the fear, the exhilaration - they were all part of the journey, and she could feel the stirrings of a deeper truth beneath the surface. "What if I am more than what I have been taught?" she mused aloud, allowing the question to linger in the stillness of the chamber. "What if the abyss is not something to be feared, but a source of strength?"

The darkness around her seemed to pulse with life, responding to her thoughts, wrapping her in its embrace. Images danced behind her eyelids - visions of the cosmos, the swirling chaos of creation and destruction, the interplay of light and shadow. She saw herself as a part of this vast tapestry, a thread woven into the fabric of existence, and the idea ignited something deep within her.

"What if," she pondered, "the path to power lies in surrendering to the chaos instead of fighting against it? What if true enlightenment comes from understanding and embracing my desires, my darkness?"

The altar shimmered in the flickering light, reflecting her inner turmoil and the potential for transformation. "Eve, your journey has only just begun," Nyx whispered, her voice like silk, weaving through the shadows of Eve's mind. "You have the power to reshape your reality, to transcend the limitations imposed upon you. But first, you must step into the abyss."

Eve took a tentative step forward, drawn to the altar, the sacred space where the past and future converged. As she approached, the air thickened with anticipation, and she could feel the weight of countless eyes - her followers, her ancestors, the very essence of existence itself - watching, waiting for her next move. "What lies beyond the veil?" she whispered, her voice barely above a breath. "What truths await me in the darkness?"

With each word, she felt her resolve strengthening, the fear ebbing away like the tide. Nyx was not merely a shadow lurking within her; she was a part of Eve, an integral piece of the puzzle that would allow her to transcend her former self. It was not about losing her identity, but about embracing the entirety of who she was - the light and the dark, the warrior and the philosopher.

"I am ready," Eve declared, the tremor in her voice replaced by a newfound confidence. "I will embrace the abyss, for in its depths, I shall find my truth."

As the words left her lips, she felt a surge of energy coursing through her, a fiery current igniting the very essence of her being.

The shadows around her danced and twisted, forming an intricate pattern that enveloped her in a cocoon of darkness, illuminating the path ahead. In that moment of surrender, Eve understood: the abyss was not the end but the beginning of a journey toward self-discovery, a chance to forge a new identity rooted in authenticity and strength.

With Nyx by her side, Eve was ready to step into the unknown, to embrace the chaos and emerge reborn, a true embodiment of the power she had sought all along.

With her heart pounding, Eve closed her eyes and took a deep breath, preparing to plunge into the depths of her own darkness. She had ignited the flame of change within the temple, but the path ahead was fraught with uncertainty. Would she be able to guide her followers through the chaos, or would the darkness consume them all?

In that moment of stillness, she felt the answer lie in her hands, ready to be grasped - the power to reshape not only her destiny but the very foundation of the temple itself. The abyss was calling, and she was ready to answer.

13

Confronting Fanaticism

The air in the temple had thickened with tension, a palpable energy that crackled like static before a storm. A council meeting was underway, with several of the high-ranking members gathered around the ornate table, their faces illuminated by the flickering light of torches. Outside, the distant rumble of conflict echoed, a reminder that the angelic invasion was not just a whisper on the wind but a roaring tempest that threatened to engulf them all.

Eve sat at the table, her heart heavy with unease as she watched the leaders rally around a singular narrative - a black-and-white portrayal of the conflict that left no room for nuance. Malen and Rhea were at the forefront, their eyes gleaming with fervor as they painted the angels as harbingers of pure evil, determined to destroy everything they held dear. The more they spoke, the more the room vibrated with their righteous zeal, and Eve felt the oppressive weight of their fanaticism closing in around her.

"Victory requires unwavering resolve," Rhea proclaimed, her voice slicing through the murmur of agreement. "We cannot falter in our conviction. The angels are a blight, and we must cleanse our realm of their presence!"

Eve's brow furrowed as she listened, her thoughts swirling like a tempest. She had witnessed firsthand the complexities of the conflict, the way both sides were prisoners of their own desires for power. It was not about good versus evil; it was a brutal struggle for dominance. But as she opened her mouth to voice her dissent, she felt a deep hesitation. The room was already charged with hostility, and she knew that challenging the traditionalists would only heighten the tension.

"Eve?" Malen's voice broke through her reverie, concern etched across his features. "Do you not agree? This is a battle for our very existence!"

Gathering her courage, Eve straightened in her seat, her heart pounding. "Malen, I do not deny the threat the angels pose, but to reduce this conflict to a simplistic narrative is to ignore the deeper truths at play. This war is not merely about good versus evil; it's about power - who wields it, who controls it, and who is willing to do anything to seize it."

A hush fell over the room, and she could feel the weight of their gazes upon her. Rhea's expression hardened, disbelief mingling with disdain. "You would suggest we empathize with our enemies? That we consider their motives?"

"Not empathy," Eve replied, her voice steady despite the mounting tension. "Understanding. To see them as more than just adversaries is to grasp the full scope of this conflict. We risk becoming like them - blind to our own desires and ambitions. Power corrupts, whether it comes from Heaven or Hell."

Her words hung in the air, thick with challenge. The council members shifted uneasily, their conviction faltering as they contemplated her perspective. Yet Rhea's face flushed with anger, and she leaned forward, her tone sharp. "You've been influenced by Nyx's madness, Eve. This isn't about philosophical musings; it's about survival! You're risking everything with your doubts!"

The accusation stung, and Eve felt the fire of Nyx stirring within her, whispering promises of liberation and strength. She took a deep breath, the taste of the confrontation igniting something primal inside her. "And what of the sacrifices we make in the name of our so-called righteousness? We must be vigilant against the very dogma we seek to uphold. To call ourselves righteous while engaging in violence and hatred is hypocrisy!"

Rhea's eyes narrowed, her jaw tightening. "Hypocrisy? You stand here questioning our resolve, speaking of nuance and understanding while our enemies slaughter our people. What would you have us do? Surrender? Sit down with them and discuss our differences?"

Eve shook her head, her frustration building. "No, Rhea. I'm not suggesting passivity. I'm suggesting clarity - an understanding that this endless cycle of dominance and submission, this fixation on winning at all costs, is a trap. It binds us to the same mentality as those we claim to oppose. Nietzsche spoke of the will to power, but not as a tool of oppression. It's about self-overcoming, not subjugation. If we only fight to dominate, to crush and control, we become slaves to the very power we seek to master."

Malen, who had been silent until now, leaned forward, his brow furrowed. "And what do you propose then, Eve? How do we fight a war like this without the resolve to win?"

Eve met his gaze, her voice softening but still firm. "It's not about losing resolve. It's about rejecting the simplistic notion that power is only about domination. Look at the angels. They believe they are justified in their actions, that their light must consume the darkness. In their eyes, we are the blight. But if we mirror their tactics, we're just repeating the same mistakes, enslaved by their definition of strength. True power, the kind that lasts, comes from balance - from understanding the chaos within and around us. It means embracing the complexity of existence, rather than reducing everything to good and evil."

"You speak in riddles," Rhea spat. "How can balance exist in war? Either we win, or we die."

Eve's frustration deepened, but she remained composed. "Balance isn't weakness. It's strength, the kind that comes from knowing when to strike and when to reflect. It's the ability to wield power without being consumed by it. We've seen what happens when those in power lose sight of this. The angels claim to bring order, but they enforce their will with a tyranny of light. If we fall into the same trap

- thinking that our way is the only way - we become no better than they are."

Her words were met with silence, the council members exchanging uneasy glances. Eve could see that some of them were listening, though doubt lingered in their eyes. The allure of simplistic narratives was strong, especially in times of war. But she had to push forward, to challenge the very foundations of their beliefs.

"We fight not just for our survival," she continued, her voice gaining strength. "We fight for what comes after. If we win by becoming what we despise, what have we truly gained? A pyrrhic victory? No. We must fight with the understanding that power doesn't have to be a zero-sum game. It's not about total domination or absolute submission. Power, real power, comes from knowing yourself, embracing your own chaos, and transcending it."

Rhea scoffed, but there was an edge of uncertainty in her voice. "And how do you propose we transcend chaos in the middle of battle?"

Eve smiled faintly, her eyes glowing with the flicker of Nyx's presence. "By acknowledging that chaos is part of the natural order. It is not something to be feared or suppressed. It is something to be harnessed, to be understood. Nietzsche spoke of the Übermensch, the one who creates their own values, who transcends the constraints of conventional morality. We must become that. Not slaves to dogma, whether it's celestial or infernal, but beings who forge our own path - who seek power not to dominate others, but to rise above our own limitations."

The tension in the room was palpable, and for a moment, Eve wondered if her words would fall on deaf ears. But then, slowly, Malen nodded, his expression thoughtful. "You're saying that we need to fight with purpose, not just for the sake of victory, but for something greater."

"Yes," Eve replied, a flicker of hope igniting in her chest. "We must fight to build something beyond this conflict. If we win by becoming monsters, then we have already lost. But if we fight with clarity, with the understanding that power is more than domination, we can create a future where we are not bound by these endless cycles of violence."

A murmur of agreement rippled through the room, though it was tentative. Rhea remained stiff, her arms crossed, but the fire in her eyes had dimmed slightly. "You ask us to walk a dangerous line, Eve. To question our own beliefs in the heat of battle. That's no easy thing."

Eve nodded, her gaze steady. "I know it's not easy. But the path to true power never is. We must be willing to confront our own darkness, to question the very foundations of our beliefs if we are to transcend them. This is not a battle for dominance - it's a battle for our souls. And if we lose sight of that, we will be no better than the angels who seek to impose their will upon us."

Silence fell once more, but this time it was not hostile. The council members were deep in thought, wrestling with the implications of Eve's words. Slowly, the rigid lines of dogma began to blur, and a new understanding began to take root.

Eve's heart swelled with a quiet sense of triumph, though she knew the battle for minds and hearts was far from over. For a fleeting moment, she glimpsed a possible path forward - one that transcended the simplistic dualities of dominance and submission, one that embraced Nietzsche's ideal of self-overcoming, where they could forge their own destiny amidst the swirling chaos.

And in that path, she sensed the promise of true freedom.

But the illusion of progress was short-lived. As the council continued to debate, tension resurfaced, and soon the room descended into chaos. Voices rose in a cacophony of anger and fear, each trying to shout down the others. The more Eve's words took root in some, the more they seemed to provoke outright hostility in others.

"Enough!" Malen shouted, his voice straining to cut through the uproar. "We must find common ground! We're fighting for the same cause!"

Yet Eve saw the truth - her words had only deepened the fault lines between her and the traditionalists. What began as a spirited discussion had evolved into a volatile clash, where the fear of change drove them back into the safety of their dogmas. Her voice had become a threat, an unsettling force that challenged the established order.

As she stood there, alone amid a rising tide of fanaticism, she felt the weight of their disdain pressing against her, trying to drown out her resolve. In that moment, Eve realized that her fight wasn't just against the celestial invaders - it was against the very mindset that refused to question itself, even in the face of its own destruction.

Just then, the ground beneath them trembled, a violent jolt that sent the council members stumbling. Dust and shards of stone fell from the temple ceiling, and the sound of battle erupted outside, like a storm breaking over the land. The clash of steel and the cries of both angels and demons echoed through the sacred halls, sending ripples of panic surging through the chamber as realization dawned - an attack was imminent.

"Prepare yourselves!" Lord Vesperion bellowed, scrambling to his feet, his obsidian eyes flashing with fury. His once-regal demeanor had been replaced by something primal, and he unsheathed a blade that seemed to hum with an energy as dark as midnight. "We must defend the temple! To arms!"

Eve's heart pounded like a drum in her ears, her senses overwhelmed by the chaos unfurling around her. The air grew thick with fear and uncertainty, and she felt the undeniable pull of Nyx's power within her, the darkness surging like a tide ready to break free from its chains. In that moment, everything seemed to slow, the din of battle fading to a distant hum as Eve closed her eyes and took a deep breath. She could feel Nyx whispering to her, the Titan's voice echoing within the depths of her soul.

"Why do you hesitate?" Nyx's voice was velvet and shadow, a caress that sent shivers down Eve's spine. "You know what must be done. Embrace me. Embrace the darkness, and I will show you the power that lies beyond your fear."

Eve felt her resolve solidify, her doubt melting away like snow under a summer sun. "Yes," she whispered, her voice barely audible amidst the tumult. "I will not be afraid." And with that, she surrendered, allowing the Titan to take control.

The transformation was both exhilarating and terrifying. Eve felt herself merging with the primordial force that was Nyx, her body dissolving and reforming as shadows poured from her skin like ink. Her senses exploded with intensity, and she opened her eyes to a world bathed in colors more vibrant, sounds more profound, and energies that crackled like lightning in the air. Every inch of her was alive, and she could feel the very pulse of the universe thrumming beneath her feet.

To the others in the room, Eve's form shifted and grew, taking on an ethereal, almost otherworldly quality. Her eyes, once a deep black, now burned with the light of a thousand stars, and her hair billowed around her like a living night sky, flecked with shimmering constellations. Darkness coiled around her limbs, tendrils of shadow that seemed to whisper and writhe, hungry for release.

In that moment of transformation, the temple around her was no longer a place of rigid beliefs; it became a battlefield - a living entity that demanded action. The air was thick with the scent of incense and blood, the flickering torchlight casting long, ominous shadows against the walls.

"Look at her!" one of the acolytes gasped, stepping back in fear. "What has she become?"

"She is Nyx!" another shouted, awe and terror mingling in their voice. "She has become the Titan herself!"

Eve surged forward, her movements fluid and predatory, each step resonating with the power of a goddess unbound. As she reached the main hall, a sight met her that made her blood boil - the angels, resplendent in their golden armor, descended upon the temple like a swarm of locusts. Their wings, radiant and blinding, cast the room into sharp relief, turning the shadows into mere slivers.

With their gleaming swords and ethereal light, they seemed invincible, a force of purity determined to cleanse the temple of its darkness. Yet, to Eve, they were invaders - self-righteous creatures who sought to impose their narrow vision of order upon a world that defied such simplicity.

The air was thick with the metallic scent of blood and the acrid stench of sulfur as the temple's defenders clashed with the radiant forces of the celestial host. Demons, mortals, and otherworldly beings of all kinds fought side by side, their roars mingling with the war cries of the angels. The sky above flickered with bursts of light and shadow, as if the heavens themselves were tearing apart from the intensity of the battle. Yet, even in the face of such chaos, the defenders held their ground, refusing to yield.

A towering demon with crimson skin and eyes like molten lava led the charge, wielding a massive, serrated greatsword that shimmered with infernal energy. His horns curled back like a ram's, and his wings were tattered, but he moved with a grace that belied his size. He swung his blade with bone-crushing force, cleaving through the shimmering armor of an angel, whose body exploded into a spray of golden light upon contact. Another angel swooped in with blinding speed, its spear thrusting forward with deadly precision, but the demon parried the strike, his muscles straining as he twisted the spear out of the angel's hands and drove his own weapon deep into its chest.

Yet even as the angel disintegrated, another took its place, and another, until the demon was forced to his knees, blood pouring from countless wounds. He roared defiantly, flames erupting from his mouth as he spat curses in an ancient tongue, refusing to submit even as the angels closed in around him. He swung his blade one last time, defiant to the end, before a flash of light consumed him, leaving nothing but ashes in his wake.

Nearby, a demoness with serpentine scales and glowing, violet eyes moved with the fluidity of a shadow, her twin daggers flashing as she darted through the ranks of the celestial host. Her movements were hypnotic, almost like a dance, as she struck with surgical precision. She severed wings with a flick of her wrist, sliced through tendons, and plunged her blades into the soft, unprotected flesh of her foes. An angel lunged at her from behind, its blade aimed for her heart, but she twisted out of the way, catching its wrist with one hand and driving her dagger into its throat with the other. The angel fell to the ground, clutching at its wound, but before it could disintegrate, she had already moved on to the next target.

Despite her skill, the sheer number of enemies began to overwhelm her. She parried blow after blow, her breath coming in ragged gasps, her scales slick with her own blood. She spun around to face a pair of angels who advanced on her, their eyes glowing with righteous fury, and prepared to make her last stand when a bolt of crimson lightning struck them down, turning them to smoldering ash. She looked up to see a fellow demon, a lithe, horned figure wreathed in crackling energy, give her a brief nod before hurling himself back into the fray.

High above the ground, a winged demon with the form of a great black crow fought against an angel wielding a sword of pure light. The two figures danced in the air, their movements blurring with speed. The crow-demon's talons scraped against the angel's armor, sending sparks flying, but each time he tried to land a killing blow, the angel's sword flickered into place, forcing him back. They clashed again and again, their forms silhouetted against the lightning-streaked sky, until the crow-demon unleashed a deafening caw and raked his talons across the angel's face, tearing it apart in a spray of golden ichor.

However, even as the defenders fought with every ounce of strength they possessed, they could not hold back the relentless tide of celestial warriors. For every angel that fell, three more took its place, and the once-mighty line of defenders began to waver. A massive, horned beast with skin like volcanic rock tried to rally the troops, his voice booming like thunder as he swung a spiked mace in great arcs, sending angels flying with each strike. But even his mighty form was slowly worn down, pierced by countless arrows of light until he, too, fell to his knees.

Amidst the chaos, a mortal warrior clad in dark armor held his ground, a testament to the power of sheer will. His eyes glowed with an infernal light as he swung his sword, cutting down angels with every strike, his face twisted in a grimace of pain and determination. Beside him, a young acolyte with trembling hands tried to conjure spells of protection, her voice cracking as she recited incantations learned from the temple's ancient tomes. A blast of angelic energy struck her, sending her sprawling to the ground, and she looked up just in time to see the mortal warrior standing over her, his shield raised to block a killing blow.

"We won't fall!" he roared, his voice carrying over the din of battle. "We are the children of the abyss, and we will not yield to the light!"

But despite their courage, despite their unyielding defiance, the defenders were pushed back, step by agonizing step. The angels advanced, their eyes burning with the light of the divine, their weapons singing with the power of righteousness. And still, the defenders fought, knowing that even if they were to fall this day, they would do so with the fires of defiance burning brightly in their hearts.

Eve's heart swelled with fury, a fire kindled by the sight of her fellow acolytes being cut down, their cries mingling with the clamor of steel against steel. "Enough!" she roared, her voice echoing through the chamber like a thunderclap. As the word left her lips, tendrils of darkness exploded from her body, spreading outward in a wave of pure chaos. The air around her vibrated with energy, and with a mere gesture, she sent the shadows crashing into the advancing angels.

The force was immense, like a tidal wave of midnight crashing against a cliff. The angels staggered, their radiant forms flickering as they struggled to maintain their footing. Some were sent sprawling, their golden armor dented and scorched by the shadowy tendrils that lashed at them like whips.

Eve moved through the fray like a tempest, striking with a precision and power that was beyond human comprehension. Her fists crackled with black lightning, and with each strike, she sent waves of dark energy ripping through the air, cutting down any angel foolish enough to stand in her way.

"You will not take this temple!" she shouted, her voice resounding with the strength of Nyx's power. "You will not impose your false light upon us!"

The clash of ideologies manifested in that moment as Eve, or rather, Nyx, faced the angelic leader head-on. The temple grounds shook under the weight of their power, and the very air seemed to ripple with anticipation, charged with the energies of light and shadow locked in eternal conflict. As Eve moved, her form blurred, flickering between the priestess and the towering titan that lay within. Her body became a silhouette of galaxies and constellations, a living nebula shifting and swirling with each step she took. The ground beneath her cracked, giving way to tendrils of darkness that writhed and snapped, eager to meet the angel in battle.

The angel's eyes narrowed, his golden wings unfurling with a brilliant intensity. "You may have deceived these lost souls," he spat, his voice echoing like thunder, "but you cannot deceive me. I see the corruption within you."

"Corruption?" Eve's voice was calm, almost mocking, as she took a step forward. "You speak of corruption as if you understand it. But tell me, is it corruption to seek one's truth, to embrace one's darkness rather than flee from it?"

The angel responded not with words but with a blinding slash of his radiant blade. The light surged forward, a wave of searing heat that incinerated everything in its path, turning stone to ash and shadows to dust. But Eve did not flinch. Instead, she raised her hand, and the darkness obeyed her command, forming a barrier that swallowed the light, devouring it as if it were nothing more than a dying ember.

"Is that all?" she taunted, eyes glimmering with a dangerous light.

In response, the angel roared, charging forward with a speed that defied comprehension. He moved like a comet streaking through the heavens, a blur of molten gold and righteous fury. His blade struck again and again, each blow a symphony of light, and each time Eve parried with tendrils of shadow, meeting his strikes with effortless grace. The sound of their collision was deafening, a thunderclap that reverberated through the temple walls, shaking loose centuries-old dust and sending fragments of stone tumbling to the ground.

The followers below watched in stunned silence, eyes wide with disbelief. Never had they seen such power, such raw, unrestrained force. Some fell to their knees, whispering prayers to Asmodeus, while others clenched their fists, feeling a spark of defiance take root within them. It was as if, in witnessing this battle, they too were awakening to the truth that Eve had long embraced: that power was not something bestowed but something seized.

With a snarl, the angel swung his blade in a wide arc, aiming to cleave Eve in two. But before he could complete the motion, she vanished, dissolving into a cloud of shadows that swirled around him like a tempest. For a heartbeat, the angel stood there, disoriented, his eyes darting from one side to the other as he tried to locate his foe.

"Up here," came Eve's voice, echoing from above.

He barely had time to react before she descended upon him, her form solidifying in mid-air as she drove her fist into his face. The impact sent him crashing into the ground, creating a crater that splintered the floor beneath him. Eve landed gracefully, her feet touching the ground with barely a sound, and she stood over him, her eyes gleaming with a mixture of pity and disdain.

"Is this your light?" she whispered. "Is this all it amounts to - violence and judgment?"

The angel snarled, blood staining his perfect features. "You... you are nothing but a shadow. A twisted reflection of what you could have been."

"And you are a slave to your own light," Eve retorted, her voice growing colder, more distant. "But even shadows can teach us something, if we are willing to learn."

The angel roared, springing to his feet with renewed fury, but before he could strike, Eve raised her hand. Instantly, the shadows around him coiled like serpents, wrapping around his arms, his legs, binding him in place. He struggled, his wings beating furiously against the restraints, but the more he fought, the tighter they grew.

"Look at them," Eve said, gesturing to the gathered followers. "Look at what they've become. Not because they were forced, but because they chose to stand against you. Against everything you represent."

As if on cue, the defenders of the temple began to rally, inspired by Eve's defiance. Where before they had fought with uncertainty, they now moved with purpose, their strikes fueled by a newfound conviction. They pushed back against the angelic forces with a ferocity that took their enemies by surprise, and for the first time, the tide of battle seemed to shift.

"Is this what you fear?" Eve whispered, leaning closer to the angel. "Not the darkness, but the possibility that they might find strength without your light?"

The angel glared up at her, and for a moment, something flickered in his eyes - doubt, uncertainty, fear. "You... you will never win," he spat, though his voice had lost some of its earlier conviction.

"I don't need to win," Eve replied, her voice softer now, almost gentle. "I just need to show them that they don't have to live in chains."

With that, she released him, the shadows retreating at her command. The angel staggered to his feet, and for a moment, it seemed as though he might attack again. But then he looked into Eve's eyes - eyes that blazed with a light of their own, a light that came not from without, but from within - and he hesitated.

"You are free to leave," she said quietly. "Take your armies and go. Return to your masters and tell them what you've seen here. Tell them that we are not afraid."

For a long, tense moment, the angel stood there, his sword still raised. Then, with a shuddering breath, he lowered it, his wings drooping in defeat. Without a word, he turned and began to retreat, his forces following him, their faces etched with disbelief and shame.

As they vanished into the distance, the defenders of the temple erupted into cheers, their voices ringing out with a triumphant cry that echoed through the night. "For Nyx! For freedom!"

Eve stood in the center of it all, her chest heaving with the effort of the battle, her heart pounding with exhilaration. She had won, but more than that, she had proven something - not just to the angels, but to herself.

In that moment, as the shadows coiled around her like a protective cloak, she felt a profound sense of peace wash over her. This was her path, her truth, and she would walk it with pride, no matter where it led.

"You have shown them," Nyx's voice murmured in her mind, softer now, almost affectionate. "You have shown them what it means to be free."

Eve nodded, a faint smile playing on her lips. "And now," she whispered, "we will show them how to live."

And as Eve stood amidst the chaos, her body a vessel for Nyx's power, she knew one thing with absolute certainty - this was just the beginning. The path to understanding and acceptance was fraught with peril, but she would not falter. Together, they would confront the fanaticism that threatened to consume them all, and they would emerge from the darkness stronger, wiser, and unbroken.

14

Communing with the Cosmos

Eve felt the transformation into Nyx becoming more instinctual, a natural response to the chaotic energies swirling around her. Each time she surrendered to the Titan's essence, she was pulled deeper into a realm that transcended the limitations of her existence in the temple. The boundaries of Hell and Heaven blurred, replaced by visions that unfurled like cosmic tapestries, revealing truths that challenged everything she had known.

One evening, as she closed her eyes in a quiet corner of the temple, the familiar sensation of being drawn into the depths of the cosmos enveloped her. Stars twinkled like distant memories, each flickering light whispering secrets of the universe. She felt herself drifting, unbound by the confines of her fallen angel form, and suddenly she was floating in a vast expanse, surrounded by swirling galaxies and pulsating energy. Here, the rigid notions of right and wrong dissolved into a spectrum of existence that was both terrifying and exhilarating.

In this ethereal realm, Nyx's voice resonated within her, a soothing echo that intertwined with the cosmic hum. "Embrace the chaos, Eve. The universe is not defined by simplistic binaries. Look beyond the illusions of morality and power."

Images flooded her mind: celestial beings dancing on the edge of black holes, the birth of stars igniting in brilliant colors, the slow decay of cosmic dust becoming the cradle for new worlds. She understood now that existence itself was a cycle of creation and destruction, a dance of forces that constantly transformed and evolved. Each moment held the potential for change, for rebirth, and for liberation from oppressive constraints.

As Eve surrendered to the pull of the vision, she felt herself drifting deeper into the cosmos, her very essence untethered, merging with the infinite expanse. The darkness surrounding her was not empty but teeming with life, a tapestry woven from the threads of time, space, and energy. She felt every atom, every particle vibrate with purpose, an orchestra of existence playing a melody only she could hear. And in that melody, Nyx's voice intertwined, guiding her to witness the truths that lay beyond mortal comprehension.

"Look closely," Nyx urged, her voice as vast as the space around them, "and see what they fear to understand."

Eve's vision sharpened, and before her stretched the birth of a star. It began as a small, trembling spark within the void, swirling with gases and particles drawn together by an unseen force. As the elements collided, their friction ignited into a radiant flame, burning brighter and brighter until it erupted into an explosion of light, painting the darkness with hues of violet, crimson, and gold. The heat was immense, yet Eve felt only warmth, a gentle reminder that even in the coldest reaches of the cosmos, life could spring forth from the ashes.

She watched as this newborn star breathed its first light into the universe, casting its glow upon the remnants of ancient, dead stars that had once ruled this space. It struck her then - the universe was not a linear path from beginning to end but an endless cycle where destruction begets creation, where death becomes the soil from which life emerges. "Creation and destruction," she murmured, feeling the truth resonate in her soul, "two sides of the same coin."

"Indeed," Nyx whispered, her tone carrying a sense of reverence, "creation is not possible without destruction, just as light cannot exist without darkness. They are eternally bound to one another, a cosmic dance that defines the universe itself."

As if responding to this insight, Eve's vision shifted again, plunging her into the heart of a black hole. The darkness swallowed everything around it, bending light and space, warping time until all that remained was an infinite void. But as she floated in this abyss, Eve felt no fear. Instead, she was overcome with awe, for within this black hole, she sensed a powerful, pulsating energy - a heartbeat that thrummed with the potential of a thousand universes. This was not an end but a beginning, a singularity from which countless possibilities would emerge.

Eve watched in wonder as, within this cradle of darkness, new stars began to form, their light piercing through the shadows, their existence defying the very emptiness that had consumed them. It was then that she understood: even in the depths of despair, there was hope, a spark that refused to be extinguished. This was the cycle of life, an eternal recurrence, a relentless surge toward becoming.

Nyx's voice echoed once more, her tone tinged with pride. "You see, Eve, power is not simply the ability to dominate or control - it is the capacity to transform, to evolve, to embrace both light and darkness as integral parts of oneself."

Eve's vision continued to expand, and she now found herself drifting past entire galaxies, each one a swirling storm of stars, planets, and cosmic dust. She saw celestial beings - great winged entities of light - dancing in the void, their movements graceful and deliberate, weaving patterns that spanned the universe. Their bodies shimmered with an iridescent glow, and as they moved, they created ripples in space, like stones cast into an infinite pond. These beings sang a haunting melody, a song that resonated with the very essence of creation, and for a moment, Eve felt herself drawn into their dance, her soul soaring alongside them.

Yet, as she drew closer, she saw something unexpected: shadows trailing behind these beings, tethered to their every step. The shadows writhed and twisted, reflecting the beings' every movement, an inseparable part of their radiant forms. "What are they?" Eve whispered, her heart aching with a strange sense of familiarity.

"They are the embodiment of duality," Nyx explained. "The celestial beings that claim to be pure light cannot escape their own darkness. It follows them, shadows cast by the very brilliance they so desperately wish to embody. It is a reminder that to exist is to possess both light and darkness, strength and vulnerability, power and fear."

Suddenly, Eve's vision shifted again, and she found herself on the edge of a dying world. The sky burned with crimson fire, and the ground trembled as volcanic eruptions spewed molten rock into the air. As mountains crumbled and seas boiled, Eve saw a solitary figure standing amidst the chaos - a giant, clad in obsidian armor, his eyes glowing with a fierce, unyielding light. With each step he took, the ground cracked, and yet he walked forward with purpose, undeterred by the destruction that surrounded him.

Eve felt her pulse quicken. "Who is he?"

Nyx's voice softened, tinged with sadness. "He is the Titan of Ruin, a force of nature, and yet, like all beings, he, too, possesses a will to endure. He walks through the flames, not to conquer but to understand, to witness the end so that he may grasp the beginning. His power lies not in his ability to destroy, but in his acceptance of the cycle, of his willingness to face the inevitable and continue onward."

As Eve watched, the Titan reached the heart of the destruction, and in a moment of profound stillness, he knelt, plunging his hands into the scorched earth. From beneath his touch, tiny green shoots emerged, pushing through the ashes, blossoming into vibrant flowers that glowed with an ethereal light. In the midst of devastation, life returned, fragile yet unyielding.

Eve's eyes filled with tears, and she whispered, "Is this the truth of power, then? To accept the cycle, to find beauty in both the creation and the destruction?"

Nyx's laughter echoed softly, a sound as ancient as the stars themselves. "Yes, Eve. True power is not about resisting the darkness or clinging to the light. It is about embracing the entirety of existence, recognizing that one cannot exist without the other. The cycle is eternal, and in that eternity lies the freedom to transform, to redefine, to rise again and again."

In the final moments of her vision, Eve stood on the edge of a great abyss. Before her stretched the universe, infinite and unknowable, each star a flickering possibility. She could see countless paths, each one winding and twisting through the vastness of space, each representing a different choice, a different life, a different version of herself. And in every path, she could see the duality that defined her - Eve and Nyx, light and shadow, fall angel and titan.

She felt Nyx's presence wrap around her like a comforting cloak, and the voice that had once been so distant now whispered directly into her ear, "You have the power to choose, Eve. You can define what you become, not by rejecting the darkness or exalting the light, but by embracing them both. In doing so, you transcend the boundaries that others have imposed upon you."

Eve took a deep breath, feeling the weight of eternity settle within her bones. The visions began to fade, the stars dimming, and the darkness receding. But even as the cosmos dissolved around her, she felt that truth - an unwavering, unyielding force - burning bright within her soul. She returned to herself, back in the quiet corner of the temple, her heart pounding with the knowledge that she had glimpsed something far greater than the dogma she had been taught.

In that moment, she understood that to be truly powerful was not to dominate or to surrender but to embrace the chaos, the uncertainty, and the infinite possibilities that lay within every choice, every moment, every breath.

As the visions began to fade, Eve found herself back in the temple, still resonating with the cosmic energies she had experienced. She could feel the remnants of those truths lingering within her, urging her to share them with the temple's followers. The chaos she had embraced was not just her own; it was a call to all who sought freedom from the dogmatic teachings that had confined them.

Eager to impart her newfound wisdom, Eve took every opportunity to weave the insights from her cosmic journeys into her rituals and sermons, infusing each word and gesture with the essence of what she had learned as Nyx. During the next gathering, as the temple's followers assembled in the grand hall, she stood before them, feeling the weight of their expectations pressing down on her shoulders. But this was not a burden; it was a challenge, one she would face head-on. The flickering torches cast dancing shadows on the walls, and the air crackled with energy, both reverent and anxious, as if the very space itself was holding its breath.

"Tonight," she began, her voice cutting through the murmurs, "I invite you to journey with me beyond the confines of our teachings. What if our understanding of good and evil is but a narrow view of a much larger tapestry? What if, instead of battling against the light and the dark, we could embrace the chaos that lies in between?"

She paused, allowing her words to settle, to take root in the minds of her followers. The silence that followed was thick with anticipation, as though the very air waited for her to continue. Eve took a step forward, the faint clinking of her jewelry punctuating the quiet. "You see, the cosmos is vast, infinite, and within it lies not a simple binary of right and wrong but an endless spectrum of possibilities. We are but fragments of that infinity, each holding within us the power to shape our destinies. We are not just servants of Asmodeus; we are agents of our own fate, capable of transcending the limitations imposed upon us!"

The hall came alive with the energy of her words. Whispers rippled through the crowd - some intrigued, others fearful. She could see the light of understanding flicker in the eyes of those who dared to consider her message, their faces illuminated by the dancing flames. There was a shift, a tremor of something raw and untamed stirring within them.

She pressed on, her passion igniting the room. "The cosmos teaches us that existence is not a simple equation but a multitude of experiences and perspectives. We cannot define ourselves by a single path, nor should we be bound by the chains of dogma. There is strength in the unknown, in the willingness to step beyond what is familiar and confront the darkness within ourselves."

As she spoke, she noticed a group of followers moving closer, drawn to the conviction in her voice. They were beginning to see Eve not as a figure of fear, but as a symbol of potential, a beacon guiding them toward their own empowerment. The idea that they could be more than mere servants - that they could be creators of their own destinies - was a revelation that sparked something deep within them. Yet, in the corners of the hall, she could also sense resistance brewing, the scowls and disapproving murmurs of those who clung to the rigid doctrines of the temple, unwilling to embrace the unknown.

Rhea, one of the most devout and unwavering followers of the old ways, stood at the forefront, her arms crossed defiantly over her chest, her eyes narrowed into slits of suspicion. "What you preach is dangerous, Eve!" she spat, her voice slicing through the air. "It undermines the very foundation of our beliefs. We cannot allow chaos to infiltrate our sanctuary!"

"Is it chaos?" Eve countered, her voice rising with fervor, the intensity of her spirit shining through her eyes. "Or is it the expansion of our understanding? We are at a crossroads, and this is our opportunity to redefine our existence. To be more than mere puppets in a cosmic play! For too long, we have allowed ourselves to be shackled by fear, by the illusion of control. But true strength does not come from hiding in the shadows of what is known; it comes from stepping boldly into the light of our potential!"

Rhea took a step forward, her fists clenched at her sides, trembling with the force of her conviction. "You speak of freedom," she hissed, "but what you offer is nothing but madness! There is safety in structure, in the teachings of Asmodeus. Without them, we are lost!"

"Safety is an illusion," Eve shot back, her voice like thunder. "The world beyond these walls is vast, chaotic, and ever-changing. We cannot hide from it. We must face it, embrace it, and allow it to transform us. It is only through embracing the unknown that we will find the strength to become something greater than we have ever been."

She gestured to the gathered followers, her eyes moving from face to face, meeting each one with an intensity that burned like fire. "Look around you," she urged. "Look at the faces of those who stand beside you. Each one of you carries within you a spark of potential, a will to power that cannot be denied. But that power can only be realized if you are willing to cast aside the chains of fear and doubt that have kept you bound to the old ways. It is not enough to simply exist; we must **thrive**, and to thrive, we must be willing to confront the darkness within ourselves, to embrace it, and to emerge stronger on the other side."

A murmur of agreement began to ripple through the crowd, faint at first, but growing stronger with each passing moment. The tension in the room was palpable, a living, breathing entity that pulsed with every heartbeat. Those who had begun to embrace these teachings rallied around Eve, emboldened by her words, while the traditionalists clung desperately to their beliefs, their fear of the unknown holding them back.

Eve took a step closer to Rhea, her voice softening, becoming almost tender. "I know you're afraid," she said, "but fear is not the enemy. It is a guide, a teacher, and it shows us the path we must take. It is through fear that we find the courage to break free from our chains, to step into the darkness, and to find the light within ourselves. You speak of structure, of safety, but what if I told you that true safety lies not in conformity, but in the freedom to explore, to question, to discover who we truly are?"

Rhea's defiance faltered, her eyes flickering with doubt. She took a step back, her gaze shifting to the floor as if searching for the answers that eluded her. Eve reached out, her hand hovering just inches from Rhea's shoulder, offering her a choice - a chance to step beyond the confines of her fear and into the unknown.

"This is not about abandoning what we have built," Eve continued, her voice a whisper that carried across the hall. "It is about evolving, about becoming more than what we were. We are not slaves to fate or destiny. We are the architects of our own lives, and it is time we started building."

The hall buzzed with the intensity of their conflicting ideologies, echoing the struggles that raged beyond the temple walls. Those who had once stood on the fringes now stepped forward, drawn by the passion and conviction in Eve's voice, their eyes shining with the promise of liberation. And in that moment, she knew that the seeds of change had been planted, that the path forward would not be easy, but it would be theirs to forge.

With a final glance at Rhea, Eve turned to face the crowd, her arms outstretched as if to embrace them all. "Let us walk this path together," she declared, her voice ringing with the strength of a thousand voices. "Let us break free from the chains that bind us and find the courage to become the masters of our own destinies!"

The tension in the room escalated, palpable and electric. Those who had begun to embrace Nyx's teachings rallied around Eve, emboldened by her words, while the traditionalists fought to maintain their grip on the established order. The hall buzzed with the intensity of their conflicting ideologies, echoing the struggles that raged beyond the temple walls.

Over the following weeks, Eve continued to hold gatherings where she encouraged the followers to explore the depths of their beliefs. She shared stories of her cosmic journeys, weaving in lessons about freedom, choice, and the limitations of dogma. The influence of Nyx began to seep into the fabric of their rituals, transforming them into opportunities for introspection and philosophical exploration.

During one particularly transformative gathering, Eve stood before her followers, her voice resonating with a newfound depth. The room was dimly lit, with flickering candles casting shadows that danced upon the walls like whispers from the past. "Tonight," she began, "we will journey beyond the limits of our minds, beyond the doctrines that have confined us. I want you to shed every preconceived notion, every fear, and every doubt. We will open ourselves to the cosmos and learn what it truly means to exist."

She paused, allowing her words to sink in, and then gestured for them to sit in a circle around her. The air thickened with anticipation as they settled, their breaths steadying, their eyes locked onto Eve's. "This will be no ordinary meditation," she warned, her tone solemn. "We are not here to seek peace, but rather to embrace the chaos, the boundless energy that courses through all things. Let us open our minds and spirits to the vastness of existence. Close your eyes, and envision yourselves as stardust, each of you a unique expression of the universe. Feel the chaos around you, and allow it to guide you."

As her followers obeyed, their eyes drifting shut, Eve began to chant softly in an ancient tongue, words that reverberated with an otherworldly power. Her voice grew stronger with each syllable, echoing off the stone walls, intertwining with the rhythm of their heartbeats. Gradually, a palpable energy filled the room, humming with a life of its own. It pulsed through the chamber, vibrating within their bones, as if the very air had come alive.

"Feel it," Eve urged, her voice a low, hypnotic whisper. "Feel the universe coursing through you. You are not separate from the stars, nor from the darkness. You are one with it all. In this moment, there is no temple, no master, no Asmodeus. There is only you and the cosmos."

As the followers surrendered to the meditation, Eve continued to guide them, her presence both gentle and commanding. She walked among them, her footsteps silent, her fingers grazing the tops of their heads as if bestowing blessings. With each touch, she whispered words of encouragement, pushing them deeper into the trance. "Feel the chaos around you," she murmured. "Let it seep into your soul. Let it show you who you truly are."

The air grew thicker, almost electric, and Eve felt the barriers of doubt and fear begin to dissolve. Some followers shivered, others sighed, and a few gasped as their consciousness expanded beyond the limits of their bodies, their souls stretching out into the vast expanse of the cosmos. For a moment, there was no separation between them and the universe - they were infinite, unbound by the chains of mortality.

One by one, they began to experience visions. A young acolyte, trembling in his place, saw himself not as the timid, subservient boy he had always believed himself to be, but as a warrior wreathed in flames, standing defiantly against the tides of fate. He could see his potential - a life of strength and courage, free from the shackles of fear that had kept him bound. Tears slid down his cheeks as he felt the fire of his own will ignite for the first time.

A priestess who had spent years trapped in the rigid expectations of her role saw herself dancing beneath a sky filled with stars, her movements wild and unrestrained, as though she were weaving the cosmos into being with every step. She felt the freedom she had always longed for, the power that came not from submission but from surrendering to her own desires. For the first time, she saw herself as more than a servant, more than a follower - she was a creator, capable of shaping her destiny.

Others saw fragments of their true selves, fragments that shimmered with possibilities they had never dared to imagine. One warrior glimpsed a future where he stood not as a mere soldier, but as a leader, his voice commanding respect not through fear but through wisdom. Another follower, who had always viewed herself as weak, saw herself holding a blade of light, standing unyielding against the darkness that sought to consume her.

Eve could feel their transformations taking root, their souls unraveling the threads of their old identities and weaving themselves into something new. And as the energy of the cosmos surged through her followers, Eve felt it, too - that familiar, intoxicating rush of power that came from breaking free of the chains that bound her. In that moment, she knew that her teachings had struck deep, that the seeds of self-empowerment had begun to sprout.

"Remember this feeling," Eve urged, her voice echoing in the silence that had fallen over the room. "Remember the strength you have found tonight, the freedom you have tasted. This is your true self - the self that no god, no doctrine, can ever take from you. You are the cosmos made flesh, and you have the power to shape your own destiny."

As the meditation drew to a close, her followers slowly opened their eyes, their gazes alight with wonder and awe. There was a tangible shift in the room, a collective understanding that they had touched something greater than themselves, something eternal. Eve looked upon them with a sense of pride and fulfillment, knowing that they had taken their first steps toward true freedom.

And in the flickering candlelight, Eve's smile was both tender and triumphant, a reflection of the journey they had all begun together. "Welcome," she whispered, "to the truth that lies beyond the darkness."

However, not all were receptive to the change. Resistance grew among the traditionalists, led by Rhea and a few others who feared what they could not control. They began to speak out more fervently against Eve, labeling her teachings as heresy, an affront to the sacred beliefs of the temple. "She seeks to lead us astray!" Rhea would declare during meetings. "If we allow her ideas to spread, we risk losing everything we've fought for!"

The schism within the temple widened, dividing the followers into two distinct camps: those who rallied around Eve's vision of liberation and those who clung to the old ways, fearful of the chaos she represented. The tension became a living entity, palpable in the air, as the struggle between liberation and oppression unfolded.

Eve felt the weight of her choices pressing down on her. Each day brought a new challenge, and as Nyx's influence grew, so did the stakes. The followers who embraced her teachings found strength in the chaos, but Eve was also aware that their rebellion could lead to fracturing the temple from within.

As she communed with the cosmic energies, she began to understand the delicate balance that lay ahead. The path toward liberation was fraught with peril, but it was a path worth walking. In the depths of her soul, she felt the call of the cosmos - a reminder that chaos was not to be feared but embraced, a force of creation that could lead to transformation.

Standing on the precipice of change, Eve vowed to guide her followers through the tumultuous waters ahead. She would be their bridge between light and dark, challenging them to transcend their fears and redefine their existence. Together, they would forge a new path, one that acknowledged the complexities of the universe and celebrated the power of their individual wills.

With Nyx at her side, she would fight for the freedom to explore the depths of existence, to commune with the cosmos, and to reshape the very foundations of their beliefs. In the heart of chaos, she would find her strength, and in that strength, she would inspire others to embrace their own truths. The journey had only just begun, and the stars beckoned her forward into the unknown.

15

Challenging the Paradigm

The tension in the grand hall of the temple crackled like a storm about to break. Eve stood at the center, the flickering torchlight casting dynamic shadows across her face, which was a mask of defiance and determination. The council of leaders, a cadre of stern figures steeped in tradition, stood before her, their expressions a mixture of fury and disbelief. The air was thick with the weight of their collective authority, and she felt the gravity of their expectations pressing down upon her.

Eve could feel that tension within the room thickening, the air charged with an intensity that electrified her very soul. The challenge was clear, and she would not back down, even in the face of such formidable opposition. She looked directly at Lord Vesperion, the demon lord's imposing figure casting a long shadow across the chamber. His crimson eyes narrowed, and his aura of authority pressed down on her, but Eve met his gaze unflinchingly.

"The principles of Asmodeus are not chains," Vesperion growled, his voice carrying the weight of centuries. "They are a path to power, a means to ascend above the chaos that you so recklessly embrace. In this structure, there is strength, and in that strength, we find our purpose."

Eve nodded thoughtfully, letting his words settle over the room before responding. "Purpose, yes. But is it truly ours? Or is it simply the purpose we've been given, handed down from one generation to the next, without question? I have walked this path, felt the call of power, and tasted the blood of my enemies on my lips. But it wasn't until I let go of that rigid path that I began to understand the true nature of power."

Erephia sneered, her voice dripping with condescension as she took a step closer to Eve. "You speak in riddles, Nyx. You claim enlightenment, but all I see is a defector, one who has turned her back on the teachings that gave her strength."

Eve shook her head, a sad smile tugging at the corners of her lips. "I haven't turned my back on them, Erephia. I've transcended them. You see, power isn't about wielding control over others, about forcing them into submission and bending them to your will. True power is about the freedom to choose, to carve your own path even when every force in the universe seeks to mold you into something else."

A murmur of uncertainty rippled through the assembly, and Eve seized upon it. She took a step forward, her eyes shining with a fierce light. "Asmodeus teaches us to seek power, to find strength in dominance and control. But what if there's another way? A path that doesn't demand the subjugation of others but instead encourages each of us to rise, to become the most authentic version of ourselves?"

Lord Vesperion's eyes flashed, and he struck his staff against the ground, the sharp crack silencing the murmurs. "You speak as though we should abandon our traditions, as if the path of Asmodeus has been wrong all these years. But you forget one thing, Eve: without structure, there is only chaos. Without hierarchy, there is only anarchy."

Eve's lips twitched into a smile that was both dangerous and alluring. "And what is so frightening about chaos, Lord Vesperion? Is it the loss of control? The fear that, without rigid lines, you might have to confront the parts of yourself that you've buried beneath layers of doctrine and duty?" She let her gaze sweep across the room, meeting the eyes of every council member. "Chaos is not our enemy. It is the crucible that forges us, that strips away our masks and reveals who we truly are."

Erephia stepped forward, her voice tinged with desperation. "You cannot dismantle everything we've built, Eve. The hierarchy of Asmodeus gives us purpose, gives us power! Without it, we are nothing."

"No," Eve said softly, shaking her head. "Without it, we are finally free to become something more." She spread her arms wide, and for a moment, the darkness that was Nyx flickered around her like an aura. "Nietzsche spoke of the Übermensch, the idea that we could transcend our limitations, that we could break free of the binary constructs of good and evil, light and dark, master and slave. This is what I offer you, not the rejection of power, but the redefinition of it."

Lord Vesperion's expression hardened. "You dare to suggest that you know better than Asmodeus himself? That you, a mere priestess, could redefine the teachings of a god?"

"I don't seek to rewrite his teachings," Eve replied. "I seek to evolve them. Power isn't static; it grows, it shifts, it changes. What was true for Asmodeus in the beginning may not be true now. And if we refuse to adapt, we doom ourselves to stagnation."

She paused, allowing her words to sink in, then continued. "Nietzsche spoke of the will to power as the fundamental driving force of life. But that power is not merely about dominance; it's about creativity, about the ability to shape our own destinies, to create meaning where there was none. It's about facing the abyss, embracing it, and then using it to craft something beautiful."

Erephia's face twisted with frustration. "And what would you have us become, Eve? Aimless wanderers, lost in a sea of possibilities with no anchor, no direction?"

"No," Eve said, her voice gentle but firm. "I would have you become seekers. Seekers of truth, of purpose, of your own power. I would have you question, challenge, and confront the very foundation of your beliefs. Because only then, when you have stripped away the illusions, can you find the true strength that lies within."

She turned to the rest of the council, her eyes burning with conviction. "You have followed the path of Asmodeus all your lives, believing it to be the only way. But I ask you now: is this truly the life you want? A life of rigid obedience, of fear and control? Or do you yearn for something more?"

Silence followed her words, thick and heavy. For a moment, Eve thought she saw a flicker of doubt in Vesperion's eyes, a crack in the armor of certainty he wore so proudly. It was small, almost imperceptible, but it was enough.

"Freedom comes with a price," Vesperion finally said, his voice barely above a whisper. "And that price is chaos, uncertainty, and the possibility of failure."

"Yes," Eve agreed, her tone unwavering. "But it is also the price of greatness. Of becoming more than what we were told we could be."

The silence stretched, each council member lost in their thoughts, wrestling with the new ideas Eve had laid before them. The Titan within her stirred, whispering of possibilities, of futures unbound by the shackles of tradition. She could feel the power within her surging, not in an attempt to dominate but to uplift, to inspire.

"Look around you," she urged, her voice softer now, almost pleading. "Look at what we have become. We stand on the precipice of something extraordinary, something that could redefine not just our temple but all of existence. Are you truly content to remain in the shadows, bound by chains you placed on yourselves, or will you take that step into the unknown and discover who you were always meant to be?"

A heavy stillness settled over the chamber, and for the first time, Eve saw something other than fear in their eyes. She saw hope, a flicker of understanding, and the faintest spark of rebellion. It was fragile, but it was there, and that was all she needed.

Lord Vesperion sighed, the sound carrying the weight of centuries. "You tread a dangerous path, Eve."

She smiled, and it was a smile of pure, unadulterated freedom. "The most dangerous paths often lead to the most beautiful destinations."

The council chamber fell deathly silent, the weight of Eve's words pressing down on every soul within. Even the air seemed to grow still, as if the very fabric of reality were holding its breath. Lord Vesperion's eyes narrowed, his expression a mixture of anger, fear, and begrudging respect. He had always been accustomed to authority, to maintaining a stranglehold over the hearts and minds of the acolytes. But Eve, standing before him, was a force he could no longer control.

"You speak as though chaos is the answer to all," he sneered, his voice dripping with disdain. "As though your rebellion against order is some noble cause. But you fail to see the destruction you invite upon us all."

Eve met his gaze with unflinching resolve. "It's not chaos I champion, Vesperion. It's liberation. It's the recognition that existence isn't confined to the binaries of good and evil, light and dark. Our power doesn't stem from blindly following the dictates of one extreme or the other. True power, true strength, comes from the acceptance of our duality - of the light and the darkness that dwell within us all."

Her words cut through the room, reverberating off the ancient stone walls like a clarion call. The council members shifted uncomfortably, some clutching their robes as if the fabric might shield them from the truth she was unearthing. Gasps of disbelief rippled through the assembly. Lysandra, the Archpriestess herself, stepped forward, her expression pinched with disapproval. Her silver hair glinted in the torchlight, and her eyes, usually calm, now burned with restrained fury.

"You speak of freedom while peddling heresy!" Lysandra snapped, her voice carrying the authority of centuries. "The teachings of Asmodeus have guided us for eons. You would throw it all away for a fleeting illusion?"

Eve's lips curved into a faint smile, and she took a step forward, meeting Lysandra's gaze without flinching. "Fleeting?" Her voice rose, cutting through the murmurs of dissent like a blade. "The illusion is not in the pursuit of knowledge but in the blind obedience to a doctrine that no longer serves us. As we stand at the brink of a cosmic battle, we must recognize the greater truths that exist beyond the light and dark."

The tension in the room grew thicker, and Vesperion's expression hardened. He stepped toward her, his towering figure casting a shadow that seemed to swallow the space between them. "You speak as if all mortals are capable of such transcendence," he growled. "What makes you so certain they even possess such strength? Most mortals are weak. They indulge in their vices without a second thought. Why should we believe they're capable of more?"

Eve held his gaze, unyielding. "Because I have seen it," she said, her voice soft but firm. "I have seen souls who, when given the chance, rise above their pain, their fear, and their guilt. They learn from their failures rather than being defined by them. But they can only do this if we allow them the freedom to try - if we stop shackling them to their past."

Lysandra's expression faltered, and for a moment, doubt flickered in her eyes. She folded her arms across her chest, a gesture more of defense than authority. "Freedom has its dangers, Eve," she said, her tone less certain. "To confront one's darkness is to risk being consumed by it. Not every soul has the resilience to emerge unscathed."

"Yes," Eve agreed, nodding. "It is a risk. But it is a necessary one. When we force them to bury their shadows, we only make those shadows stronger. If they face it, if they stare into the abyss and confront their deepest fears, they can learn to master it. They can turn their darkness into something powerful - something that serves them, instead of the other way around."

Vesperion's eyes narrowed, suspicion lacing his tone. "You speak as if you believe they all possess this courage."

"They do," Eve replied, her voice tinged with sadness and hope. "It may be buried beneath layers of fear and conditioning, but it is there. And when we allow them to confront their darkness, that courage begins to surface. It is not an easy path, but it is the only path that leads to true freedom."

"And what if their darkness consumes them, Eve?" Vesperion challenged, taking another step forward, his voice dripping with disdain. "What if, in giving them this freedom, we unleash something far worse than what they already are?"

Eve didn't flinch. "Then that is the risk we must take. For even in the face of failure, there is growth. Every step, even a misstep, brings them closer to understanding. And it is through understanding that they find the strength to rise above their circumstances."

Lysandra tilted her head, her tone softer now, as if she were testing Eve's resolve. "You believe they can transcend their suffering? That they can move beyond the mistakes that damned them?"

"Yes," Eve whispered, her heart swelling with conviction. "Because I have seen it happen. I have seen mortals rise from the depths of despair and transform into something magnificent. Not because they were punished into submission, but because they were given the chance to find their own strength. To see themselves not as victims or sinners, but as beings capable of change."

Vesperion's lip curled in disdain, but there was a flicker of something else in his eyes. Curiosity, perhaps. Or doubt. "And you think this is the path we should take? That we should guide them not through fear, but through understanding?"

"Yes," Eve said, her voice growing stronger. "Fear binds them to their past; understanding frees them to create their future. If we truly want them to transcend, to overcome that which has damned them, we must allow them the chance to confront their darkness, to learn from it, and to emerge stronger. We must trust that they are capable of more than we have ever allowed them to be."

For a long moment, there was silence. Lysandra looked at Eve, her gaze searching, and then, slowly, she nodded. "You would have us trust them," she murmured. "Trust that they will find their way, even when all we see are their failures and flaws."

Eve smiled. "Yes. Because within those flaws lies the seed of greatness. A mortal's greatest mistake can become their greatest teacher if they are allowed to learn from it."

Vesperion sighed, rubbing his temples. "And you think we can learn from them as well?" he asked, his voice tinged with reluctant curiosity.

"I do," Eve said. "For we are not so different from them, are we? We, too, have our own shadows to face, our own demons to overcome. Perhaps it is in helping them transcend that we find the strength to do the same."

Vesperion stared at her, and for a moment, the hardness in his eyes softened. He stepped back, folding his arms across his chest. "You are either a fool, Eve, or the most dangerous visionary we have ever seen."

Eve chuckled, the sound echoing softly in the chamber. "Perhaps I am both," she said. "For it takes a fool to dream of change, but it takes a visionary to make that change a reality. And I believe that together, we can forge a path that leads not to damnation, but to the liberation of every soul willing to take that first, terrifying step toward the light."

Lysandra looked at her for a long moment, and then, with a slight, almost imperceptible smile, she nodded. "Then let us see if your vision can stand against the darkness, Eve. For I suspect you may have more to teach us than we ever imagined."

Eve bowed her head in gratitude, feeling Nyx's power thrumming in her veins, and for the first time, she felt that perhaps, just perhaps, they were ready to listen.

Eve took a step forward, her eyes glowing with the dark energy of Nyx. "Strength built on fear is a brittle thing, Lysandra. You believe we are strong because we enforce submission and dominance, but what kind of strength is that if it collapses the moment someone dares to question it? The angels we face... they are no different from us in that regard. They, too, are prisoners of their absolutes."

"Then what would you have us do?" another council member spat, his voice tinged with desperation. "Shall we welcome the angels with open arms? Embrace them as brothers?"

Eve shook her head. "No. This isn't about surrendering or submitting to them. It's about understanding that they are as much a part of this struggle as we are. If we continue to fight them from a place of fear, then we are no better than they are. We become what they accuse us of being - mindless, soulless creatures clinging to dogma."

She could see the confusion spreading across their faces, but there was something else too - curiosity. It was the first crack in the armor of their certainty, the first sign that they were truly listening. Nyx's voice whispered within her, urging her forward, and she obeyed, drawing from that endless well of strength.

Eve continued, her voice growing softer, more intimate, as if sharing a sacred secret. "A being who transcends the confines of morality, who forges their own path, their own truth. This is not a call to become ruthless or devoid of compassion. It's a call to rise above the limitations we've placed upon ourselves. To acknowledge that power isn't about bending others to our will, but about mastering ourselves. It's about overcoming, time and time again, until we stand as beings of true autonomy."

"But what of the weaker ones?" Rhea interjected, desperation creeping into her tone. "What of those who cannot rise as you do? Are they to be left behind, discarded in this quest for individual strength?"

Eve's gaze softened as she turned to Rhea, and for a moment, her stern demeanor melted away. "No, Rhea. That's not the point. This path isn't about abandoning anyone. It's about showing them that they, too, have the power to rise. That they, too, can confront their shadows, their fears, and emerge stronger on the other side. True strength isn't about domination - it's about lifting others up, even as we climb."

A murmur rippled through the chamber. She could see the internal struggle playing out on their faces, the war between old beliefs and this new, frightening possibility. Lord Vesperion, however, was not swayed. His lips curled into a sneer, and he took a step toward Eve, towering over her with all the menace he could muster.

"You preach ideals that will get us killed," he hissed, his voice dangerously low. "This temple has stood for centuries on the foundation of dominance. It is that very doctrine that has protected us from being obliterated by the forces that seek our destruction. And you would dismantle it all because you believe in some fantasy of self-empowerment?"

Eve did not back down. Instead, she stepped closer, so close that she could feel the heat radiating from him, her gaze never wavering. "Yes, Vesperion, I would dismantle it. Because it is a lie. A lie that has kept us shackled to an illusion of power, while true strength lies just beyond our reach. We claim to be beings of darkness, but we have allowed ourselves to be ruled by fear. By tearing down these false walls, we make room for something greater - for a power that doesn't need to dominate, but simply **is**."

Vesperion's eyes flashed with fury, but Eve could see the doubt creeping in, the seed of uncertainty taking root. Before he could respond, one of the younger acolytes, a boy no older than sixteen with a mop of unruly hair, stepped forward. His hands were trembling, but his eyes shone with determination. "I... I want to follow you," he said, his voice barely more than a whisper. "I want to understand what it means to be free."

His words acted like a catalyst. More acolytes began to step forward, their movements hesitant but resolute, drawn by the truth in Eve's words. One by one, they gathered around her, forming a small circle in the center of the council chamber. Each face told a story - stories of doubt, of longing, of a desire to break free from the chains that had bound them for so long.

"You see," Eve said softly, gesturing to those who had joined her, "I am not alone in this. There are others who feel as I do, who yearn for something beyond what we've been given. This is not a rebellion for the sake of rebellion. It is a call to awaken, to rise, and to carve out a path that is truly our own."

Lord Vesperion's fists clenched at his sides, the veins in his neck standing out like cords. "You will destroy us all," he growled. "You will bring ruin to everything we have built."

"Perhaps," Eve conceded, a small, knowing smile tugging at her lips. "Or perhaps I will set us free."

For the first time, Vesperion had no retort. He could only stare at her, his eyes burning with a mixture of fear, rage, and, just maybe, a sliver of hope. Eve turned her back on him, her followers forming a protective circle around her as they made their way toward the temple's exit.

As they passed through the arched doorway, Eve paused, looking back one last time. "The choice is yours," she said, her voice echoing through the chamber. "You can remain chained to the past, or you can step into the unknown and discover what lies beyond."

And with that, she turned and walked away, her heart swelling with a newfound sense of purpose. Behind her, she could feel the weight of their eyes, the sense of a world on the brink of change. And as she stepped into the night, Nyx whispered in her ear, a promise of what was yet to come.

"Together, we will transcend."

Erephia's eyes widened with disbelief, her voice rising in desperation. "You will regret this betrayal! You will lead them to their doom!"

Eve met her gaze with unwavering resolve. "It is not betrayal to seek truth. It is cowardice to cling to falsehoods."

With that, she turned back to the assembly, now a vibrant tapestry of divided loyalties. "Together, we will explore the vastness of existence, challenging the paradigms that have held us captive for far too long. I invite you to embrace your individual strength, your unique will, and to reject the fear that has kept you from realizing your true potential."

The murmur of dissent transformed into a low roar of agreement as more followers stepped forward, emboldened by Eve's words. The council's authority waned in the face of the undeniable power of choice that resonated through the hall. Eve could feel the energy shifting, the very air vibrating with potential.

Yet she knew that this was only the beginning. The path ahead would be fraught with challenges as the temple leadership would not take her defiance lightly. With each step forward, she felt the weight of responsibility pressing on her shoulders. This was not merely about her own transformation; it was about the future of her followers and the very fabric of their beliefs.

As the council members looked on, their expressions shifting from disbelief to anger, Eve understood that she had crossed a threshold from which there was no return. She had embraced her identity as Nyx and would no longer allow herself to be constrained by their rules. The time had come to redefine the very concept of power.

"Let this be a lesson to all of you," she declared, her voice resonating through the hall. "Power is not about dominance; it is about choice. It is about the courage to confront one's own beliefs and to embrace the unknown. Together, we will forge a new path - a path that celebrates individuality, freedom, and the rejection of the dogmas that have kept us in chains."

With those words, Eve felt a surge of energy wash over her, the embodiment of Nyx igniting a fire in the hearts of her followers. The shift in the temple's dynamics was palpable, and she could sense the excitement mingling with the fear. They were on the cusp of a revolution, and she was determined to lead them through the chaos.

As the meeting disbanded, Eve turned to her followers, a wave of warmth spreading through her as she saw their faces alight with newfound determination. "We will gather again at the next moon's cycle," she instructed, her heart racing with anticipation. "Come prepared to explore the depths of our existence together. Let us challenge the status quo and uncover the truths that await us."

With that, Eve stepped back into the shadows of the temple, her heart racing. She had challenged the very foundation of their beliefs, and now the real work would begin. There would be those who would resist, those who would fight to maintain control, but she was ready. With Nyx at her side, she would face the storm, guiding her followers into a new era of understanding.

As she walked away from the hall, Eve felt the power of her choice reverberating within her. The future was uncertain, but for the first time, she felt truly alive, ready to embrace the chaos that lay ahead. The seeds of change had been sown, and with each passing moment, she could feel them growing, ready to burst forth into a new reality.

16

Deepening the Bond

The dim light of the temple's library filtered through the ancient windows, casting elongated shadows across the worn stone floor. Dust motes danced in the air, and the musty scent of old scrolls filled Eve's nostrils as she prepared for her session with Liora. Today felt different; a palpable energy pulsed between them, suggesting that the younger acolyte was on the brink of a breakthrough.

Eve sat at a large, wooden table cluttered with scrolls, their delicate fibers whispering secrets of the past. She had taken a personal interest in Liora's development, recognizing her potential to challenge the temple's entrenched teachings. The girl was bright, eager, but still tethered to the rigid moral constructs that defined her upbringing. It was time to guide her into the deeper waters of philosophical inquiry.

Liora entered, her eyes wide with curiosity and a hint of apprehension. "I hope I'm not late," she said, brushing her hair behind her ear.

"Not at all," Eve replied, her voice warm yet firm. "Today, we dive deeper into the concept of the Übermensch. Are you ready?"

Liora nodded, though uncertainty flickered in her eyes. They settled into their seats, the atmosphere charged with expectation. Eve took a moment to gauge Liora's state of mind. She could see the conflict within her, a struggle to reconcile the teachings of Asmodeus with the burgeoning philosophies that Eve had been introducing.

"Let's begin with a fundamental question," Eve proposed, leaning forward. "What does the idea of the Übermensch mean to you?"

Liora hesitated, her brow furrowing as she searched for the right words. "I think... it's about strength and power, right? Someone who is above the ordinary, who sets their own rules."

"Exactly," Eve encouraged, "but let's dig deeper. To be an Übermensch, one must transcend conventional morality, yes? It's about creating your own values rather than accepting those imposed by others. Can you see how this might challenge the teachings we've followed?"

Liora bit her lip, clearly struggling. "But how can we just... ignore what has been established? Doesn't that lead to chaos? Without some form of morality, how do we know what's right?"

Eve smiled gently, recognizing the familiar resistance. "You're right to question it. Think of morality not as an absolute truth, but as a construct - an agreement among people to maintain order. But what happens when that order becomes oppressive or limiting? Can you not envision a scenario where the true power lies in the freedom to choose your own path?"

Liora's gaze dropped to the table, the weight of Eve's words pressing upon her. "I guess... I've never really thought about it like that. It feels dangerous."

"Dangerous, perhaps, but also liberating," Eve responded softly, leaning back in her chair. "The fear of chaos often blinds us to the potential for growth and understanding. The journey of the Übermensch is a journey of self-discovery, of finding strength within oneself. Let's explore this through your own experiences."

Eve paused, allowing Liora to gather her thoughts. "Think about moments in your life when you've felt confined by rules or expectations, whether from the temple, society, or even family. Have you ever questioned whether those rules truly reflected your own desires, or were they imposed upon you?"

Liora frowned, reflecting on Eve's words. "I suppose there were times I felt like that. But I never thought of questioning those rules. It felt... wrong."

"And why do you think it felt wrong?" Eve pressed, her eyes searching Liora's face. "Was it because you genuinely believed in those rules, or because you were taught to accept them without question?"

Liora hesitated, her inner conflict palpable. "I... I think it was fear. Fear of what would happen if I didn't follow the rules. Of what others would think."

Eve nodded knowingly. "Fear is a powerful force, and it often keeps us shackled to beliefs that no longer serve us. But the Übermensch, the one who transcends, learns to overcome that fear. They rise above the expectations of others and carve out their own path, one that reflects their true nature."

The words hung in the air, and Liora's gaze flicked up to meet Eve's. "But how do you know what your true nature is? What if you make the wrong choice?"

"That's part of the journey," Eve said. "To be an Übermensch is to accept responsibility for your own existence, even in the face of uncertainty. It's not about following a predetermined path, but about having the courage to forge your own. And yes, sometimes that means making mistakes. But those mistakes are part of the process. They teach you, help you grow, and refine your understanding of yourself."

Liora leaned back, exhaling slowly. "It sounds overwhelming. Like... there's no safety net."

"There isn't," Eve agreed, her tone unwavering. "But that's where true strength comes from. You see, the Übermensch is not merely someone with power in the conventional sense. It's not about dominance over others. It's about self-mastery. It's about the realization that you are the creator of your own values, your own meaning, and your own life. And that's the greatest form of freedom."

"Self-mastery..." Liora repeated softly, as if testing the words on her tongue. "But doesn't that lead to isolation? If everyone is just following their own path, doesn't that tear society apart?"

Eve shook her head, her expression thoughtful. "It's a common misconception. The Übermensch doesn't reject others or society outright. What they reject is the idea of blind conformity. By discovering their own truth, they actually bring something new and authentic into the world. They don't destroy, they create. Think of it this way: a society full of individuals who are true to themselves, who are driven by purpose rather than obligation, would be far stronger and more vibrant than one where everyone simply follows the same rigid rules."

"But what about morality?" Liora asked, her brow furrowing again. "If everyone's just doing what they want, isn't that dangerous?"

Eve leaned in slightly, her gaze intense. "Morality, as we've been taught, is often a tool of control. It serves a purpose, yes - to keep order. But what happens when that morality is no longer relevant or becomes a tool of oppression? The Übermensch transcends that, not by rejecting morality outright, but by creating a new, higher morality that reflects their deeper understanding of life. This isn't about indulgence or anarchy. It's about evolution."

Liora sat quietly for a moment, her thoughts swirling as she processed Eve's words. "So, the Übermensch is like... a guide to what we could become if we stopped letting fear and tradition dictate our lives?"

"Exactly," Eve said, her smile returning. "It's about embracing the unknown, about seeing life as something fluid and ever-changing. The Übermensch isn't bound by the past or by dogma. They are the architects of the future, constantly reshaping themselves and the world around them."

A spark flickered in Liora's eyes. "That sounds... powerful. But also lonely."

Eve's smile softened. "It can be. The path of the Übermensch is not easy, and it's not for everyone. But for those who are brave enough to walk it, the rewards are profound. They find a sense of meaning and fulfillment that transcends the superficial pleasures and constraints of ordinary life."

Liora nodded slowly. "I think I'm beginning to understand. It's not just about power, is it? It's about becoming something more... something greater."

"Yes," Eve said quietly. "Something greater. Not just for yourself, but for the world around you. The Übermensch, in their pursuit of self-mastery and truth, becomes a beacon for others. They show that there is a way beyond fear, beyond limitation. They don't just transcend - they transform."

Liora's expression shifted, the uncertainty slowly fading, replaced by a glimmer of curiosity and resolve. "I want to learn more. I want to understand this fully."

Eve's eyes gleamed with approval. "Good. This is only the beginning, Liora. The path is long, and there will be challenges, but remember this: true power comes not from domination over others, but from the mastery of yourself. And that journey, though perilous, is worth every step."

Liora smiled faintly, the weight of Eve's words settling over her like a cloak of understanding. She was beginning to see the world in a new light - a light that, though uncertain, was filled with infinite potential.

Eve leaned back, observing Liora as she contemplated the question. "Think of a moment where you felt constrained by the temple's teachings. What was it that held you back?"

Liora looked up, her expression shifting from confusion to contemplation. "Last week, during the council meeting, I disagreed with how we handled a conflict between two acolytes. They were arguing about the morality of helping a human who had stumbled into the temple grounds. Everyone was so quick to dismiss him as unworthy, but I felt he deserved compassion."

"And what stopped you from voicing your thoughts?" Eve probed gently.

"I didn't want to go against the council. I feared their judgment and what it would mean for my standing here," Liora admitted, her voice a mere whisper.

"Ah, the fear of judgment," Eve said knowingly. "But that's exactly the point. The council's authority is not inherent; it is derived from a set of beliefs. You have the power to redefine your response to such situations. Remember, Liora, true strength lies in your ability to choose your own values and act upon them."

A spark ignited in Liora's eyes. "So, if I had spoken out, I could have created my own path?"

"Precisely. You could have chosen compassion over dogma. Now, let's put this philosophy into practice." Eve leaned forward, her demeanor shifting to one of playful seriousness. "I have devised a series of challenges for you. Each will require you to make decisions based on your instincts rather than established dogma."

Liora's brow furrowed in curiosity and apprehension. "Challenges? What kind?"

Eve smiled, relishing the moment. "For our first challenge, I want you to find an opportunity to defy an established norm within the temple. Look for an instance where the rigid teachings could be reinterpreted. Observe how your decisions impact those around you."

Liora blinked, the gravity of the task settling over her like a heavy cloak. "Defy an established norm?" she repeated, her voice tinged with both curiosity and apprehension. The temple had always been a place of unyielding structure, a sanctuary where order was prized above all else. To question that structure felt like stepping into dangerous, uncharted territory. The weight of tradition pressed down on her, a tangible force that had shaped her entire existence.

Eve's smile remained steady, her eyes unwavering. "Indeed. It's about testing the limits of your convictions. Remember, the goal is not to rebel for the sake of rebellion, but to discover what you truly believe and how it aligns with your emerging sense of self." Eve's voice was calm, yet her words carried an intensity that sparked something within Liora. This was more than a challenge - it was an invitation to reshape her own identity, to test whether the beliefs she had been taught were truly her own or just the echoes of others.

Liora felt her pulse quicken. In the temple, there was a norm for everything: the way you prayed, the way you spoke, even the way you interpreted the sacred texts. Each aspect was governed by a system of rules designed to maintain order and control. The thought of breaking away from that was exhilarating but terrifying. What would the others think? What would the Archpriestess say if she noticed?

As if reading her mind, Eve continued, her voice softening just slightly. "You'll find that breaking with tradition often stirs discomfort in those around you. It's human nature to cling to what feels familiar. But discomfort is a sign that growth is happening, both in you and in them. You're not aiming to dismantle the temple, Liora, but to question whether every aspect of it is in line with your own path. Sometimes, the greatest growth comes from the smallest acts of defiance."

Liora glanced toward the grand doors that led deeper into the temple, imagining the weight of its rituals, the hum of whispered prayers, the heavy scent of incense. For so long, the temple had been her entire world - a place where the rules were sacred, where deviation was seen as a threat to stability. What Eve was asking of her wasn't just a small act of defiance - it was a radical shift in how she would engage with the temple, with herself, and with the world around her.

"But how will I know what's right?" Liora asked, her voice faltering slightly. "If the teachings have guided us this far, how do I trust my own judgment against them?"

Eve leaned forward, her gaze piercing but kind. "That's exactly the challenge. You won't always know what's right, and that's the point. The Übermensch does not rely on external validation to determine their path. They trust their inner compass, and even when they falter, they learn from the missteps. The only way to truly discover your values is to question the ones handed to you. Each challenge will reveal a part of who you are."

Liora's breath caught in her throat. The idea of acting without the safety net of established rules left her feeling exposed, vulnerable even. But Eve's words also stirred something deeper, a flicker of excitement beneath the trepidation. There was a possibility here - an opportunity to shape her own destiny, to step into a role that was not dictated by the temple's traditions but by her own will.

"I'll do it," Liora said, her voice carrying more conviction than before. The words felt strange, almost foreign, as they left her lips, but they carried a weight that resonated deep within her. She would step out of the mold, if only for a moment, to see what lay beyond it.

Eve's expression softened, the edges of her lips curving into an approving smile. "Good. It doesn't need to be grand or disruptive - often, the most profound shifts come from the quietest moments. Find a teaching, a ritual, or a custom that doesn't sit right with you. Approach it with intention, not recklessness. Remember, this is about discovery, not destruction."

Liora nodded, a flurry of thoughts swirling in her mind. Which norm would she defy? Would it be something subtle, like refusing to chant during morning prayers? Or something more noticeable, like questioning the Archpriestess during a council meeting? Each idea seemed bold, yet filled with potential.

"And when you do," Eve added, her voice a calm anchor, "pay attention to the reactions around you. How do others respond to your challenge? How do **you** respond to the discomfort it brings? This is part of the growth process. You're not just learning about the temple - you're learning about yourself."

Liora took a deep breath, her resolve slowly hardening. She knew this would be a defining moment, one that could change the way she interacted with the temple and her place within it. But the fear of failure, of judgment from her peers, loomed large in her mind. What if she made the wrong choice? What if her act of defiance was met with scorn or punishment?

"Trust yourself," Eve said, as if sensing Liora's hesitation. "There will always be fear when you step outside the boundaries of what's comfortable. But growth doesn't happen within the confines of comfort. It happens when you push beyond it, when you dare to question."

Liora nodded again, the apprehension still there, but now it was accompanied by a spark of determination. She would find a way to test the limits of the temple's teachings, not to dismantle them, but to see whether they truly reflected what she believed. Eve had given her a challenge, but more importantly, she had given her permission to explore, to question, to grow.

The room fell silent for a moment, the weight of the conversation settling between them. Liora's mind raced as she considered her next move, the possibilities unfolding before her like the pages of an unwritten story. It was her story now, one she would write on her own terms.

Eve, ever observant, watched as the conflict and curiosity warred within Liora's eyes. This was only the beginning. The seed of doubt had been planted, and soon it would grow into something far more powerful - an understanding of what it meant to be truly free, to transcend the limitations imposed by external forces, and to create one's own path in life.

"Excellent. But first, we'll discuss the next steps." Eve felt a surge of pride for her pupil. Liora was beginning to awaken, and the journey would only deepen from here.

As the hours passed, Eve and Liora delved deeper into the intricacies of the Übermensch, their conversation evolving from abstract philosophy to tangible, real-world applications. To make the concept more relatable, Eve wove in examples of artists, thinkers, and leaders who had defied societal norms, crafting their own values in the face of adversity.

One of the first stories Eve shared was about Friedrich Nietzsche himself, the philosopher who had coined the term Übermensch. She recounted how Nietzsche had been dismissed by his peers, his works largely ignored during his lifetime. "He lived in a time when the Christian morality dominated Europe," Eve explained. "To speak out against it was seen as blasphemy, yet Nietzsche believed that humanity could transcend this slave morality. He envisioned a future where people would reject the imposed definitions of good and evil and create their own values. Despite the rejection, he pressed on, driven by a vision that was ahead of his time. Now, his works have reshaped entire fields of philosophy. Can you imagine the courage it took to stand alone against the dominant culture of his day?"

Liora listened intently, her mind racing with the implications of such radical defiance. Eve, sensing her interest, transitioned to a more recent figure: Pablo Picasso, the revolutionary artist who reshaped the world of painting. "Picasso didn't just paint," Eve continued. "He challenged the very way people saw art. At the time, classical realism was the accepted norm. But Picasso? He broke those rules. His cubist paintings were initially ridiculed, but he wasn't trying to follow tradition. He created art that reflected his vision of the world, not society's expectations. And because of that, he became one of the most celebrated artists in history. His defiance of norms wasn't just rebellion for the sake of rebellion - it was an act of creation, of bringing something entirely new into existence."

Liora's eyes widened as the stories unfolded. The idea of challenging established systems felt daunting, yet the thought of being part of that lineage of creators and thinkers stirred something deep within her.

Eve smiled, sensing the spark within Liora begin to ignite. "Creating your own values requires courage," she said, her voice steady but full of conviction. "But it also brings clarity. You begin to see that the rules others follow are not sacred. They're just agreements people made at one point in time, based on their own fears and needs. Once you realize this, you understand that you have the power to rewrite those rules, to shape your own reality."

To make the point even more personal, Eve shared her own experience. "When I was younger in the temple, I faced a decision between blind obedience to tradition or carving my own path. There was a ritual - one everyone had to perform to prove their loyalty. It wasn't dangerous, but it was a way for the temple to ensure that everyone fell in line. I knew, deep down, that it was just a way to control us, to weed out anyone who dared to question. So, I refused." Eve's voice took on a reflective tone. "The backlash was immediate. I was isolated, scorned by those I thought were my allies. But what I gained in that moment was far greater than their approval - I gained clarity. I understood then that power wasn't something granted by an institution, but something you claim for yourself when you refuse to conform."

Liora, who had been silently absorbing the stories, finally spoke. "But how did you... how did you know it was the right thing to do? What if you were wrong?"

Eve smiled gently. "There is no 'right' answer, Liora. That's the very essence of the Übermensch - rejecting the need for external validation. I didn't know for sure that it was the right choice at the time. What I did know was that I wasn't going to live by rules that felt hollow. I was going to live by my own truth, even if it meant walking alone for a while. And you will face that same uncertainty. That's where trust in yourself comes in. The more you trust your instincts, the more you'll realize that you possess the power to shape your own reality."

Liora sat back, absorbing the weight of Eve's words. She thought of her own life, the countless times she had felt trapped by expectations - by the temple, by her family, by the society she lived in. For the first time, she realized that those constraints didn't have to define her. She could choose to break free.

Sensing the shift in Liora's understanding, Eve continued, her tone more urgent now. "This isn't just about defying norms for the sake of it. True rebellion isn't about chaos or destruction - it's about creation. It's about building a life that reflects who you truly are, rather than living out someone else's vision for you."

Eve shared the story of Rosa Parks, the woman who defied segregation laws in America. "Parks wasn't trying to start a revolution when she refused to give up her seat. But in that moment, she embodied the Übermensch - by choosing to stand by her own moral compass rather than the unjust laws that surrounded her. She wasn't concerned with how others viewed her actions. She did what she knew was right. And that act of defiance rippled outwards, changing the course of history."

As the examples flowed, Liora could feel the weight of the challenge ahead of her, but it no longer felt impossible. It felt like a path she could choose, a path she **wanted** to choose.

As their session drew to a close, Eve could see the transformation in Liora. The flicker of understanding had grown into a steady blaze of determination. Her shoulders were no longer slumped in doubt, and her eyes held a new light - a readiness to face the unknown.

"I'm ready to face the challenge," Liora declared, her voice steady and resolute.

Eve nodded, her expression soft but serious. "Remember, it won't always be easy. The path of the Übermensch is not one free of obstacles. You will face resistance, both from within and outside. People are comfortable with what they know, and they'll challenge you when you break from that comfort. But trust in yourself, and you'll discover strength you never knew existed."

Liora stood, her mind now filled with possibilities. The temple, once a symbol of rigid tradition, had suddenly become a canvas on which she could begin painting her own path. The stories of Nietzsche, Picasso, Parks, and Eve herself now served as guideposts, lighting the way forward. She knew that defying the norms wouldn't come without consequence, but for the first time, the fear of stepping out of line was outweighed by the excitement of discovering who she could become when those lines no longer mattered.

As she left the room, Eve watched her go with a quiet sense of satisfaction. This was the first step on a long journey for Liora, but it was a step in the right direction - towards becoming an Übermensch, towards claiming her own power.

With a newfound sense of purpose, Liora left the library, her steps light as she ventured into the depths of the temple, ready to confront the very teachings that had defined her life thus far. Eve watched her go, a wave of hope washing over her.

In that moment, Eve realized that she wasn't merely shaping Liora's journey; she was paving the way for a new generation of seekers - those who would challenge the established norms and forge their own paths, unafraid to explore the complexities of existence. And as Nyx's essence intertwined with her own, she felt the power of transformation rippling through the temple, setting the stage for a profound evolution that would resonate through the ages.

17

The Rejection of Pity

The temple buzzed with an uneasy tension, the aftermath of a recent skirmish resonating through its stone halls. Whispers of discontent filled the air, and shadows flickered like memories on the walls. The once-calm atmosphere felt charged, as if the very walls were brimming with the unspoken fears of those who resided within them. Eve stood near the edge of the courtyard, her gaze sweeping over the stone structures, listening to the dissonance that now permeated her sanctuary. This place, once a bastion of strength, now felt fragile, as though a delicate balance was teetering on the verge of collapse.

Liora approached from the far end of the courtyard, her steps hesitant, the weight of the news she bore visible in her troubled expression. Concern and confusion played across her features, her usual grace tempered by the events that had unfolded.

"Did you hear what happened?" Liora asked, her voice barely above a whisper. The heaviness in her tone matched the oppressive energy in the air. "The weaker demons... they were left behind during the last raid. It was brutal."

Eve nodded, acknowledging the information without reacting emotionally, her demeanor calm and collected. She gestured for Liora to sit beside her on a low stone bench that lined the courtyard. Liora hesitated for a moment before settling beside Eve, her gaze shifting between the elder priestess and the distant fires of Hell that burned perpetually beyond the temple's grounds.

"I did hear," Eve said after a moment, her voice soft but steady. "It's a harsh reality we must face."

The cold truth hung in the air, the implications sinking in for Liora. She clenched her hands in her lap, visibly struggling to reconcile what she had heard. Eve let the silence stretch between them, not rushing to fill it. She knew that silence often allowed the deeper truths to rise to the surface, that the discomfort could bring clarity.

As the sun dipped lower on the horizon, casting long shadows across the courtyard, Eve's eyes flickered to the distant line where the fiery glow of Hell mingled with the darkening sky. She allowed the weight of the moment to settle between them, as if the shifting sky mirrored the turmoil within the temple. Only then did she break the silence with a question designed to cut through Liora's uncertainty.

"What do you feel when you think about those demons?" Eve's voice was calm, yet probing, encouraging Liora to look inward.

Liora blinked, taken aback by the directness of the question. She had expected sympathy or perhaps instructions on how to assist those who had suffered. Instead, she was met with a question that demanded reflection, something far deeper than the immediate situation called for. She glanced down at her hands, her brow furrowed in thought.

"I feel..." Liora began, her voice trembling slightly, "I feel like I should help them. They need us. The ones who were left behind - they didn't stand a chance." Her words were filled with compassion, but also with a certain helplessness, as though she didn't quite know how to process the enormity of the suffering she had just described.

Eve nodded, her expression thoughtful, yet unreadable. "Compassion is a noble impulse," she said, her tone measured. "But what form does your help take? Pity? Charity? Those can often be deceptive traps."

Liora looked up, her brow furrowing in confusion. "What do you mean?" she asked, genuinely curious but clearly struggling to understand the direction of Eve's thoughts.

"Pity is a subtle poison," Eve explained, her voice low but firm. "It disempowers those who receive it, reinforcing the belief that they are weak and incapable of change. Pity doesn't elevate - it imprisons. Instead of offering true strength, it fosters dependency. What they need is not sympathy, but the tools to rise above their circumstances."

Liora's frown deepened. "But they're suffering. How can I turn my back on them when they need us?" Her voice wavered, caught between the compassion she felt and the confusion wrought by Eve's words.

Eve turned slightly to face her, her dark eyes sharp, cutting through Liora's doubt. "You must understand that your first instinct to help can sometimes come from a place of condescension, even if it's unconscious. The real gift you can give is not your pity, but the opportunity for them to find their own strength. It is far more difficult, but it is the only way they can truly rise. Instead of comforting them in their weakness, teach them how to fight back, how to claim their power."

Liora's expression grew troubled, her mind racing to understand the depth of Eve's point. "But how?" she asked, her voice thick with uncertainty. "How do I teach them when I'm still learning myself?"

Eve smiled faintly, as though recognizing the echo of her own past struggles in Liora's question. "By embodying the lessons you are learning," she replied. "You don't have to have all the answers right now. But you can guide them, just as you are being guided. Show them that weakness is not their fate. Strength is built through struggle, not through the easy comfort of pity. When you face hardship, embrace it. Use it to grow, not to cower."

A stillness settled between them, the quiet intensity of Eve's words sinking into Liora's soul. The young woman's breath hitched as she tried to process the implications of what she was being told. Eve was right - offering comfort and pity was easier, but it did little to change the reality of suffering. Real help, real empowerment, would require much more than simple gestures of kindness.

Eve stood, her posture commanding, as if drawing strength from the very stones of the temple beneath her feet. "The choice is yours, Liora. Do you want to be the one who comforts the weak, or do you want to be the one who helps them find their own strength? Only one of those paths leads to real change."

Liora looked away, her gaze settling once more on the distant horizon where the infernal glow of Hell flickered ominously. The weight of Eve's words seemed to press down on her, yet at the same time, they sparked something deep within. The demons she had once viewed with pity now appeared in a different light. Instead of helpless souls needing rescue, they were individuals capable of growth and transformation - if given the right tools. But the path Eve was pointing to wasn't easy. It demanded more of her than mere kindness. It required her to lead by example, to confront her own fears and uncertainties before she could truly help others do the same.

"You must be willing to let them suffer," Eve continued, her voice soft but resolute. "Not because you enjoy their pain, but because suffering is often the crucible in which strength is forged. If you constantly shield them from hardship, you deny them the opportunity to grow. It's a difficult balance, but it's necessary if you truly want to help them rise."

Liora nodded slowly, the conflict in her eyes now mixed with something new - determination. The concept was still foreign, even uncomfortable, but there was a logic to it that she couldn't deny. To help others, she had to stop seeing them as weak and in need of saving. Instead, she had to view them as capable of becoming strong, as long as they were given the chance to struggle and overcome.

Eve watched her closely, noting the shift in her posture, the way her shoulders squared slightly as if preparing for a new burden. "This won't be easy," she said softly, almost as if reading Liora's thoughts. "There will be times when you'll want to step in, to offer comfort. But remember, true strength doesn't come from avoiding pain - it comes from facing it head-on."

Eve knew how difficult this lesson was, especially for someone like Liora, who had always been driven by compassion. But Liora needed to understand that there was a delicate balance between compassion and empowerment, and that the two were not always synonymous. Pity could feel like kindness, but in the end, it could rob people of their agency.

Liora sighed, the realization settling heavily on her shoulders. "I understand," she said quietly, though there was still hesitation in her voice. "But it's hard. It feels... cruel to just stand by and watch someone suffer."

"It's not about standing by," Eve corrected. "It's about guiding them through the suffering, helping them see that they can overcome it. You're not abandoning them; you're giving them the greatest gift - belief in their own strength. But you have to be strong enough to let them fight their own battles. That's true leadership, Liora. That's what the Übermensch embodies."

For a moment, they both sat in silence, the weight of the conversation hanging between them like the still, heavy air of the underworld. Liora's mind churned with the implications of Eve's words. The fiery landscape of Hell seemed less ominous now, not because it had changed, but because her perception of it had. It was no longer a realm of hopeless torment but a place where the strong could be forged in the crucible of suffering.

Finally, Liora stood, her expression resolute but contemplative. "I think I understand now," she said, her voice steady. "I need to stop seeing them as victims. I need to help them see their own strength."

Eve smiled, rising to stand beside her. "Exactly. And in doing so, you'll find your own strength as well. This path is not just for them - it's for you too. Every time you face your own struggles, every time you refuse to succumb to pity or weakness, you are becoming stronger. And that strength will ripple out to those around you."

"Come," Eve said, walking away from the bench. "Let's witness the aftermath of that skirmish together. I want you to see what happens when pity prevails."

Liora hesitated but followed Eve as they made their way toward the temple's edge. The scene that unfolded before them was grim. The weak demons, those who had fallen during the raid, were huddled together, their expressions vacant and defeated. Some nursed wounds, while others simply sat in despair.

"Do you see?" Eve gestured toward the group. "What has become of them?"

Liora's heart ached at the sight. "They look so lost," she murmured.

"Exactly. They are lost because they have been taught to rely on others to save them. Pity has stripped them of their will to fight. If you approach them now, what will you offer? Comfort? Words of sympathy?"

"I... I guess so," Liora admitted, uncertainty still lingering in her voice.

"Then let's watch," Eve said, her gaze unwavering. "Observe how they respond to your pity."

Tentatively, Liora stepped forward, her heart racing as she approached the group of demons huddled together in the shadowy corner of the temple courtyard. The air was thick with despair, their gaunt faces etched with years of hardship, yet a flicker of hope gleamed in their eyes as they noticed her presence. "I'm here to help," she said, her voice steady but soft, trying to convey strength without overstepping the delicate balance between assistance and pity.

A few demons looked up, their weary eyes glistening with a mix of hope and resignation, as though they had heard such promises before, only to be disappointed. "Can you save us?" one of them asked, his voice hollow and broken, the weight of lifetimes of suffering evident in his tone. It was a plea that carried the burden of countless souls crushed under the yoke of oppression.

Liora felt the pull to reach out and offer words of comfort, to tell them everything would be alright, but Eve's presence loomed large in her mind, reminding her of the lessons they had discussed. To comfort them now would be to fall into the very trap Eve had warned her about - the trap of pity that disempowers rather than uplifts. Instead, she swallowed the urge and spoke carefully. "I can't save you," she said slowly, each word carefully measured. "But I can help you find your strength again."

A murmur rippled through the gathered demons, a mix of disbelief and confusion spreading like wildfire. Some exchanged skeptical glances, their doubt heavy in the air. Liora could feel the weight of their expectations pressing down on her, the temptation to give in and promise them easy answers, but she steeled herself, drawing on the inner resolve she had begun to cultivate. "You have to choose to rise," she continued, her voice growing more confident with each word. "I can show you how to train, how to fight back against those who would seek to oppress you. But you have to take the first step."

Her words hung in the air like a challenge. A deep silence fell over the group as the demons processed what she had said. Liora watched their faces closely, noting the subtle shifts in their expressions - uncertainty, yes, but also a flicker of something else. Perhaps defiance, or even a spark of hope long buried under layers of despair. One demon, a female with dark, smoldering eyes, stepped forward, her face twisted with bitterness. "You think we can just stand up and fight?"

she demanded, her voice sharp with anger and disbelief. "Look at us! We're nothing."

Liora's heart clenched at the rawness of the demon's words. It was a stark reminder of just how deep their suffering had gone, how profoundly they had been conditioned to believe in their own inferiority. But she did not falter. She had to hold firm, not only for their sake but for her own journey toward understanding strength. "No," Liora countered, her voice firm and unwavering. "You are not nothing. You are stronger than you believe. It won't be easy - no one is handing out victories - but if you let pity keep you down, if you allow yourself to believe that this is all you are, then you will remain in chains forever."

The bitterness on the female demon's face softened slightly, replaced by a flicker of doubt. It was clear that Liora's words had hit a nerve. The chains she spoke of were not just physical - they were the mental and emotional bonds that kept them subservient to their circumstances. Liora could see that some part of them wanted to believe, but centuries of suffering didn't fade overnight. "I can't promise you victory," Liora continued, her tone resolute. "But I can promise that we will train together, and we will fight. Not because someone else will save us, but because we will save ourselves."

Eve, who had been standing quietly in the background, observed the exchange with growing pride. She could see the transformation happening within Liora - the initial hesitance giving way to conviction. It was a small but pivotal shift. Liora was no longer the unsure apprentice questioning her role; she was stepping into the mantle of leadership by empowering those around her rather than seeking to rescue them. Eve had known this moment would come, and now that it had, she could feel a quiet sense of satisfaction settling over her.

Slowly, the demons began to respond. Some murmured among themselves, exchanging hesitant glances as the embers of hope ignited within them. One of the older demons, his face lined with scars from battles long past, stepped forward. "You really think we can fight?" he asked, his voice rough with skepticism but tinged with a trace of curiosity. The challenge in his tone was evident - he had heard many promises before, and he was not easily swayed by empty words.

Liora met his gaze without flinching. "I believe we can," she replied, her tone growing stronger as she spoke. "It's not going to be easy. But strength doesn't come from comfort. It comes from struggle. We will start training together, and I will help you find your strength. But you have to want it. You have to believe that you are more than what your circumstances have made you."

The silence that followed was heavy with contemplation. The demons, for so long accustomed to their chains, were beginning to see that perhaps those chains were not as unbreakable as they once believed. Slowly, they began to straighten their postures, their once-defeated body language shifting as they looked at Liora with a mixture of cautious hope and curiosity. The bitter resignation that had once defined them was starting to crack, replaced by the faintest glimmer of defiance.

Eve stepped forward, her voice clear and purposeful as she addressed Liora. "This is what I meant, Liora," she said, her tone filled with both pride and instruction. "You're not here to save them; you're here to empower them. Pity has no place in strength. It's not enough to feel sorry for their suffering - you must help them discover their own will to rise. True leadership is not about carrying others; it's about teaching them to stand on their own."

The atmosphere in the courtyard shifted, the oppressive weight of despair beginning to lift. The demons' eyes, once filled with defeat, now gleamed with the faintest spark of possibility. They weren't saved, but they weren't broken either. The battle ahead would be long, and the road to reclaiming their strength arduous, but in this moment, something had changed. A ripple of energy passed through the group, subtle but undeniable, as they began to stand a little taller, their gazes turning toward Liora with a new sense of trust and hope.

As they turned to one another, murmuring quietly, Eve couldn't help but feel a deep sense of satisfaction. Liora had taken the first step toward embodying the ideals of the Übermensch - not by being a savior, but by guiding others to discover their own strength. This was the path of the Übermensch: not to lord over others or seek to impose one's will, but to inspire others to rise above their limitations and claim their power.

"Now," Eve said, breaking the stillness that had settled over the courtyard. "You've begun a journey, Liora. But remember, this is just the beginning. You must continue to confront the discomfort of true strength, even when it means rejecting the comforts of pity."

Liora nodded, her features shifting from uncertainty to determination. The weight of Eve's words hung in the air, but it was clear that Liora had absorbed them. Her posture straightened as if the realization of what lay ahead had finally sunk in. "I understand. I'll help them find their strength, and in doing so, I'll find mine."

This was no small revelation. The distinction between pity and empowerment that Eve had drilled into Liora was not just about these demons - it was about Liora's own development, her potential as a leader, and her evolution toward something greater than herself. Pity, as Nietzsche had argued, was not a virtue to be praised but a vice to be eradicated. It was an insidious force that, under the guise of kindness, reinforced weakness and stagnation.

As they turned to leave the demons behind, Liora glanced back, her eyes filled with a mixture of empathy and resolve. The challenge was clear: she could no longer view their suffering as something to be soothed or alleviated through soft gestures or comforting words. These demons did not need to be saved from their misery; they needed to be shown the way out of it through their own strength, their own will to power. Eve knew this was a turning point for Liora, a pivotal moment in which she would either rise to meet her potential or fall back into the easier path of false charity.

Eve's thoughts drifted to the core of Nietzschean philosophy, the rejection of pity as a moral imperative. Nietzsche despised pity because he saw it as a way of keeping the strong down and the weak comfortable in their weakness. In the world of Hell, where the strong were constantly tested, the concept of pity was poisonous. It created a cycle where the suffering of others became a crutch, not a call to action. For Liora, learning this lesson wasn't just about helping these demons; it was about understanding that true compassion lies in fostering self-reliance.

"You see," Eve began as they walked back toward the heart of the temple, her tone taking on the cadence of a mentor deep in philosophical instruction, "pity seems noble on the surface, but it is a deceptive force. When you pity someone, you are telling them that they are beneath you, that they are too weak to rise on their own. It strips them of their agency and reinforces their suffering."

Liora's brow furrowed in thought. "But if we don't offer comfort, don't we risk becoming cold? Detached?"

"Not at all," Eve replied. "Compassion and pity are not the same. Compassion can drive you to guide others, to challenge them, to give them the tools to improve. But pity... pity is the hand that holds them down. Think of the demons back there. If you had told them that they were helpless and needed you to save them, what would have happened?"

"They would've relied on me," Liora said slowly, the realization dawning on her. "They wouldn't have tried to find their own strength."

"Exactly. And that is the problem with pity. It fosters dependence and weakness. When we pity others, we are, in essence, comforting ourselves more than we are helping them. We're making their suffering about our need to feel righteous, to feel like saviors. That's the dangerous allure of pity - it offers comfort to both the giver and the receiver, but in doing so, it destroys the potential for growth."

As they moved further from the courtyard, the temple's towering spires cast long shadows over them, the fiery glow of Hell reflecting off the dark stones. Eve glanced at Liora and could see the wheels turning in her mind. The young woman was wrestling with the implications of this new philosophy, as Eve had expected she would. This was no easy path, but it was a necessary one if Liora was to become more than just another follower of the temple's teachings.

"Think of it this way," Eve continued. "What we're doing isn't about rejecting compassion - it's about rejecting false compassion. True strength comes from hardship, from facing challenges that force you to grow. If we coddle these demons, if we offer them only pity and sympathy, they will never rise. They will remain weak, reliant on others, and stuck in their suffering. But if we teach them to fight, if we show them that they have the power to shape their own fate, then we've truly helped them."

"I see," Liora said, her voice steady. "So, it's not that we shouldn't care - it's that we should care enough to help them grow."

"Precisely," Eve said, nodding approvingly. "And that applies to you as well. You're not just learning this to help others - you're learning it to help yourself. You are on your own journey of strength, of self-overcoming. And along the way, you'll face temptations to fall back into old habits, to offer comfort instead of challenge, to seek the easy path. But if you keep this lesson in mind - if you remember that true growth only comes through struggle - then you will continue to grow into the leader I know you can be."

Liora remained silent for a moment, her gaze fixed on the path ahead. Eve could see the determination settling into her features, the resolve to embrace this philosophy not just in words but in action. It was a rare thing, to see someone so young understand such a difficult concept, but Liora had shown promise from the beginning. Now, that promise was beginning to take shape, and Eve knew that this was just the beginning of her transformation.

The temple loomed ahead, its dark stone walls etched with runes of power and ancient wisdom. As they approached the entrance, Eve felt the winds of change stirring around them. Something had shifted in the air, an energy that seemed to vibrate with potential. In this world of darkness, where suffering was a constant companion, Eve and Liora were nurturing something different - something stronger. They were planting the seeds of resilience, of strength, and of self-reliance.

As they stepped through the massive doors, Eve turned to Liora one last time. "Remember, this is a path few have the courage to walk. You will face resistance - from others and from yourself. The temptation to fall back into the comfort of pity will always be there, but if you can reject that and embrace the discomfort of growth, you will become more than you ever imagined."

Liora nodded, her eyes alight with understanding and determination. "I won't forget. I'll keep pushing, even when it's hard."

Eve smiled, a rare warmth in her otherwise stoic expression. "Good. That's the first step toward true strength."

As they made their way deeper into the temple, the atmosphere around them shifted. The echoes of their footsteps seemed to resonate with purpose, the flickering torches casting long shadows on the stone walls. Together, they were forging a new path - one that rejected the easy comforts of pity in favor of the hard-earned power of self-reliance. In this, they were not only reshaping the lives of those around them but the very foundation of the temple itself.

18

The Embrace of Individual Will

The temple's great hall echoed with an energy that simmered like a brewing tempest. Shadows danced along the walls, flickering with the movement of flickering candles that lined the stone alcoves. Eve stood at the center, her presence commanding as she awaited Liora's arrival. Today was not merely another lesson; it was a challenge that would shape the path Liora was forging.

As the heavy doors creaked open, Liora stepped in, her expression a blend of anticipation and apprehension. The hall felt alive, vibrating with the weight of philosophy, and she could sense the pivotal nature of what was to come.

"Welcome, Liora," Eve said, her voice smooth yet intense. "Today, we engage in a philosophical duel. You will articulate your understanding of freedom, power, and responsibility. Are you ready to confront your own beliefs?"

Liora hesitated, her heart racing. "A duel? What if I can't articulate my thoughts clearly?"

Eve stepped closer, her gaze piercing yet supportive. "The point of this exercise is not perfection, but exploration. You will learn more about yourself through this challenge. Embrace it."

Taking a deep breath, Liora nodded. "I'm ready."

"Good. Let's begin," Eve replied, moving to a circle of stone chairs that had been arranged in the center of the hall. They took their seats, the atmosphere thick with the gravity of the moment.

"First question: What does freedom mean to you?" Eve asked, her voice steady, urging Liora to find her footing.

Liora paused, the silence amplifying her thoughts. "I think... freedom is being able to make choices without outside interference. It's the ability to pursue what I want."

"Interesting," Eve said, tilting her head slightly. "But is it only about the absence of constraints? Or is there more to it?"

Liora furrowed her brow, wrestling with the concept. "It's also about having the strength to follow through on those choices. If I'm free but too weak to act, am I truly free?"

"Precisely," Eve responded, a hint of approval in her tone. "But what about the responsibility that comes with freedom? If one is truly free, must they not also embrace the weight of their choices?"

Liora shifted in her seat, the question resonating deeply within her. "Yes, I suppose that means I'm responsible for the consequences of my actions. But that can be terrifying. What if I choose wrong?"

Eve's eyes softened for a moment as she saw the vulnerability in Liora's expression, but her words remained sharp. "Ah, and there's the heart of it. True freedom is terrifying. It is not the absence of constraints alone, but the realization that with that freedom comes the burden of responsibility. The world is full of people who wish to be free, but few are prepared to accept the consequences of their own autonomy."

Liora sat back, considering this. "So, freedom is more than just doing what I want... it's about owning every outcome, even the ones I didn't expect?"

"Exactly," Eve said, her voice taking on a more intense note. "The Übermensch, the one who transcends, is not afraid of the consequences of their choices. They do not look to others to validate their decisions. This is the essence of power, Liora - not just the ability to act, but the strength to live with the results, good or bad."

Liora frowned, her mind grappling with this idea. "But isn't that dangerous? What if someone abuses that power, making decisions that hurt others just because they're free to do so?"

Eve leaned forward, her eyes gleaming with the weight of the conversation. "This is where responsibility comes in. Power without responsibility is mere tyranny, a hollow mockery of strength. True power - true freedom - is found in the ability to wield it with wisdom. To harm others recklessly is the path of the weak, not the strong. The Übermensch seeks to rise above, not by crushing those beneath them, but by elevating themselves to a plane where they no longer need to dominate. They transcend the petty morality of 'good' and 'evil,' recognizing that their actions shape reality."

Liora looked uncertain. "But if we reject 'good' and 'evil,' what guides our choices? How do we know what's right?"

Eve smiled, knowing this was the crucial moment. "You must decide for yourself what is right, based on the values you create. This is why the path of the Übermensch is so demanding. It requires you to look within, to wrestle with your own beliefs, your desires, and your ambitions, and to shape your own moral code. No external law or divine decree will tell you what is right. Only you can define that."

"But... what if my values conflict with those around me? What if they don't understand?" Liora's voice wavered, revealing the deep-rooted fear of isolation.

Eve's gaze hardened slightly, though her voice remained calm. "That is the price of true freedom. The Übermensch walks a lonely path, often misunderstood by the masses who cling to convention. You must be prepared to stand alone if necessary, to face rejection from those who do not share your vision. But in doing so, you achieve something far greater than mere acceptance - you achieve self-mastery."

Liora sighed, her mind racing with the implications. "It sounds... lonely."

"It can be," Eve admitted. "But it is also empowering. When you stop seeking validation from others, you begin to trust in your own power, your own judgment. And when you find those rare individuals who can walk alongside you, not because they need you but because they choose to, that connection will be far deeper and more meaningful than any superficial bond."

Liora fell silent for a moment, the weight of the lesson settling over her. "So, freedom isn't about running away from responsibility, but embracing it fully. And power isn't about control - it's about self-mastery."

"Precisely," Eve said, satisfaction clear in her tone. "The weak seek control over others because they lack control over themselves. But you, Liora, must aspire to something greater. You must learn to control yourself, to shape your own destiny, without fear of what others might think or say."

Liora nodded slowly, beginning to understand. "But what about when we make mistakes? When we choose wrong? Doesn't that prove we're not ready for this kind of power?"

Eve smiled, her eyes softening once more. "Mistakes are inevitable. Even the Übermensch stumbles. The difference is how they respond to those mistakes. The weak crumble under the weight of failure, retreating into self-pity or blame. But the strong - those on the path to true freedom - learn from their failures. They do not let mistakes define them. Instead, they grow stronger because of them. Every wrong choice is an opportunity to refine your values, to become more in tune with who you truly are."

Liora's face brightened slightly at this. "So failure isn't the end - it's part of the journey?"

"Exactly," Eve said, nodding approvingly. "In fact, failure is often the most powerful teacher. It strips away illusions and forces you to confront the truth about yourself. If you can embrace failure without letting it defeat you, you will become unstoppable. This is why the path of the Übermensch is not for the faint of heart - it requires relentless honesty, both with yourself and with the world around you."

A flicker of realization crossed Liora's face. "I think I'm beginning to understand. It's not about avoiding mistakes or controlling others. It's about controlling myself - my actions, my reactions, my choices."

Eve smiled, seeing the shift in Liora's perspective. "Now you're getting it. Freedom is not a gift - it's a responsibility. Power is not a weapon - it's a tool. And the more you understand yourself, the more capable you become of using both wisely."

Liora's brow furrowed in concentration as she absorbed Eve's words. "But how do I start? How do I take the first step toward this kind of freedom and power?"

"The first step," Eve said, her voice low and deliberate, "is to challenge your own assumptions. Question everything you think you know - about yourself, about the world, about what is right and wrong. Don't accept anything at face value. Think critically, deeply, and without fear. Only by confronting your own beliefs can you begin to shape them."

Liora nodded, determination flashing in her eyes. "I'm ready to try."

"Good," Eve said, rising from her chair. "But remember, this is a lifelong journey. There will always be more to learn, more challenges to face. You will stumble, you will fall, but each time you do, you will rise stronger than before. That is the way of the Übermensch."

Eve leaned forward, her expression earnest. "The essence of power lies in the mastery of oneself. To embrace freedom is to accept that risk. Power is not about controlling others; it's about controlling your own fate. Do you see the connection?"

Liora nodded slowly, her thoughts coalescing into a clearer picture. "So, freedom and responsibility are intertwined. I can't truly be free without acknowledging what comes with that freedom."

"Exactly," Eve said, her voice infused with encouragement. "Now, let's delve deeper. What does it mean to pursue your own path?"

Liora took a moment, her mind racing. "Pursuing my own path means following my instincts and beliefs rather than simply adhering to what others tell me. It's about discovering who I am outside the expectations of the temple or the teachings I've learned."

"Good," Eve said, her eyes shining with approval. "But what if that path leads you into conflict with those very teachings?"

Liora felt a surge of determination. "Then I must be willing to challenge them. If I believe something different, I can't shy away from that truth, even if it makes me uncomfortable. I need to find my voice."

"Very well said," Eve replied, a hint of pride evident in her expression. "Your voice is your power. Now, let's shift the focus a bit. What is the role of suffering in this journey toward freedom?"

Liora frowned, the question stirring a multitude of thoughts. "Suffering... it's hard. It feels like an obstacle, something to be avoided. But I guess it also teaches us, doesn't it? It shapes who we are."

Eve nodded, sensing that Liora was beginning to grasp the intricacies of her journey. "Exactly. Nietzsche believed that suffering is an inherent part of life. He argued that it's through suffering that we gain strength and resilience. Without adversity, we cannot truly grow. Would you agree?"

"Yeah, I can see that," Liora said slowly. "When I reflect on my own experiences, the moments of pain and hardship often pushed me to confront my fears, to dig deeper into my own convictions. It's like they forced me to grow up faster than I wanted."

"Precisely," Eve replied, leaning forward, her expression intense. "Think about it. In moments of suffering, we are stripped of our illusions. We are confronted with our limitations, our weaknesses. This can be frightening, but it is also liberating. It compels us to confront reality, to take responsibility for our choices, and ultimately to assert our will."

Liora nodded, absorbing this. "So, suffering isn't just something we endure. It can be a catalyst for change, a push toward self-discovery?"

"Exactly," Eve said, her voice rich with conviction. "Suffering can be transformative if we allow it to be. It teaches us that we are not invincible, that life is complex and often painful. But in that pain, we find our strength. We learn to embrace our vulnerabilities and recognize that they do not define us; rather, they are part of our journey."

Liora's brow furrowed, as she considered this. "But if we embrace suffering, doesn't that mean we're accepting the status quo? What if we suffer for reasons beyond our control? Doesn't that just perpetuate the cycle of pain?"

"An excellent point," Eve acknowledged. "But embracing suffering does not mean passively accepting it. It means actively engaging with it. We are not merely victims of our circumstances; we have the power to shape our responses. When we suffer, we have a choice: we can allow it to defeat us or use it as a stepping stone toward our own empowerment."

"Right," Liora said, her voice gaining strength. "So, it's not about avoiding pain at all costs, but rather facing it head-on and learning from it. It's about using that experience to fuel my journey."

"Absolutely," Eve encouraged, her eyes sparkling with pride. "This is where the concept of the Übermensch becomes crucial. The Übermensch embraces suffering as an integral part of existence, seeing it not as a barrier but as a challenge to overcome. They cultivate their will to power, finding strength in adversity and turning pain into purpose."

"Wow," Liora replied, her voice almost a whisper. "I never thought of it that way. It's like reframing the narrative. Instead of seeing suffering as a punishment, I can view it as an opportunity to grow."

"Exactly," Eve said, her voice resonating with excitement. "This reframing allows you to reclaim your power. Rather than being defined by your struggles, you define them. You choose how to respond to them, how to transform them into something greater. This is the essence of taking control of your life."

Liora leaned back, a smile spreading across her face. "So, if I encounter suffering on my path, I can ask myself what it can teach me, rather than just wishing it away?"

"Yes!" Eve exclaimed, the intensity of the moment electrifying the air between them. "And in doing so, you begin to recognize the value of resilience. You develop a deeper understanding of yourself and your values. Suffering becomes a teacher, not a tyrant. This is where you will find freedom - not in the absence of suffering, but in your response to it."

Liora considered this, her expression thoughtful. "But how do I learn to respond positively? What if I get overwhelmed? It's easy to say I can use suffering to grow, but in the moment, it's so hard to see clearly."

Eve smiled knowingly. "That's the challenge of life, isn't it? But this is where preparation and self-awareness come into play. You can cultivate a mindset that embraces growth, that seeks to learn from every experience, especially the painful ones. Journaling, reflection, and honest conversations like this one help you process your feelings and thoughts. The more you engage with your own experiences, the more equipped you become to handle suffering when it arises."

"I see," Liora replied, her voice contemplative. "It's about building resilience over time. I need to practice responding positively, so that when the tough moments come, I'm ready to face them."

"Exactly," Eve reiterated, pride blooming in her chest. "Resilience is like a muscle; the more you exercise it, the stronger it becomes. But remember, strength doesn't mean you won't feel pain. It means you will acknowledge it, confront it, and ultimately rise above it."

Liora sat in silence for a moment, absorbing Eve's wisdom. "It's a powerful lesson," she said finally. "I think I've always seen suffering as something to be avoided, something that takes away my freedom. But now I see it can be a part of my journey to freedom."

Eve smiled warmly, appreciating Liora's growing insight. "Yes, and as you embark on your own path, remember that freedom comes from within. It is not dictated by your circumstances or by the actions of others. You have the power to shape your reality, even in the face of suffering."

"Thank you, Eve," Liora said, her voice sincere. "This discussion has opened my eyes to so many things I hadn't considered before. I feel more prepared to face whatever comes my way."

Eve's expression softened further, her heart swelling with pride. "You're welcome, Liora. But remember, this is just the beginning. You have the tools to confront your beliefs, to embrace suffering, and to find your path. The true journey is just beginning, and I look forward to seeing how you continue to grow."

As the debate continued, Liora's confidence began to swell. She articulated her thoughts with increasing clarity, drawing from her own experiences, her struggles, and the teachings of Eve. They debated fiercely, each point met with counterpoints that pushed her to think critically about her beliefs.

Hours passed as they engaged in this intellectual dance, the flickering candlelight casting long shadows across the hall. Finally, Eve leaned back, a satisfied smile gracing her lips. "You've done well, Liora. You've wrestled with these ideas and emerged stronger for it. Now, it's time to solidify your commitment to these principles through a rite of passage."

Liora's heart raced at the mention of the ritual. "What does it entail?"

Eve rose, her movements fluid and purposeful. "You will undergo a trial that tests your understanding of freedom and responsibility. This will challenge your will, pushing you to apply everything you've learned today."

"Are you sure I'm ready?" Liora asked, her voice tinged with uncertainty.

Eve nodded, her gaze unwavering. "You are more prepared than you realize. Trust yourself."

With a deep breath, Liora followed Eve deeper into the temple, past intricate carvings and ominous murals that told tales of power and sacrifice. They entered a sacred chamber where the air buzzed with energy, an ancient ritual space reserved for transformative experiences.

"Here, you will confront your own limitations," Eve explained, gesturing to a circular platform at the center of the room. "You will face a vision that embodies your doubts, your fears, and your aspirations. Overcome it, and you will emerge with a renewed sense of purpose."

Liora stepped onto the platform, her heart pounding in her chest. "What will I see?"

"Whatever you need to confront," Eve replied, her tone encouraging. "Embrace it, and let it guide you toward your truth."

As Liora closed her eyes, the world around her began to blur and fade away. It felt as though the walls of reality were melting into a mist, drawing her into a different realm, a place that existed beyond the tangible and the known. She was no longer confined to the physical space of the temple; instead, she floated in a vast expanse, where swirling shadows danced with blinding beams of light. The contrasting forces ebbed and flowed, creating an atmosphere thick with tension and possibility.

In this ethereal space, a figure began to emerge from the chaos - a silhouette forged from her deepest fears. Liora felt her breath catch in her throat as the figure took shape, an unsettling amalgamation of her self-doubt, her perceived weakness, and the remnants of pity that still clung to her like shadows at dusk.

"Who are you?" Liora demanded, her voice steady despite the tremor of uncertainty echoing in her heart. She squared her shoulders, attempting to project confidence in a moment that threatened to consume her.

"I am the embodiment of your hesitations," the figure replied, its voice resonating like distant thunder rumbling in a storm. "I am everything that holds you back."

Liora took a deep breath, summoning her inner strength. "No. You do not define me."

The figure let out a hollow laugh that reverberated through the expanse, as if mocking her. "You think you can escape me? Every moment of doubt, every time you've felt powerless - I am your shadow. You cannot rid yourself of me."

With her resolve ignited, Liora charged at the figure, a fierce roar escaping her lips. "I am more than my fears! I choose to embrace my strength, to claim my freedom and my will!" Her heart raced, each beat echoing her determination.

As she lunged toward the figure, Liora felt the surge of energy coursing through her veins, a reminder of every lesson she had learned from Eve - the wisdom that had guided her to this moment. The figure flickered, momentarily startled by the intensity of her conviction. Liora would not succumb to the darkness that had haunted her for so long.

The shadow loomed larger, twisting and morphing into familiar faces: the doubters who had once whispered words of inadequacy, the moments of hesitation that had anchored her in fear. Yet, with every advance she made, Liora began to realize something crucial. This figure was not merely an enemy to be defeated; it was a part of herself that she had long neglected, a fragment of her journey that needed acknowledgment and integration.

"You are a part of my journey, but you do not dictate my path," Liora declared, her voice ringing clear, unfaltering in the tempest of doubt surrounding her.

The figure trembled, its form shifting as Liora's resolve deepened. Memories washed over her - moments of pain, sorrow, and disappointment - but within those memories lay the seeds of growth. "I embrace you," she continued, her words gaining strength, "but I will not be ruled by you. I will not allow my fears to define my existence."

With each proclamation, Liora felt a lightness spreading through her being, the shadows receding slightly in the face of her acceptance. The figure began to waver, its features softening, as if responding to her newfound clarity. It was a dance of power, a revelation that the darkness could coexist with her light, but it did not have to dominate.

The figure's laughter faded, replaced by a whisper - a recognition of her journey. "You are strong," it murmured, a hint of reverence lacing its tone. "But strength is forged through struggle, and I am a testament to that struggle. Without me, you would not know your true power."

In that moment of realization, Liora saw herself reflected in the figure - her past, her pain, and her perseverance. She understood now that the shadows represented not just her fears but the trials she had faced and overcome. They were not obstacles to be eliminated but integral parts of her identity, essential for her growth.

As the understanding deepened, a blinding flash of light erupted from within her. The figure began to disintegrate into a cascade of shimmering particles, each one a representation of the lessons learned through suffering and strength. The air was alive with energy as the remnants of her fears dissolved, leaving behind a sense of liberation and empowerment.

Liora stood tall, her heart swelling with newfound power and clarity. The particles swirled around her, bathing her in warmth and light, filling the void that had once been occupied by self-doubt. She felt lighter, as if the burdens she had carried were being replaced by a profound understanding of her capabilities.

"From now on, I will not run from my fears. I will acknowledge them, learn from them, and use that knowledge to fuel my journey," she whispered, the words a solemn vow to herself. She felt an urge to move forward, to embrace the path ahead with courage and intention.

As the swirling shadows and lights began to dissipate, Liora opened her eyes, her surroundings slowly coming back into focus. The room was unchanged, yet she felt transformed. She was no longer just a student of philosophy; she was a warrior ready to confront her reality with newfound strength.

Eve stood before her, a knowing smile gracing her lips. "Welcome back, Liora. How do you feel?"

"Changed," Liora replied, her voice steady with conviction. "I understand now that my fears are part of me, but they do not control me. I am more than the shadows; I am the light that can rise above them."

Eve nodded, pride shining in her eyes. "You've taken a significant step on your journey, Liora. Remember, this lesson doesn't end here. Each day presents a new challenge, a new opportunity to confront and integrate the parts of yourself that you once feared."

Liora felt a wave of exhilaration wash over her, a sense of clarity that sharpened her focus. "I understand now. True freedom is the courage to face oneself and to claim one's path."

Eve nodded, pride evident in her eyes. "You are no longer just a student, Liora. You are an acolyte, capable of forging your own destiny. Remember this moment as you move forward. Let it be a reminder that your will is your greatest ally."

As they left the chamber, Liora felt the weight of the world shifting beneath her feet. She was ready to embrace her individuality and the responsibilities that came with it. In the temple of Asmodeus, she had found her voice, her strength, and a commitment to freedom that would guide her into whatever challenges lay ahead.

With that, they stepped back into the familiar rhythm of their lives in the temple, the air thick with potential and the promise of change. Liora knew that the journey ahead would be fraught with difficulties, but she also understood that she was equipped to navigate it with strength and resilience. Together with Eve, she would forge a new path, not just for herself but for those who looked to her for guidance.

Act 3: The Transformation

19

Embracing the Shadows

The air in the temple pulsed with tension, dense and charged with an electric energy, as Eve stood at the center of the grand chamber. Flickering torches cast long shadows against the stone walls, and the gathered priests and priestesses formed a semi-circle around her, their expressions a mix of awe and apprehension. Today was different; today, she would not just channel Nyx - she would embody her.

As she closed her eyes, the familiar sensation of power surged through her, a dark tide rising to meet the moonlit sky. With each breath, the essence of Nyx intertwined with her own, reshaping her features, sharpening her senses. Her skin glimmered like starlight, and her hair flowed like liquid night, cascading around her shoulders. When she opened her eyes, they gleamed with an intensity that commanded respect and fear.

"Today, we will transcend the limitations of our doctrine," Eve declared, her voice resonating with an echo that seemed to come from the very depths of the cosmos. "Power is not bound by rigid teachings; it is found in the chaos of existence itself."

Murmurs rippled through the assembly, some intrigued, others troubled. The traditionalists exchanged glances, their disapproval palpable. They were accustomed to the well-worn paths laid out by Asmodeus, but Eve, as Nyx, was not one to tread lightly.

"Nyx challenges the idea that strength lies solely in obedience," she continued, feeling the thrill of her words as they took flight. "True strength is the ability to break free from the chains of dogma and forge one's path. We must learn to embrace the shadows within us, for they are as much a part of our power as the light we seek."

The High Priest, Mordred, stepped forward, his expression darkened with concern. "Eve, or should I say Nyx, what you propose undermines the very foundation of our beliefs. Asmodeus teaches that power is derived from adherence to his doctrine. To deviate from it is to invite chaos and corruption."

Eve's heart raced at the challenge. "You speak of chaos as if it is something to be feared. But I say it is the crucible of creation. Without chaos, we remain stagnant, bound by fear and ignorance. We must dare to explore what lies beyond the confines of our teachings."

"Your words are seductive, but they are a lie!" Mordred shouted, his voice rising above the murmurs of the crowd. "You risk leading our followers astray! What you call freedom may only be a descent into madness."

Eve felt a surge of defiance within her, fueled by the very essence of Nyx. "Madness? Or is it awakening? To reject the dogma that has held us captive for so long is not insanity; it is liberation."

The tension in the room escalated, an electric current of conflicting ideologies. Some followers were captivated by Eve's conviction, nodding in agreement, while others stood firmly against her. Mordred's face twisted with fury, and Eve knew that he would not back down easily.

"Enough of this blasphemy!" he bellowed, his eyes blazing with righteous anger. "I will not stand by while you corrupt our sacred teachings. You must submit to the will of Asmodeus, or face the consequences!"

The challenge hung heavy in the air, and Eve felt the stirrings of power within her - a tempest ready to be unleashed. "If it is a confrontation you seek, then so be it. But know this: Nyx is not a force to be contained. She is freedom incarnate, and I will not submit to the chains of fear."

With that, the air shimmered with energy as Eve fully embraced her transformation. She felt the overwhelming presence of Nyx coursing through her, invigorating every fiber of her being. The shadows coalesced around her, swirling like a dark halo as she prepared to defend her newfound beliefs.

Mordred lunged forward, his movements fueled by fury, his eyes alight with conviction as he called upon the temple's energy to amplify his strike. He felt the familiar surge of power flowing through him, igniting his core as light crackled from his outstretched hand, coalescing into a beam aimed directly at Eve. It was a radiant force, a manifestation of the temple's doctrine, its rigid truths hardened into weaponized light.

But Eve had anticipated the strike. In the split second before the blast could reach her, her body shifted with the effortless grace of shadow, dissolving into fluid darkness as she sidestepped. Nyx's influence pulsed within her veins, guiding her every movement with a precision beyond mortal capability. The beam hurtled past her and exploded against the stone wall, illuminating the chamber in a dazzling flash, splintering stone and scattering dust into the air.

"Is this the best the temple's doctrine can offer?" Eve's voice rang out, mocking yet calm, cutting through the noise of the chaos that enveloped them. "You cling to a script, Mordred, reciting verses that no longer hold meaning. I have discarded such chains. I am the embodiment of existence itself."

Her words hung in the air as she raised her hand, fingers curling as dark energy gathered at her fingertips. It surged forward like a storm of shadow, swirling with the raw force of freedom and rebellion. Mordred's eyes widened in panic, but before he could react, the wave of darkness enveloped him. He stumbled backward, the shadowy storm disorienting him, stripping away the sense of control he had always relied on.

The room erupted into pandemonium. Followers of the temple scattered, some seeking refuge behind the stone pillars, while others remained frozen in place, their gazes fixed on the spectacle of the battle. The clash between Mordred and Eve, or Nyx as many were beginning to see her, was more than a physical contest - it was an ideological war played out in front of them, the old and the new colliding in a violent burst of power.

Eve advanced, her body alive with the pulsing energy of Nyx, her form ethereal yet commanding. Every step she took resonated with the essence of the freedom she had come to embody, the path that defied the constraints of the temple's dogma. She could feel the eyes of the onlookers on her, their fear and awe blending into one as they witnessed her command over the shadows. But this was not about instilling fear; it was about something deeper, something more profound.

"You've become a slave to the past, Mordred," Eve declared, her voice carrying the weight of centuries of cosmic knowledge. "While you cling to the familiar comforts of your doctrine, I have embraced what lies beyond. You speak of control and authority, but those are mere illusions. Power is in freedom, in the choice to carve one's path, to reject the shackles of expectation."

Mordred, regaining his composure, pushed himself to his feet, his mind racing as he summoned another wave of energy, this time brighter, more concentrated, born from desperation. He hurled it at Eve with all the force he could muster, shouting, "You speak of freedom, but all I see is chaos! You cannot defeat the light of Asmodeus!"

Eve raised her hand in response, her dark energy forming a barrier that absorbed the light's force, dissipating it like smoke against the wind. The chamber groaned under the pressure of their power, the very walls trembling as if caught in the crossfire of their clashing ideologies. Yet Eve stood firm, unyielding, her presence unwavering.

"Asmodeus?" Eve's voice was calm but resolute. "You invoke his name as if his teachings are static, as if power can only be understood through the narrow lens of dominance. But Asmodeus is more than just a force of control. His path is about seizing one's will, shaping destiny, and embracing strength. I do not reject him; I see beyond the rigid chains you've forged in his name. True power is not just in subjugation, but in the freedom to redefine it."

The tension in the room mounted as Eve gathered her energy, her power swelling as she drew upon the full might of Nyx. Stars seemed to flicker within the darkness she wielded, a cosmic force that transcended mortal comprehension. Her final strike, the culmination of her transformation, was imminent.

Mordred braced himself, his heart pounding, knowing that this next move would decide the battle. He attempted to summon more energy, but he could feel his reserves waning, the cracks in his faith showing. He glanced at the followers who remained, their faces twisted in a mixture of fear and uncertainty. His power no longer inspired the devotion it once did.

With a fierce cry, Eve unleashed her attack. A swirling vortex of shadow and starlight erupted from her hands, crashing into Mordred with unrelenting force. The chamber shook violently as the vortex consumed him, its sheer intensity overwhelming his defenses. Mordred struggled to hold his ground, his body wracked by the force of Eve's power, until finally, he collapsed, defeated, gasping for breath as the darkness closed in around him.

When the storm of shadows subsided, silence fell over the room. The air, once crackling with the tension of battle, now felt still, the dust settling as the onlookers gazed upon the scene in awe. Mordred lay on the ground, defeated, his strength sapped. Eve stood above him, her form now fully Nyx, the embodiment of chaos and freedom, radiant and terrifying in her power.

"You see now," she said, her voice calm, resonant with the authority of someone who had transcended the boundaries of fear. "Power is not to be feared. It is to be embraced. I do not stand before you as a threat but as a beacon of what we can become when we choose to break free of the past."

The followers who had remained in the chamber stared at her, their minds racing, their beliefs unraveling. Eve had shattered the illusions that had held them captive for so long. This was not about the defeat of Mordred or the victory of Nyx. It was about something far more transformative - the realization that the old ways no longer served them, that they could choose to walk a new path, one where power was found not in domination but in the freedom to create their truth.

Eve turned, leaving Mordred on the ground, knowing that the seeds of change had been planted. The temple, and its people, would never be the same.

As she surveyed the faces of the assembly, she saw the spark of transformation in some, while others still clung to their fear. But Eve knew that seeds had been planted - seeds of doubt that would grow into questions, debates, and perhaps even a revolution within the temple.

"We are not bound by the past," she continued, her tone resolute. "We are the architects of our destiny. It is time for us to forge a new path, one that honors both power and freedom."

Eve stepped back, allowing the shadows to recede as she regained her composure. The confrontation had solidified her authority, not just as Eve but as Nyx - a symbol of the struggle against dogma and the celebration of individuality. The path ahead would be fraught with challenges, but she was ready to embrace the shadows and lead her followers into the unknown.

As the murmurs of the assembly grew louder, an overwhelming force swept through the chamber. The air grew thick with an ancient, electric energy that sent shivers through the crowd. An aura of authority and power filled the room, and then, from the depths of shadow, Lord Asmodeus himself appeared. His presence was immense, commanding an awe that silenced every voice in the temple. His dark figure, framed by an ethereal glow, radiated a blend of danger and allure that made the crowd instinctively part to allow him passage.

Eve stood still, her heart racing, but not from fear. It was a cocktail of emotions - anticipation, exhilaration, and a strange, intoxicating thrill at the prospect of standing in her truth before Asmodeus. The lord's eyes locked onto hers, a gaze so intense it felt as if he could see through her very soul. The world outside the chamber seemed to fade, leaving only the weight of this moment between them.

"As you can see, my dear Eve," Asmodeus began, his voice like velvet over steel, "your new teachings have borne unexpected and remarkable fruit." His words echoed with a mix of approval and subtle challenge as he gestured toward the crowd, who watched in stunned silence. "By embracing the chaotic essence of Nyx and daring to question the rigid structure of our dogma, you have achieved what few thought possible."

A murmur of disbelief rippled through the congregation, but Asmodeus's gaze remained unwavering. "More souls, both mortal and infernal, have ascended to greater heights than ever before. Your teachings have not weakened the temple; they have expanded our reach, brought new power to our fold."

Eve blinked, her heart skipping a beat. Could it be? Was this not only acknowledgment but an endorsement from a Lord of the Nine Hells himself? "You support my vision?" she asked, her voice carefully controlled despite the thrill coursing through her.

"Support?" Asmodeus repeated, his lips curling into a knowing smile. He took a step closer, his presence suffocating in its intensity, yet invigorating. "I do more than support you, Eve. I recognize evolution when I see it. The teachings of Asmodeus are not stagnant. Power is not static. You have tapped into a deeper truth - a truth that power, control, and freedom are intertwined, but never simply about dominance. It is a much broader tapestry, woven with chaos, freedom, and the courage to transcend boundaries."

He looked around at the assembly, his voice lowering to a near whisper that somehow filled the entire chamber. "You, Eve, have grasped the essence of our existence in a way most here are too blind to understand. Chaos, far from weakening our influence, has only sharpened it. In questioning the old ways, you've opened doors thought long sealed. New realms of power await us."

The silence was palpable as the followers processed his words, their expressions shifting from confusion to dawning realization. Asmodeus wasn't merely tolerating Eve's new path; he was embracing it, encouraging it.

Eve's excitement swelled, but she kept her composure. "You see the strength in questioning," she said, her voice steady with new-found certainty. "The temple's rigid interpretation of power limits us. It's not enough to control others - we must first master ourselves, embrace chaos as a force for growth, and teach others to forge their own destinies."

Asmodeus smiled darkly, his approval evident. "Exactly. You challenge the status quo, and in doing so, you push our influence beyond Hell's borders. Let the traditionalists cling to their dogma," he said, casting a brief glance at Mordred and others who looked shocked by his words. "Their fears only prove how much they misunderstand the teachings of Asmodeus. What you have tapped into, Eve, is the true heart of your lord's philosophy: the power to evolve, to shape the world not through blind obedience but through strength, cunning, and will."

Eve's pulse quickened as she felt the weight of his words. This was more than support - it was a mandate. Her approach was not just tolerated; it was necessary for the temple's future. "So, we move forward, embracing both order and chaos," Eve declared, emboldened by Asmodeus's blessing. "Power is not to be feared, but explored. Our followers will not simply submit; they will rise, stronger, more autonomous, and prepared to face any force that stands in their way."

Asmodeus nodded, a glint of pride flickering in his eyes. "The time for blind loyalty has passed. This temple will no longer be confined to the traditions of the past. We will break free from those chains, and in doing so, we will forge a new order - an order that embraces chaos and commands respect through sheer will." He raised his hand, and the shadows surrounding him seemed to pulse with life. "Chaos is not the enemy, but the path forward. It strengthens those who wield it with purpose."

The followers exchanged glances, their faces a mixture of shock, intrigue, and excitement. It was clear that everything was changing. Their understanding of Asmodeus, their place in the temple, even their very concept of power, was being reshaped in this moment.

Asmodeus gestured to the assembly, his voice now booming with authority. "Look at them," he said to Eve. "They are beginning to see what you have shown them. You have ignited the flames of curiosity and ambition in their hearts. They see now that true power is not bound by rules but is defined by those bold enough to claim it."

Eve stood taller, the weight of her responsibility heavy yet exhilarating. This was the moment she had been moving toward. "Together, we will shape the temple into something far greater," she said, meeting Asmodeus's gaze with unwavering conviction. "A place where strength is measured not by domination but by the will to challenge and the courage to evolve."

The energy in the room shifted once more. What had begun as a confrontation had transformed into a declaration of a new era for the temple. Asmodeus and Eve stood united, their vision of the future clear: a temple of Asmodeus that embraced both chaos and freedom, where power came not from blind allegiance but from the audacity to forge one's own path.

The chamber throbbed with potential, and Eve knew that this was just the beginning. The followers, now watching with reverence, would soon become the torchbearers of this new philosophy, guiding others toward a future free from the limitations of the past. Together, they would rise, unchained and unyielding, ready to embrace whatever came next.

Eve looked out at the assembly, her heart racing with the prospect of what lay ahead. "Together, we will redefine our existence," she proclaimed, her voice echoing with newfound conviction. "No longer will we be bound by fear or dogma. We are the architects of our destiny!"

As the echoes of Asmodeus's words settled into the stone walls of the chamber, a new weight hung in the air - an unspoken question. The followers had seen the angels' relentless attacks, their aggression growing fiercer with each passing day. They had whispered in the halls, unsure of what had driven these divine beings to such fury. Now, with Asmodeus standing before them, they hungered for answers, for an explanation that made sense of the chaos engulfing their world.

As if sensing their collective unease, Asmodeus's gaze darkened, and his lips curved into a knowing smile. He stepped forward, the shadows parting for him like water, and the room seemed to hold its breath. His voice, calm yet full of power, cut through the silence.

"You wonder why the angels strike at us with such fervor, don't you?" Asmodeus's tone was laced with something akin to amusement, as if the answer was so obvious it bordered on ridiculous. "You see them as agents of Heaven, pure in their mission, driven by righteousness. But I tell you now, their rage is not born of divine will. It is born of pride."

The crowd murmured in confusion. Pride? Could it be true? They had always been taught that angels fought to maintain the balance of good, to purge evil from the world. But to hear Asmodeus describe their motives as sin, as something base and corrupt, challenged everything they had believed.

"Yes, pride," Asmodeus continued, his eyes narrowing as he surveyed the assembly. "Pride, one of the very sins they claim to fight against. The angels, in all their supposed purity, have become blinded by their own arrogance. Their attacks on us - on this temple, on Hell itself - are driven not by the will of their Father, but by the festering pride that has grown within them like a disease."

Asmodeus raised a hand, and with a flick of his fingers, a swirling vision appeared in the air before them - a battle between angels and demons, light and shadow clashing in a brutal dance. But as the angels fought, their faces twisted in something beyond righteousness. Their expressions were filled with wrath, with a rage so deep it bordered on madness.

"Look at them," Asmodeus commanded. "Do these appear to you as beings of grace and serenity? Do they resemble the peaceful shepherds of light they claim to be? No. They fight because they fear us. They fear what we are becoming. They fear the power we now wield."

He turned his gaze toward Eve, and she felt the weight of his focus like a physical presence. "It is because of you, Eve. Because of the path you've chosen. They see the strength you've awakened, not just in yourself, but in this temple. You've shown them a truth they cannot unsee - that the line between light and dark is not so clear, that their own existence is built on a fragile lie."

The room remained eerily still, as though the very stones were listening. Eve met Asmodeus's gaze, her own confidence building with each passing moment. The angels' assaults weren't a sign of their righteousness - they were proof of their fear.

"But fear is not their only sin," Asmodeus continued, his voice dropping to a near whisper, making every word feel like a secret revelation. "They are also driven by rage. They see themselves as above such things, but in truth, their wrath burns hotter than Hell's fires. And in their pride and anger, they have become the very thing they claim to despise. Sins, in the eyes of their Father."

Eve's eyes widened at his words. The angels - those supposed paragons of virtue - were guilty of the very sins they condemned. It was a revelation that felt both shocking and inevitable. For too long, the temple had seen the angels as unyielding symbols of purity. Now, under Asmodeus's piercing analysis, they stood revealed as deeply flawed beings, no better than the demons they fought.

Asmodeus stepped closer to Eve, his presence dominating the space between them. "And that, my dear Eve, is where we have the upper hand. They are bound by their hypocrisy, chained by their pride and rage. They fight because they cannot accept a world where the lines between good and evil blur. But you, and this temple - what we represent - is something far greater than their narrow understanding."

He gestured toward the congregation, his voice rising with conviction. "We do not fear chaos. We do not cling to rigid definitions of right and wrong, of light and dark. We understand that the world is far more complex, that true power lies not in choosing a side but in embracing the whole. And that is why we will succeed. That is why this new path - your path, Eve - will bring balance."

Eve felt a surge of energy ripple through her as Asmodeus's words took root. This was what she had always known, deep in her soul, but had never fully articulated. The temple's future was not about domination, nor was it about adhering to the binary of light and dark. It was about balance, about understanding that existence was a spectrum of forces, all of which could be wielded in the pursuit of true freedom and power.

"The angels fight out of pride and rage," Asmodeus repeated, his voice now booming with authority. "But we? We fight for something far greater. We fight for balance. We fight for the freedom to embrace both light and shadow, for the power to rise above the petty morality of Heaven and Hell alike."

He looked around the room, his gaze sweeping across the assembly like a wave of fire. "This new path will not be easy. It will challenge everything you've ever known, everything you've been taught. But it is the only way forward. It is the only way to break free from the chains that have bound us for centuries. It is the only way to achieve true power."

Eve's heart raced as she stepped forward, feeling the eyes of the congregation on her. She could feel their uncertainty, their fear, but also their curiosity. They were at a crossroads, torn between the old ways and the new, between the security of dogma and the allure of freedom.

"And what Asmodeus speaks is the truth," Eve said, her voice steady, yet filled with the fire of conviction. "The angels' attacks are proof that they fear what we are becoming. They know their time is ending, that their rigid ways can no longer hold sway over the hearts of mortals or demons alike."

She raised her hand, and shadows danced at her fingertips, swirling and pulsing with the energy of Nyx. "We will embrace the chaos they fear. We will walk the line between light and dark, and in doing so, we will find a balance that neither Heaven nor Hell can offer."

Asmodeus nodded approvingly, stepping back to let her words settle over the crowd. "This is the future of the temple," he declared. "A future where balance is our guiding principle, where we are not slaves to either order or chaos, but masters of both."

The followers exchanged glances, some hesitant, others filled with a newfound sense of purpose. Slowly, a murmur of agreement began to ripple through the crowd, growing louder with each passing second.

Eve smiled, feeling the momentum building. "We will not be constrained by old ideas, nor will we allow the angels' pride and rage to dictate our path. We are forging a new way forward, one where power is defined not by the domination of others, but by the mastery of ourselves."

The chamber thrummed with energy as Asmodeus and Eve stood together, their vision clear, their purpose united. The future of the temple was no longer a question of control or submission - it was a question of balance, of finding the strength to wield both light and shadow in harmony. And in that balance, they would find true power.

With Asmodeus by her side, Eve felt unstoppable, ready to lead her followers into a future filled with potential. The shadows that once loomed over her now felt like a cloak of power, wrapping her in the knowledge that she was not alone in this fight. The transformation had only just begun, and together, they would forge a new reality - one where freedom reigned and individuality thrived.

20

The Bridge Between Realms

Eve sat cross-legged in the heart of the temple, surrounded by flickering candles casting elongated shadows on the stone walls. The air was thick with incense, a rich blend of myrrh and sage that filled her senses and grounded her in the moment. Yet, beneath that grounding was a turbulent sea of confusion. As she closed her eyes, she felt the familiar pull of Nyx, the Titan of Night, whispering in the recesses of her mind.

"I am not merely a vessel for chaos," Eve murmured, her voice a blend of determination and doubt. "I am Eve, a priestess of Asmodeus, yet I feel tethered to something far beyond this temple and its rigid doctrines."

In her mind's eye, she envisioned the duality of her existence: Eve, the Battle Priestess, wielding the teachings of Asmodeus, and Nyx, the embodiment of chaos and liberation. Both were integral to her identity, yet they pulled her in opposing directions. How could she reconcile the duty to uphold the traditions of her temple with the desire to forge a new path that embraced the complexities of existence?

As Eve sank deeper into meditation, the boundaries between her two selves - priestess and Titan, Eve and Nyx - began to blur, the distinctions she had once held so rigidly in place dissolving like mist in the early morning light. The flickering candlelight in the temple chamber danced and twisted, casting shadows that seemed to move of their own accord. They swirled in tandem with the soft glow, merging together in an intricate ballet of illumination and darkness until they became one. It was as if the room itself mirrored the duality within her, creating a space where opposites could converge, where light and shadow were no longer enemies, but parts of a greater whole.

It was here, in this liminal space between night and day, chaos and order, that Eve sought communion with forces greater than Hell or Heaven, greater than even Nyx's immense power. She was no longer content with the narrow confines that defined existence in terms of good and evil, right and wrong. The doctrine of Asmodeus had given her power, structure, and a sense of place, but now she could feel something far larger calling to her, something infinite. This meditation was her bridge, her passage beyond the constraints of those who saw the cosmos in black and white. Here, in the quiet stillness, she felt the pull of the universe, of something beyond Hell's fiery depths and Heaven's blinding light.

With a steady, deliberate breath, she envisioned herself reaching outward into the vast, inky void that lay beyond the realms of gods and demons. Her essence, tethered momentarily to her body, began to spiral outward, expanding through the cracks between reality. She felt herself weaving through the very fabric of the universe, like a thread pulled through the cosmic loom. She could feel the stars - brilliant, distant, and ancient - glistening like diamonds against the velvet black of space. Each one pulsed with potential, not as points of light in the heavens, but as entire worlds unto themselves, brimming with power, possibility, and chaos.

The void welcomed her. It did not judge or demand allegiance. In it, there were no rulers, no followers, no decrees of how existence should be. The void simply **was**, infinite and unfathomable, filled with forces that existed long before Heaven and Hell began their eternal conflict. As Eve drifted further into this abyss, she felt the presence of these ancient forces. They were not like the angels, with their rigid codes, nor like the demons, with their thirst for power. These energies existed beyond such trivial concerns. They were the primordial forces of creation and destruction, chaos and order, spinning endlessly in a dance older than time.

"Embrace me," a voice echoed from the vastness, deep and resonant. It was not the voice of a god or a demon, nor even of Nyx. Yet, in its tone, Eve heard the familiarity of Nyx's ancient wisdom, intertwined with something far greater. This was the voice of the cosmos itself, a force that transcended individual identities and spoke to the essence of existence. "Reject the confines of expectation and allow yourself to be the bridge between realms."

For a moment, Eve hesitated. The teachings of Asmodeus had given her power, yes, but they had also given her limitations, even if she had not seen them as such. As Nyx, she had power beyond comprehension, but that too came with expectations, with the weight of an ancient legacy tied to the dark and chaotic forces of Hell. Now, though, standing at the edge of the void, she saw these identities for what they were - vessels, not prisons. She could be both, and neither. She could be **more**.

Eve surrendered to the call of the cosmos, allowing the vast, swirling currents of the universe to flow through her. She let go of the identities she had clung to for so long, the fears of betraying her purpose as a priestess, the doubts about whether she was truly Nyx, the Infernal Titan of Night. As these burdens lifted, she felt her being expand, becoming both infinite and infinitesimal at once. She was no longer confined to the dichotomy of Heaven and Hell. Here, in the embrace of the void, she was part of the everything - the chaos, the order, the creation, the destruction.

As she opened herself to these ancient forces, Eve saw visions flicker before her, stretching across the span of time and space. She saw worlds in the process of being born, stars bursting into life with a brilliance so powerful it brought tears to her eyes. She saw others winking out of existence, collapsing into the cold embrace of the void. Civilizations rose and fell in the blink of an eye, each one following its cycle of chaos and order.

In these cosmic visions, she understood a deeper truth: existence was not about the victory of one force over another. It was about balance, about the eternal dance between creation and destruction, between chaos and order, freedom and structure. The universe itself thrived not on dominance or submission, but on the interplay between opposites. Without chaos, there could be no creation. Without order, there could be no growth. It was a constant, infinite cycle, and in this cycle, everything had its place.

"You are the bridge," the cosmic voice whispered again, and Eve felt its words vibrate through her very soul. "Through you, these forces shall converge. You are neither bound to the light nor the dark. You are both. You are balance."

Eve's heart swelled with understanding, her thoughts now clear and sharp. Her role as a priestess of Asmodeus had never been about rejecting the teachings of the dark lord, but about seeing them for what they truly were: a reflection of one part of the universal whole. Asmodeus represented control, order, and structure, but those could not exist without the chaos she now embraced as Nyx. Her teachings could be the bridge between the dogma of Hell and the freedom of chaos.

In this moment of unity with the cosmos, Eve saw the true potential of the temple she had served for so long. It did not need to be confined to Hell's rigid rules. Her role was to guide her followers in understanding this broader truth: that chaos and freedom were not enemies of order, but necessary complements to it. She could teach them to see beyond the binary definitions of good and evil, to embrace the complexity of existence, and to find strength in both the light and the dark.

The power of this realization surged through Eve, filling her with purpose. She was not abandoning her path as a priestess. She was evolving it. Nyx's chaos and Asmodeus's structure would not conflict within her - they would harmonize. And in that harmony, she would guide her followers to a new era of understanding.

Slowly, Eve opened her eyes, the candlelight still flickering around her. But now, she saw it differently. The light was not in opposition to the shadow. They were two parts of the same whole, dancing together in the endless, cosmic cycle of existence.

Her path was clear. She would lead the temple into the future - not by rejecting what it had always been, but by helping it embrace all that it could become.

Her gaze locked onto the candle flames before her. The shadows danced as if in agreement, and a surge of energy pulsed within her. It was time for a symbolic act - one that would redefine her journey and signify the union of light and darkness.

Eve stood, the flickering candles casting a radiant glow around her. She gathered the celestial and infernal energies within her, channeling the essence of both Asmodeus and Nyx. As she began to move, her body flowed gracefully, a dance that intertwined the fluidity of night with the strength of infernal fire.

The temple vibrated with energy, each step a challenge to the conventional beliefs held within its stone walls. Eve felt the eyes of her followers upon her, their expressions a mixture of awe and uncertainty. They were witnessing something unprecedented, a ritual that defied the rigid doctrines they had been taught.

The temple was heavy with anticipation as the followers gathered closer, their eyes fixed on Eve standing at the altar. She stood alone in the center, bathed in a dim, ethereal light. Her presence commanded reverence, but tonight, there was something different. Tonight, she was not just Eve, the priestess of Asmodeus. She was also Nyx, the Titan of Night, and the boundaries between the two identities had all but disappeared.

"Today, I stand before you as both Eve and Nyx," she declared, her voice reverberating through the temple. The resonance of her words silenced the murmur of whispers, filling the vast chamber with a stillness that was almost palpable. Her tone was imbued with a strange mix of authority and vulnerability, a balance of the cosmic and the mortal. "I reject the binaries of good and evil, light and dark, and embrace the complexity of existence. I invite you to join me in this journey of self-discovery and empowerment."

Her followers shifted in place, their faces illuminated by the flickering candles scattered throughout the room. Some looked unsure, others captivated. This was not the usual sermon or ritual, not a recitation of doctrines they knew by heart. Tonight was a reckoning, an offering of a new path. A chance to unravel the old dogmas and weave something new from the tapestry of chaos and order.

Eve moved with purpose, every step deliberate and graceful. She raised her arms, and with that motion, the air around her began to stir. The energies of the temple - long attuned to the infernal powers of Hell - shifted. The infernal power still crackled with its usual intensity, a deep red aura simmering just beneath the surface. But now, new energy entered the chamber. Celestial light began to filter in, not in opposition to the infernal energies, but alongside them. The celestial essence glimmered like starlight, weaving through the infernal as if the two had always been destined to coexist.

Her hands traced complex, unfamiliar symbols in the air, and with each gesture, the celestial and infernal forces spiraled together, forming a vortex of light and shadow. It whirled around her, enveloping her form in a luminous, chaotic embrace. Eve could feel it in her bones - this was more than a performance, more than a ritual. She was shifting the temple's very ideology, reshaping its foundation to align with the cosmic truths she had glimpsed in her meditation.

The vortex expanded, filling the temple chamber with its presence. The followers gasped, some stepping back in awe, others leaning forward as if drawn by an unseen force. The energies crackled and pulsed, humming with life. They were no longer separate, no longer at odds. Light and darkness, infernal and celestial, swirled together in perfect harmony, a manifestation of the philosophy Eve had embraced.

The air itself was alive, electric with potential. Every breath Eve took seemed to charge the space around her, amplifying the tension. Her heart raced, not with fear but with the sheer magnitude of what was unfolding. The temple had always stood as a testament to Asmodeus' teachings - power through control, dominance through submission - but now, in this moment, it was transforming into something more. The rigid dichotomies that had defined its doctrine for centuries were being unmade, replaced by the fluidity of chaos and freedom.

Eve's movements became more fluid, each gesture punctuated by purpose. She reached into the swirling energy, drawing it closer, letting it pass through her as if she were the conduit between realms. Her fingers sliced through the air, parting the light and shadow in perfect synchronicity. As she moved, she channeled the wisdom of the cosmos, the ancient forces that existed beyond the boundaries of Hell and Heaven.

"True strength," she proclaimed, her voice resonating with cosmic power, "does not lie in rigid adherence to doctrine. It lies in the willingness to question, to evolve, to redefine one's beliefs in the face of change. Power is not static - it is dynamic, ever-changing, like the cosmos itself."

The air grew thick with energy, almost tangible. The followers could feel it - a shift in their very souls, a stirring of something long dormant. Many had come to the temple seeking power, seeking to climb the ranks of Hell's hierarchy or to harness the infernal forces for their own ends. But now, standing before this vortex of light and shadow, they began to understand that there was more to power than dominance. There was freedom in chaos, in the ability to choose one's path, to embrace the complexity of existence rather than submit to a singular truth.

Suddenly, the candles flickered violently before dimming altogether. The temple was plunged into a strange twilight, neither fully dark nor fully light. The vortex of energy around Eve shifted, its colors now swirling in a kaleidoscope of hues, each representing a different facet of existence. Red and gold, silver and black, purple and green - all danced together, creating an otherworldly spectacle.

As the lights swirled, Eve felt the presence of something beyond, something vast and ancient. The void she had communed with in her meditation had taken notice. Powerful beings, forces that existed beyond the understanding of mortals and even gods, had been drawn to the chaos she was weaving. Whispers echoed through the chamber, disembodied voices that seemed to come from everywhere and nowhere. They reverberated against the stone walls, filling the temple with the hum of the cosmos itself.

Eve's voice remained steady, though she could feel the weight of these presences bearing down on her. "You feel it, don't you?" she asked, her eyes sweeping over the gathered followers. "The universe has taken notice. It watches us now, not as Hell watches, not as Heaven judges, but as a force beyond our comprehension. The cosmos sees what we do here, and it approves."

Her words hung in the air, heavy with meaning. The followers exchanged glances, their expressions a mix of awe, fear, and curiosity. Eve could see the seeds of understanding beginning to take root. They were not just witnesses to this ritual - they were participants in a transformation, a rewriting of the very principles that had governed their lives.

Eve raised her arms higher, drawing the energies closer to her body, letting them wrap around her like a second skin. "We are not slaves to Heaven or Hell," she continued. "We are not bound by their binaries, their endless war of light versus dark. We are more. We are the bridge between realms, the balance between chaos and order, the embodiment of the cosmic dance."

As she spoke, the swirling energies began to pulse, growing brighter, more intense. The power in the room was palpable, almost suffocating in its intensity. Eve could feel it in her bones, in her blood - a connection to something infinite, something far greater than herself.

"Today, we embrace this power," she declared, her voice rising to a crescendo. "Not as followers of Hell, not as enemies of Heaven, but as beings who understand the true nature of existence. We are the balance, the chaos, the freedom. We are the future."

With that, the vortex of light and shadow collapsed inward, rushing toward Eve in a final burst of energy. For a brief moment, everything was silent. Then, slowly, the lights in the temple began to flicker back to life. The swirling colors faded, leaving only Eve standing at the center, her body still humming with the remnants of the cosmic power she had wielded.

The followers stared at her, their faces a mixture of awe and newfound understanding. Eve had not just performed a ritual. She had ushered in a new era - one where the boundaries between light and dark, good and evil, were no longer chains but doors to be opened.

As the temple's lights flickered back to life, the energy from the ritual still reverberating in the air, Eve's followers remained spellbound. They had witnessed something unprecedented - a glimpse into a cosmic truth that extended beyond the infernal doctrines they had known. Eve, standing at the center of it all, allowed the moment of silence to linger before speaking once more, her voice now calm yet filled with a new authority.

"What you have witnessed today is not just a shift in our temple's ideology. It is an invitation - a call to action," she began, her gaze sweeping across the room, locking eyes with each of her followers. "As for the mortals who have found themselves in Hell, you are no longer bound to the singular pursuit of power for power's sake. That path is narrow, limiting, and it feeds into the very binaries that keep us chained. But now, with this new direction, there is a greater purpose before you."

She paused, letting the weight of her words settle. The mortals in Hell had always been conditioned to believe that power was the ultimate goal - domination over others, the endless struggle for rank, to climb the infernal hierarchy. But Eve was offering something more than the relentless quest for superiority.

"In this new era, the goal for mortals in Hell is not merely to rise within its ranks but to transcend the rigid structures that confine you," Eve continued. "The teachings of Asmodeus have always been about control, and that control has brought you strength. But strength alone is not enough. You must learn to wield that strength with purpose, with clarity, and with the understanding that true power lies not in the domination of others but in the mastery of yourself."

Her voice grew more impassioned, her words infused with the cosmic wisdom she had touched during the ritual. "You must reject the false dichotomy that pits Heaven against Hell, light against darkness. Both realms are driven by their own forms of tyranny - one through rigid order, the other through endless chaos. But in between these extremes lies the truth: that existence is a spectrum, and that your journey through Hell is not meant to break you, but to free you."

The followers began to shift, exchanging glances as they tried to comprehend the enormity of what Eve was saying. For centuries, their goals had been simple: survive Hell, rise through its ranks, gain power, and avoid eternal torment. But now, Eve was painting a picture of something much grander.

"Your time in Hell should not be seen as punishment," she declared, her voice rising in intensity. "Nor should it be seen merely as a test of endurance or a proving ground for your worth. It is an opportunity - a chance to break free from the constraints that both Heaven and Hell have placed upon you. To question, to evolve, to transcend. The goal is not to become slaves to power, but to find balance within yourselves. To rise not just through Hell's ranks but beyond its limitations."

Eve walked closer to her followers, her eyes blazing with a fire that reflected her newfound purpose. "Hell teaches control through suffering, and Heaven demands obedience through its promises of salvation. But in this new path, you are asked to embrace chaos as a tool for transformation. The suffering you endure here is not an end - it is the means by which you strip away the illusions that bind you. The rage you feel, the fear, the pain - these are your teachers. But instead of succumbing to them, you must learn to transcend them."

She gestured to the temple's altar, which had long been a symbol of submission to Hell's infernal order. Now, it was a testament to something more. "You have the power to shape your own destiny. Not by playing into Hell's endless games of domination or Heaven's empty promises of salvation, but by embracing the chaos within yourselves. By learning that the only true goal worth pursuing is the freedom to choose your own path."

The mortals began to murmur, some nodding in agreement, others still processing the enormity of the idea. Eve sensed their hesitation, their uncertainty. "I know this is difficult to grasp," she said softly, her tone shifting to one of empathy. "For so long, you have been taught that your only options are submission or rebellion, control or chaos. But in this new path, you are offered something different: the opportunity to become your own masters. To embrace the complexity of your existence, to question the false binaries, and to find strength in that ambiguity."

She raised her hands again, summoning a spark of energy that flickered between her fingers. "This is what the cosmos has shown me. That your time in Hell is not a curse, nor is it a simple stepping stone to some higher rank. It is a journey - a journey through which you can discover who you truly are, beyond the labels of mortal, demon, or sinner. In this new direction, your goal is not to conquer Hell, but to conquer yourself. To balance the forces within you, to understand that both chaos and order are tools at your disposal, and to wield them with purpose."

Eve's voice lowered, becoming almost a whisper, but her words carried a weight that filled the room. "The mortals of this temple will no longer be defined by the old ways. You will be seekers of balance, agents of transformation. Your journey through Hell will no longer be about surviving its torments, but about finding the truth of your own existence within the chaos. That is your new goal - to transcend the limitations of this realm and become something greater."

The air in the temple seemed to vibrate with the power of her declaration. The followers, once unsure, now began to understand. Eve was offering them more than just survival or power within Hell's hierarchy. She was offering them the chance to break free from the cycles of suffering and domination that had defined their existence.

"Look within yourselves," Eve urged, her eyes burning with conviction. "Find the balance between the light and the dark, the infernal and the celestial. That is where your true strength lies. Not in submission to Hell or the pursuit of Heaven, but in the freedom to define your own destiny."

The temple fell silent, the weight of Eve's words settling on the gathered souls. The goal for mortals in Hell had shifted. No longer were they bound by the simplistic ambitions of control or power. Now, they had a higher calling - a journey toward self-mastery, toward balance, and ultimately, toward the freedom that came from embracing the chaos within themselves.

Eve closed her eyes again, surrendering to the energies that surrounded her. The vision of Nyx expanded within her, revealing the infinite realms beyond the temple, realms where the rigid definitions of good and evil did not exist. It was a landscape of possibility, a place where one could forge their destiny without the weight of dogma holding them back. The energy in the temple seemed to pulse with her heartbeat. Her voice, rich and resonant, rose from deep within, filling the chamber with an ethereal melody.

> *In the heart of fire, we've walked so long,*
> *Taught to bow, taught what's right, what's wrong.*
> *But the shadows whisper a different tune,*
> *Not just darkness under Heaven's moon.*
> *In the chaos, there's a spark of light,*
> *A flame that burns through eternal night.*
> *We're not just sinners or slaves to sin,*
> *There's a deeper power waiting within.*
> *We rise beyond the chains, break free from Hell's domain,*
> *No more the fear, no more the shame, we'll never be the same.*
> *Through chaos, we will find, the balance in our minds,*
> *We'll walk the line between the stars, our destiny designed.*
> *Beyond the chains, beyond the pain,*
> *We choose the path that we create.*

The room shimmered as her voice weaved through the air, harmonizing with the flickering lights around her. The followers, entranced by her song, felt the weight of their doubts lifting, replaced by a shared hope.

> *Not just Hell that holds us tight,*

Not just Heaven's blinding light.
We are more than angels and fiends,
More than power, more than dreams.
Through the storm, we see the truth,
There's no divide, no lies, no proof.
Just the freedom to rise or fall,
To find our place beyond it all.

Eve's voice swelled with the energy of her convictions, igniting a spark within each listener, urging them to rise from their confines.

We rise beyond the chains, break free from Hell's domain,
No more the fear, no more the shame, we'll never be the same.
Through chaos, we will find, the balance in our minds,
We'll walk the line between the stars, our destiny designed.
Beyond the chains, beyond the pain,
We choose the path that we create.

The shadows danced, swirling around her, mirroring the emotions rippling through the gathered crowd. They felt her resolve, her defiance against the confines of tradition and dogma.

Through the flames, through the night,
We'll dance in shadows, we'll find our sight.
In the ashes, we are born anew,
Both light and dark, we'll follow through.
No masters here, no one to please,
Only freedom on the cosmic breeze.
We're the architects of our own fate,
In the chaos, we elevate.

With each note, Eve felt the weight of the temple's history shift, the very fabric of their beliefs bending to the strength of her song.

We rise beyond the chains, break free from Hell's domain,
No more the fear, no more the shame, we'll never be the same.
Through chaos, we will find, the balance in our minds,

We'll walk the line between the stars, our destiny designed.
Beyond the chains, beyond the pain,
We choose the path that we create.

Her voice soared, blending with the echoes of the cosmos, calling forth the energy of the universe to fill the temple. The followers began to sing along, their voices rising in a powerful chorus, uniting in a shared purpose.

So let the shadows guide us home,
No longer lost, no longer alone.
Beyond the chains, beyond the flame,
We'll write our story, we'll claim our name.

As the final notes hung in the air, Eve opened her eyes, revealing a brilliance that resonated with the strength of her newfound identity. She was met with a sea of expressions - some filled with fear, others ignited by hope. The temple's followers were beginning to understand that change was not something to be feared but embraced. Eve could see the seeds of doubt being planted in the minds of those who once adhered strictly to tradition.

As she completed the ritual, a powerful burst of energy erupted, shaking the very foundation of the temple. The light and darkness converged, creating a harmonious balance that resonated with the cosmos. In that moment, Eve knew she had stepped beyond the role of a mere priestess; she had become a bridge between realms, a beacon for those seeking liberation from the confines of their beliefs.

With her heart full of determination, Eve stood at the center of the chamber, Nyx's essence intertwining with her own. The journey ahead would not be easy, but she was ready to embrace the shadows and lead her followers into a new understanding of power and existence. The cosmos had spoken, and she was prepared to heed its call.

21

Ascension Beyond Divisions

The grand chamber of the temple loomed before Eve, its walls adorned with intricate carvings that depicted the long history of Asmodeus and the principles of the temple. Yet today, those symbols felt heavy with expectation, a weight she had long since begun to challenge. She stood at the entrance, her heart racing, knowing she was about to confront Archpriestess Lysandra - one of the highest authorities in the temple and a staunch guardian of its traditions.

As she stepped inside, the air was thick with tension. Lysandra was already waiting, her piercing gaze locked onto Eve as if she were measuring the depths of her resolve. The archpriestess exuded an aura of authority, dressed in robes that seemed to shimmer with an ethereal light. There was both intrigue and wariness in her expression, a recognition that the winds of change were blowing through the temple.

"Eve," Lysandra began, her voice firm but not unkind. The air in the chamber was thick with tension, the flickering candlelight casting dancing shadows on the stone walls as the followers gathered around, their expressions a mixture of curiosity and concern. The Archpriestess's gaze bore into Eve, a mixture of authority and a flicker of uncertainty in her eyes. "You have stirred a tempest within these walls. Nyx's influence grows stronger with each passing day. Tell me, what do you seek?"

Eve took a deep breath, summoning the strength that Nyx had instilled in her. The voices of her followers filled her ears, their whispered doubts and fears echoing around her like a cacophony, but she silenced them with conviction. "I seek a new understanding of power and freedom, Archpriestess. The teachings of Asmodeus have served us, but they limit our true potential. Power is not merely about control; it is about the mastery of oneself and the acceptance of chaos as a fundamental part of existence."

As she spoke, she noticed the way some of her followers leaned in, their interest piqued, while others crossed their arms defensively, skepticism etched across their faces. Lysandra's brow furrowed, the weight of her position evident. "And you believe that embracing chaos will strengthen our resolve? That it will unite us?"

"Yes," Eve replied, her voice gaining confidence as she gestured to the assembled followers. "The rigid dichotomy of good and evil stifles growth. If we are to transcend our limitations, we must be willing to question our beliefs and embrace the complexities of existence." The energy in the room began to shift, a palpable buzz as her words resonated with some, igniting a flicker of hope.

Lysandra raised an eyebrow, her interest piqued but caution still radiating from her. "You challenge the very foundation of our faith, Eve. Many would see your words as heresy." She took a step closer, the archway of the temple framing her silhouette against the flickering flames. "What you propose could shatter the very essence of our community. How can we stand strong if we abandon the principles that bind us?"

"Perhaps," Eve conceded, meeting the archpriestess's gaze with unwavering resolve, "but what is heresy if it leads us to a greater truth? I do not wish to dismantle our faith; I wish to expand it, to allow our followers to explore the full spectrum of their existence. We can be both light and dark, both structured and chaotic." She felt the energy of the temple shifting in response to her words, some followers nodding in agreement while others appeared visibly torn.

The archpriestess regarded her for a long moment, weighing Eve's words carefully. The silence in the chamber grew thick, an almost tangible entity as every pair of eyes rested upon them, awaiting Lysandra's response. "If you are to convince me, you must prove your commitment to this new philosophy. Are you prepared to undergo the Rite of Acceptance?"

Eve's heart quickened at the mention of the ritual. It was a trial that tested one's essence, forcing the participant to confront their past and future, to reconcile the duality within. "I am ready," she declared, the words spilling forth with determination.

Around them, the followers whispered among themselves, some expressing excitement, others fear. The Rite of Acceptance was not to be taken lightly; it required a willingness to lay bare one's soul, to face the shadows lurking within. Eve could feel the weight of their gazes, the burden of expectation settling heavily on her shoulders, yet she knew this was a necessary step. If she was to embody this new philosophy and lead them toward a more profound understanding of existence, she had to embrace her own darkness.

"Very well," Lysandra replied, her tone softening slightly, perhaps recognizing the resolve in Eve's eyes. "The Rite will take place at the hour of twilight, when the veil between our world and the cosmic forces is thinnest. Prepare yourself for the journey ahead. You will face your past, confront your fears, and accept the chaos within you." The archpriestess's voice rang with authority, but there was a hint of respect in her tone that made Eve's heart swell with gratitude.

As Lysandra turned to address the assembly, Eve could see the flicker of uncertainty in the eyes of some followers, the fear of what this new direction might bring. "You must all understand the gravity of what Eve proposes. To embrace chaos is to abandon the safety of our traditions. It is a path filled with uncertainty, but it is also a path to empowerment. Each of you must decide where you stand."

Whispers rippled through the crowd, some voices filled with trepidation, others sparking with excitement. "What if we lose ourselves?" a voice called out from the back. "What if we become lost in this chaos?"

Eve raised her hand to quiet the murmurs, her voice steady as she addressed her followers. "The fear of losing ourselves is what has kept us chained to the old ways. But I believe we are capable of so much more. Embracing chaos doesn't mean surrendering to it; it means understanding it, integrating it into our being. We must learn to dance with it, to navigate its unpredictable currents. Only then can we truly master our own destinies."

The chamber grew still again, the weight of her words settling upon the group. Eve could feel the energy shifting, the tension mingling with hope. Lysandra stepped back, her expression contemplative. "You have much to prove, Eve. I will hold a council tonight to discuss your proposal, and we will see how the others feel about your path."

Eve nodded, feeling the gravity of the moment. The next steps would be critical; she had stirred a storm within the temple, and the outcome was uncertain. Would they accept this new philosophy, or would they cling to the old ways, fearful of what lay beyond their comfort zones?

As the assembly began to disperse, Eve felt a mix of emotions swelling within her - excitement, fear, and an undeniable sense of purpose. She had taken a step into the unknown, and now she would have to prove that her vision for the future was not just a fleeting thought but a pathway to liberation.

In the hours leading up to the Rite of Acceptance, she prepared herself, meditating on the teachings of Asmodeus while embracing the lessons of Nyx. It was a delicate balance, a tightrope walk between the comfort of tradition and the allure of chaos.

As twilight descended upon the temple, Eve stood at the altar, the sigil of her duality etched into the stone beneath her feet. She could feel the energies of the cosmos swirling around her, beckoning her to embrace her full essence. The flickering candles cast long shadows, the walls of the chamber pulsating with life.

With every heartbeat, she steeled herself for what was to come. She would confront her past, face her fears, and embrace the chaos within. It was not just a personal trial; it was a pivotal moment for her followers, a chance to redefine their understanding of power and freedom.

Eve closed her eyes, centering herself in the now, ready to dive into the depths of her soul and emerge transformed, a beacon of hope and possibility for all who followed. The Rite of Acceptance awaited, and with it, the dawn of a new era for the Temple of Asmodeus.

Lysandra nodded, her expression serious. "Let us begin."

The chamber transformed around them, the stone walls shimmering as the ritual's energies took hold. An intricate sigil appeared on the ground, pulsing with a soft light that filled the room. Eve stepped into the circle, feeling the warmth envelop her, grounding her in the moment yet propelling her into the depths of her soul. The air thickened with anticipation, every breath laden with the weight of what was to come.

As the ritual commenced, visions began to unfurl before her eyes. She saw herself as Eve, the devoted Battle Priestess, fighting fiercely in battles to protect the temple's ideals, her heart full of conviction but also blind adherence. Memories of struggles against angels and demons alike flooded her mind, and she felt the weight of expectation pressing down on her. The shouts of her comrades echoed in her ears, their faces obscured but filled with determination. The thrill of combat surged within her as she recalled each clash of steel, each fervent prayer, the promise of victory brightening her resolve.

But the scene shifted, and she found herself transformed into Nyx, the Titan of Night. She soared through cosmic realms, embracing the chaos and freedom of her new identity. The stars twinkled like scattered jewels on a black velvet canvas, each one a universe unto itself, bursting with potential. In this form, she was untethered, a being of pure potential, wielding the power to reshape not only her own destiny but that of those around her. She felt the currents of existence thrumming beneath her, a symphony of chaos and order that danced at her fingertips.

Yet, the visions twisted again, presenting her with a stark choice. The light of the temple and its traditions beckoned her back, offering comfort and certainty. Golden beams of light cascaded from an unseen source, illuminating the familiar stone altar, the figures of her mentors hovering in the background with expectant smiles. They were the embodiment of the teachings she had clung to, the pillars of strength and guidance that had supported her through the darkest times. But as she stepped closer, she felt the pull of their expectations, the chains of their beliefs wrapping around her heart like tendrils of ivy, squeezing tighter with each heartbeat.

On the other side lay the dark void of chaos, promising liberation but also uncertainty. Shadows flickered, swirling like smoke, whispering of freedom from the chains that bound her. It was a tantalizing invitation, one that echoed the very essence of Nyx, yet it also held the abyssal weight of isolation and the fear of losing herself completely in the dark. The contrast was stark - comfort and safety versus chaos and the unknown. She stood on the precipice, her heart racing as she faced the contradictions of her existence, her mind spiraling with doubt.

"You cannot serve two masters," a voice echoed, familiar and haunting. It was the voice of Asmodeus, a reminder of her allegiance and the teachings that had shaped her. "Choose wisely, Eve. Power is a double-edged sword." The words echoed in her mind, a mantra of caution that urged her to consider the consequences of her choice.

As she lingered in the dichotomy, the visions began to intensify, pulling her deeper into the core of her conflict. She saw the faces of those who had fought beside her - their trust in her unwavering, their belief in her strength resolute. But then the visions darkened, showing the corruption within the temple, the dogma that stifled growth, the moments when her adherence to tradition had blinded her to the suffering around her. Each face morphed into a mask of disappointment, questioning her choices, demanding conformity.

In that moment, Eve realized that her true power lay not in choosing one path over the other but in merging them, in transcending the binaries that had defined her journey thus far. The wisdom of both her past and her future coalesced within her, forming a singular, potent force. She understood that to fully embody both Eve and Nyx was not to abandon her history but to honor it while forging a new destiny. It was the acceptance of contradictions that would propel her forward.

"I will not be confined," she declared within the vision, her voice echoing through the void, infused with a fierce determination. "I am both Eve and Nyx. I am chaos and order, light and darkness. I embrace the entirety of my being!" The words reverberated through the chamber, breaking the silence and shattering the confines of her identity.

With those declarations, the sigil glowed brighter, a blinding light enveloping her as the boundaries of her identity shattered. Eve felt her essence merging, the two halves of her spirit coming together in harmony, a dance of power and freedom that was both exhilarating and terrifying. The light wrapped around her like a cocoon, and in that radiant embrace, she felt the fear of judgment dissipate.

But just as quickly, doubt surged back in, threatening to unravel her newfound clarity. What if she failed? What if the merging of her identities brought chaos that consumed her? The memories of those who had come before her, the failed attempts to challenge the status quo, weighed heavily on her mind. Each voice echoed warnings, each face reminding her of the cost of defiance.

As the light dimmed, Eve emerged from the ritual transformed. Her features bore the unmistakable marks of Nyx, yet they were now softened by the wisdom of Eve. She stood tall, an embodiment of balance, a bridge between the realms, resonating with a newfound authority.

Yet, the challenges remained. The followers before her looked on, their expressions a blend of awe and apprehension. Would they accept this new path? Would they follow her as she ventured into the unknown? The silence hung heavy, pressing against her, as if the weight of their collective expectations rested on her shoulders.

"Do you fear what lies ahead?" she asked the assembly, her voice steady, but within her, a storm raged. "Do you fear the chaos of creation, the uncertainty of a world where we are not bound by doctrine but guided by our own will?"

Their faces reflected a myriad of emotions - fear, hope, curiosity. Some nodded, while others hesitated, caught between the safety of the known and the allure of the unknown.

"Let me show you," she urged, her heart pounding with urgency. "Let me show you that within chaos lies the opportunity for rebirth, for growth! Together, we can forge a new understanding of power, one that transcends the chains of our past."

As her words hung in the air, Eve felt a shift within her. It was as if the very essence of the temple resonated with her call, the stones vibrating with the truth of her proclamation. And within that moment of connection, she realized her path was not hers alone. It was a collective journey toward empowerment, a shared awakening that would echo through the realms of Hell and Heaven.

Eve took a deep breath, centering herself as she looked into the eyes of her followers. "Together, we will redefine what it means to wield power. We will no longer be pawns in a game played by the gods. We are the architects of our destiny, the weavers of our reality."

With each word, the energies in the chamber swelled, harmonizing with her spirit. And as they responded, Eve understood that her journey was only just beginning. The complexities of her existence would be her greatest strength, guiding her as she embraced the duality within herself and among her followers.

With renewed determination, she lifted her arms, welcoming the energy swirling around her, the forces of chaos and order blending into a powerful tide. "Let us step into the void together," she declared, her voice a clarion call for those willing to take the leap. "Let us embrace our true selves and discover the extraordinary potential within each of us!"

As the echoes of her declaration resonated through the chamber, she felt the burgeoning energy of the cosmos envelop her, inviting her into the vastness of possibility. In that moment, Eve was not just a priestess or a titan; she was a beacon of hope, a force of transformation, ready to forge a new reality from the fabric of existence itself.

Lysandra gazed at her with a mixture of awe and apprehension. "You have undergone a profound transformation," she said, her voice barely above a whisper. "What will you do now?"

"I will lead," Eve/Nyx declared, her voice strong and unwavering, echoing through the chamber like a clarion call. "Not as a mere priestess of Asmodeus, but as a philosopher-queen who challenges the very foundations of our beliefs. We will forge a new path forward, one that transcends the limitations of our dualistic nature." The weight of her words hung in the air, igniting a flicker of hope in the hearts of her followers.

Just as the fervor began to ripple through the gathered crowd, Lysandra stepped forward, her expression a blend of pride and resolve. "Eve/Nyx, your vision resonates deeply, and it has stirred something within me. I have spoken with the council, and they share our vision. They have agreed to embrace this new direction."

A collective gasp swept through the temple, reverberating against the stone walls. The followers exchanged glances, disbelief and excitement mingling in their expressions. This was not merely a shift in leadership; it was a transformation of the temple's very essence.

"Your willingness to challenge convention has opened a door that many thought was sealed," Lysandra continued, her voice steady but imbued with emotion. "The council understands that we are at a crossroads, and clinging to old doctrines may lead us into stagnation. Our world is changing, and so must we. We must embrace the complexities of our existence to thrive."

Eve/Nyx felt a swell of elation at Lysandra's words, the pulse of the temple's energy echoing her own heartbeats. The moment was electric, charged with the potential for a brighter future. "Together, we will redefine our teachings, forging a doctrine that encompasses the full spectrum of our existence," she replied, her gaze sweeping over her followers. "We will not merely serve the will of Asmodeus; we will expand upon it, turning the temple into a beacon of empowerment and self-discovery."

Lysandra nodded, her eyes glistening with pride. "The council sees your potential, Eve/Nyx. They acknowledge that your duality, your ability to weave chaos with order, is not a threat but a strength. As we embark on this journey together, we will unite our voices to spread this message beyond these walls."

Eve/Nyx felt the truth of Lysandra's words resonate within her, and a newfound determination surged through her veins. "We will host gatherings, open discussions, and rituals that allow our followers to explore their inner complexities. They will no longer be bound by rigid definitions of good and evil, light and darkness. They will learn to wield their power through choice, embracing their true selves."

Lysandra's gaze hardened with resolve. "The council stands behind you, but know this: the path ahead will be fraught with challenges. There will be traditionalists who oppose our vision, who see change as a threat to their beliefs. Are you prepared to confront them?"

Eve/Nyx straightened, her voice unwavering. "I am ready. I understand that growth comes with resistance, but I believe in the potential of our followers. They possess the strength to question and evolve, just as I have. Together, we will show that this temple is not a prison of ideals but a sanctuary of freedom."

A wave of energy rippled through the chamber, and Eve/Nyx could feel the unwavering support of her followers behind her. The council's approval had given her words a newfound gravity, and now the temple stood on the precipice of a bold new era, ready to embrace a future where the complexity of existence would be celebrated, not shunned.

With the council's endorsement, the stage was set for the Temple of Asmodeus to rise as a bastion of empowerment, challenging the status quo and forging a path where every voice could be heard. A new chapter awaited, and Eve/Nyx was ready to lead them into the light.

As Eve/Nyx stepped out of the ritual circle, she felt the eyes of the temple upon her - those who had once feared her, now intrigued, perhaps even inspired. The air was thick with anticipation, a palpable energy swirling around her as she embraced her newfound identity. A new era was dawning, and with her ascension came the promise of liberation and self-discovery.

"Together," she continued, raising her arms to encompass the gathering, "we will embrace both our light and our shadows, redefining what it means to be followers of Asmodeus. We will show the realms that power is not merely about dominance; it is about choice, freedom, and the courage to embrace the unknown."

A hush fell over the crowd, their faces a tapestry of emotions - curiosity, fear, and, above all, a yearning for something more profound. Eve could see the flicker of belief igniting in their eyes, a longing to break free from the constraints of traditional dogma. It was a beautiful sight, one that fueled her determination.

The archpriestess regarded her with a newfound respect, stepping closer, her voice low yet resolute. "Then lead us, Eve/Nyx, and may the cosmos guide your path." But there was something more in her gaze, an unspoken connection, a bond that transcended mere mentor and disciple.

"Eve," Lysandra began again, her tone softening, "as I look at you now, I see not just a follower but a daughter." The weight of those words settled between them, and Eve felt her heart swell with emotion. "I have watched you grow, struggle, and transform into something extraordinary. I cannot turn my back on that, nor can I ignore the power that lies within you."

Eve/Nyx was taken aback, her mind racing as she processed this new revelation. "Daughter?" she echoed, her voice tinged with disbelief and gratitude. "You would adopt me?"

"Absolutely," Lysandra affirmed, her gaze steady and full of warmth. "You embody the essence of what it means to challenge and transcend. I have been a guardian of our traditions, but it is time for me to step aside and empower the next generation. Your vision for our temple reflects the true spirit of Asmodeus - one of change, growth, and evolution."

A deep sense of belonging surged within Eve. She had spent so long wrestling with her dual identity, feeling like an outsider in both the mortal and celestial realms. Now, here in this sacred space, she found a familial bond, a sense of home she had long craved. "Thank you, Archpriestess. I will strive to honor this bond and guide our followers with the wisdom we both carry."

Lysandra smiled, and for a moment, they stood united, a bridge between the old and the new. "Then let us stand together, as mother and daughter, to usher in this new era. We will reshape our beliefs and redefine our purpose."

With a shared sense of purpose, they turned to face the assembly. The murmurs of the crowd grew louder, curiosity bubbling to the surface. "What now?" one follower called out, her voice laced with hope.

"Now, we embrace our destiny," Eve/Nyx proclaimed, her heart racing. "We will embark on a journey of self-discovery and empowerment, exploring the depths of our being. The Rite of Acceptance will be the first of many steps toward unveiling the truth hidden within our shadows."

A ripple of energy surged through the room, igniting the crowd's enthusiasm. Eve could feel the swell of collective spirit, the burgeoning sense of unity among them. "We will hold councils, share our struggles, and forge connections that transcend the superficial divisions that have long kept us apart. Together, we will explore the duality of existence and uncover the latent power that resides in each of us."

Lysandra stepped forward, her presence commanding the attention of the followers. "This is not merely Eve's vision; it is ours. We will transform the temple from a bastion of rigid tradition into a sanctuary of exploration and freedom."

Eve could feel the weight of the moment, the gravity of their shared purpose. She glanced at her followers, seeing their faces transform from skepticism to determination. "Will you join us?" she called out, her voice ringing with conviction.

"Yes!" the crowd erupted, voices rising like a tide. "We will follow you!"

"Then let us begin," Eve declared, a sense of exhilaration surging through her veins. "Let us embrace the chaos and order within us, the light and darkness that define our existence. Together, we will weave a tapestry of understanding that transcends the binaries of this world."

As she spoke, the sigil beneath her feet began to pulse with radiant energy, resonating with the collective will of the temple. The air crackled with potential, a tangible force that enveloped them, igniting their spirits with a sense of empowerment and purpose.

In that moment, Eve/Nyx felt a profound connection with each follower gathered before her. She was no longer just a priestess or a titan; she was a leader, a daughter, and a beacon of hope. The temple was on the cusp of transformation, and she would stand at the forefront, bridging the realms of light and dark, chaos and order.

With the power of Nyx and the wisdom of Eve coursing through her, she embraced her role as the philosopher-queen. The whispers of doubt that once plagued her began to fade, replaced by the clarity of purpose that resonated within her soul. This was her moment, her time to shine and guide others toward the liberation they all craved.

As the crowd cheered, their voices echoing through the temple, Eve raised her arms in triumph, feeling the energy of the cosmos swirl around her. "Together, we will change the course of our destinies," she proclaimed, her voice carrying on the winds of transformation. "Together, we will reclaim our power!"

And with that, a new dawn broke for the Temple of Asmodeus, where the promise of freedom and self-discovery gleamed like a distant star on the horizon, beckoning them to stretch out and seize it.

22

The Angelic Challenger

The air in the Temple of Asmodeus sparked with tension, the walls vibrating as if they sensed the imminent arrival of a storm. Eve, now fully embodying Nyx, stood at the center of the grand hall, surrounded by her followers. They had gathered, drawn by the promise of a new era - a time when they could explore their identities beyond the confines of rigid morality.

But the atmosphere shifted suddenly, dark clouds swirling above as an otherworldly light broke through the temple's entrance. The ground trembled, and a piercing, golden beam illuminated the space. As it faded, a figure emerged: Seraphael, a powerful angel known for his zealous adherence to divine law and morality. Clad in shimmering armor, his wings spread wide, casting an imposing shadow that darkened the temple's sanctity.

The chamber buzzed with tension as Seraphael's booming voice echoed across the stone walls. His towering frame, haloed in a golden light, radiated a terrifying divine presence. The followers, many of them trembling in awe and fear, stared wide-eyed at the celestial being who had intruded upon their sacred temple. Even those who had questioned Eve's leadership and her connection to Nyx could not deny the power standing before them. Seraphael was a warrior of Heaven, a symbol of rigid order and righteousness.

Eve, standing at the center of the room, felt the weight of their gazes upon her. They had placed their hopes and doubts in her hands, waiting to see how she would respond. Nyx's power surged through her veins, grounding her in the present but also stirring something ancient within. She had faced many adversaries - angels, demons, even the internal struggles that had once threatened to tear her apart - but this confrontation was different. Seraphael represented everything she had fought against: the suffocating chains of dogma, the tyranny of control masquerading as divine order.

Seraphael's luminous eyes narrowed as he pointed a condemning finger at her. "You stand accused of corrupting the very essence of Hell," he declared, his voice resonating with an undeniable authority. "Your teachings of chaos and freedom threaten the balance of all realms. I have come to restore order."

The air crackled with the intensity of the moment. Eve's followers, who had once looked upon her transformation into Nyx with uncertainty, now shifted uneasily. Whispers swept through the crowd, the words too hushed to make out but laden with fear and curiosity. The angel was a symbol of celestial power - his mere presence could topple their fragile sense of security. Could Eve, or Nyx, truly stand against him?

Eve took a step forward, her darkened eyes locking onto Seraphael's. The room felt smaller, the energy between them dense and volatile. She was no longer just Eve, the battle priestess - she was Nyx, the Titan of Night, and she would not back down. "Seraphael," she replied, her voice calm yet unwavering, "you seek to impose your rigid morality upon us. What you call order is nothing more than control. I embrace the chaos of existence, for it is in chaos that we find our true strength."

A few gasps echoed through the room at her bold words, though some of her followers, the ones who had stood by her transformation into Nyx, nodded in agreement. The temple was not just a place of worship anymore - it was becoming a crucible for new ideas, a battleground of philosophies. And Eve was at the forefront of this war.

Seraphael's lips curled in disdain. "Chaos is a breeding ground for weakness," he countered, his voice thick with contempt. "Without moral absolutes, humanity and demonkind alike will descend into depravity. I cannot stand by while you lead them astray."

Eve's eyes blazed, and she could feel the ancient power of Nyx swirling within her, growing stronger with each passing second. She glanced around the room, meeting the gazes of her followers - some fearful, some intrigued, others cautiously hopeful. This was no longer just a battle between angel and demon; this was a battle for their souls, for the very foundation of their beliefs.

She raised her chin, speaking not just to Seraphael but to everyone in the chamber. "Morality, Seraphael, is a construct. It is not an absolute truth handed down by the divine, but a tool wielded by those in power to manipulate the masses. You speak of righteousness, yet it is your own belief system that fosters oppression."

Her words struck like lightning. The crowd shifted, some nodding thoughtfully, others muttering under their breath. It was clear that Eve's transformation had done more than alter her physical appearance; it had granted her a new perspective, one that challenged everything the temple had once held sacred.

Seraphael's expression darkened, and the very air seemed to tremble with the force of his divine conviction. "You betray your heritage, Eve," he said, his voice carrying a sharp edge of disappointment. "As a daughter of Hell, you were meant to embody the power of Asmodeus, not this misguided philosophy that leads to ruin. Do you not fear the consequences of your rebellion?"

The angel's words hung heavy in the air, and for a brief moment, there was silence. Eve's eyes never left his, her mind clear, her resolve unshaken. She had once feared rebellion, feared losing herself in the process. But now she knew that fear was the very thing that kept them all chained - chained to dogma, chained to old ways of thinking, chained to the limited perception of power.

"I fear nothing," Nyx's voice rang out, rich with authority. Her words reverberated through the chamber, resonating with the ancient power that now infused her very being. "The only thing I fear is the stagnation of thought and spirit. The followers of Asmodeus deserve the freedom to define their own paths. Power should not be an imposition but a choice."

Seraphael's eyes hardened, and Eve could see the inner conflict simmering beneath his rigid exterior. He was not accustomed to such defiance - especially not from a being he believed should submit to Heaven's moral absolutism or Hell's brutal law of dominance. But Eve was neither angel nor demon anymore. She was something else, something that transcended both realms. And that terrified him.

"Then let us settle this," Seraphael finally said, his voice dropping into a dangerous calm. The crowd held its collective breath, the tension mounting with each heartbeat. "Not with words but with actions. I will purify your spirit and rid this temple of your corrupting influence."

The challenge had been issued. The angel took a step forward, his hand reaching for the gleaming sword at his side. The celestial weapon shimmered with divine energy, its blade humming with the promise of obliteration. But Eve did not flinch. She met Seraphael's gaze head-on, her dark aura growing, enveloping her in a cloak of shadows that seemed to pulse with life. The power of Nyx surged within her, wild and untamable, but she held it with a steady hand. She had control now - not over others, but over herself.

"I welcome the challenge," Eve said, her voice low, almost a whisper. But there was no mistaking the power behind her words. She would not be purified. She would not be controlled. The battle that was about to unfold would be a reckoning, not just for Eve and Seraphael, but for the very nature of power and freedom within the temple.

With a final look at her followers, Eve stepped forward, her stance strong and unyielding. The battle had begun - not just for the temple, but for the soul of what it could become.

Eve's heart raced, a thrill of anticipation coursing through her. "You may attempt to fight me, but know this: I will not be bound by your definitions of right and wrong. This clash is not merely physical; it is a battle for the very essence of freedom."

Seraphael's wings unfurled in a blur of light as he surged forward, his gleaming sword arcing toward Eve with lethal precision. The sheer force of his attack sent shockwaves throughout the chamber, rattling the stone walls and shaking the ground beneath them. Some of the assembled followers staggered back, shielding their faces from the burst of energy that crackled between the two combatants.

But Eve - no, Nyx - stood firm. The chaos within her was a storm, and it answered to her command. Shadows flickered around her like serpents, weaving through the air in response to her will. Her dark aura absorbed the impact of Seraphael's assault, pushing back against the oppressive light he wielded. The temple, once a place of unchallenged order and tradition, now became a battleground of raw, primal forces.

Seraphael's sword cut through the air with a blinding speed, its radiant edge humming with the power of divine judgment. The very fabric of reality seemed to warp and tremble as it collided with Nyx's defenses - a swirling shield of black energy that rippled and bent with every strike. Sparks flew in every direction, bright and fierce, as the two forces met in a brilliant flash of light and darkness.

With each blow, Seraphael's frustration grew. He wielded the weapon with the confidence of a seasoned warrior, his attacks sharp and precise, but Nyx moved with an unsettling fluidity. She was not bound by rigid forms or predictable patterns. Her every step, every twist of her body, was a manifestation of chaos itself. She flowed like water, adapting effortlessly to his every strike, her movements unpredictable and beyond the understanding of traditional combat.

"You cannot escape the judgment of Heaven!" Seraphael roared, his voice echoing with divine fury as he pressed forward, trying to break through her defenses. His wings beat with a powerful rhythm, sending gusts of wind through the chamber. He swung his sword again, this time with even more force, a burst of radiant light exploding from the blade as it crashed against Nyx's shield.

But Eve, calm and resolute, met his onslaught with equal power. "I am not bound by your judgment!" she shouted, her voice cutting through the din of the battle. Summoning her chaotic energy, she thrust her hands forward, sending a surge of darkness that rippled like a tidal wave. The energy struck Seraphael head-on, forcing him to skid backward across the floor, his celestial light momentarily dimmed by the intensity of her power.

The crowd gasped as they watched the clash unfold, their eyes wide with awe and disbelief. Seraphael, the embodiment of Heaven's order and might, was being matched - no, overwhelmed - by the very chaos he sought to destroy. Eve's followers, those who had once questioned her transformation, now saw with their own eyes the strength that came from embracing the abyss. Nyx was not merely a demon; she was something far greater, a force that defied categorization.

Seraphael recovered quickly, his wings snapping open as he regained his footing. With a furious cry, he launched himself back into the fray, swinging his sword in a wide arc that cleaved through the air with terrifying force. Eve ducked under the strike, her body twisting in a blur of motion. She retaliated with a flurry of strikes, her hands crackling with dark energy as she weaved through his defenses, landing blow after blow on the angel's armor.

For every strike Seraphael delivered, Nyx countered with equal ferocity. Her hands moved like lightning, conjuring waves of shadow that danced around her, slashing through the air and forcing Seraphael to retreat. His sword cut through the darkness, but it could not cut through her. She was chaos incarnate, her form constantly shifting, evolving, adapting to every move he made.

With a roar of frustration, Seraphael raised his sword high, summoning a blinding light that illuminated the entire chamber. The sword gleamed with celestial power, pulsing with divine energy. It was clear he was preparing for a final, decisive strike, one that would obliterate everything in its path.

Eve narrowed her eyes, sensing the shift in his intent. This was no ordinary attack - it was a divine judgment, one meant to erase her from existence. The air itself trembled as Seraphael brought the sword down with a ferocious cry, a beam of pure, radiant energy erupting from the blade and tearing toward her like a bolt of lightning.

But Eve was ready.

In the heartbeat before the energy reached her, she raised both arms, her eyes glowing with the power of Nyx. Shadows swirled around her, coiling tighter and tighter until they formed a barrier - a void of darkness that absorbed the incoming light. The two forces collided with a deafening crash, sending shockwaves that reverberated through the entire temple.

For a moment, it seemed as though the light would break through. The divine energy surged against the shield of darkness, pushing forward inch by inch. But Eve held her ground, her expression calm and focused. She could feel the chaotic power within her growing stronger, feeding on the celestial energy, bending it to her will.

With a fierce cry, she unleashed her full power. The dark barrier exploded outward, swallowing the radiant beam whole and turning it into nothingness. Seraphael staggered back, his face a mask of disbelief as his ultimate attack was absorbed and dissipated like mist in the wind.

Eve did not let the moment pass. In an instant, she was upon him, her body moving with supernatural speed as she delivered a devastating strike to his chest. Her hand, crackling with chaotic energy, slammed into his armor, sending him flying backward across the chamber.

Seraphael crashed into the stone wall with a thunderous impact, the force of the blow cracking the very foundation of the temple. He slumped to the ground, his sword slipping from his grasp. Blood trickled from his mouth as he looked up at Eve, his expression a mix of fury and disbelief.

Eve approached slowly, her dark aura swirling around her like a living shadow. She stood over Seraphael, her power undeniable, her presence commanding. "You came here to purify me," she said softly, her voice echoing through the silent chamber. "But it is not purity that we need. It is freedom."

She raised her hand, the dark energy pulsing around it, ready to deliver the final blow. But then, she hesitated. For a brief moment, her eyes softened, and the power within her seemed to calm.

"You are wrong, Seraphael," she whispered, lowering her hand. "I do not seek to destroy you. I seek to transcend what you represent."

In the midst of their confrontation, Eve seized the opportunity to address her followers. "Look at what this battle represents! It is not just a fight between an angel and a demon; it is a struggle for the freedom to define ourselves. Will we accept the chains of dogma or embrace the chaos that leads to true power?"

Her words resonated in the hearts of her followers, igniting a fire of conviction within them. Some began to chant her name, their voices rising in unity, affirming their choice to stand beside her in this fight for self-definition.

Seraphael, sensing the shift in the atmosphere, narrowed his eyes. The tension between them crackled in the air, heavy and electric. With a guttural roar, he lunged again, his wings creating powerful gusts that knocked some of Eve's followers off their feet. His divine sword sliced through the air with terrifying precision, its radiance burning with holy fire.

Nyx met his attack head-on, her form gliding effortlessly as she parried the blow with a barrier of shadow. The clash of their powers sent a tremor through the temple, causing chunks of stone to crack and fall from the ceiling. Sparks flew as the two forces collided, light and dark warring against one another in a chaotic dance.

"You will never understand, Seraphael," Nyx said, her voice sharp with conviction, "because you are chained by your own beliefs. You fight for a false order, blind to the possibilities beyond your narrow understanding. I will show you that true strength lies not in domination, but in the acceptance of the entirety of existence!"

With a sudden shift in momentum, Nyx stepped back and raised both hands, her eyes glowing with an otherworldly light. The energy of her dual nature - cosmic and infernal - began to pulse through the chamber. Her arms stretched outward as she summoned a powerful surge of energy, weaving the light of the cosmos and the shadows of Hell into a single, harmonious force.

The energy spiraled between her hands, a vortex of creation and destruction that seemed to bend reality itself. With a sweeping gesture, she hurled the combined force toward Seraphael. The collision created a shockwave that shattered the pillars of the temple, sending debris flying in all directions and forcing Seraphael to stagger backward. Several acolytes scrambled for cover as the ground beneath them cracked, threatening to swallow them whole.

Seraphael's eyes widened in disbelief. His wings faltered, and for the first time, uncertainty flashed across his divine visage. He had faced countless demonic foes before, but Nyx - this combination of Eve's mortal understanding and the primordial chaos of Nyx - was something entirely different. She wasn't merely a demon or a celestial force gone rogue; she transcended the very laws of the universe.

"This cannot be!" he exclaimed, shaking off the debris and regaining his footing. His voice was tinged with disbelief, but also a growing desperation. "You cannot defeat the divine! The will of Heaven is absolute!"

But Eve/Nyx stood tall, her form brimming with a power that defied the boundaries of their world. The storm of chaos and freedom swirled around her, wild and untamable. She smiled grimly, her eyes fixed on Seraphael. "You mistake my strength for weakness, Seraphael. I am not bound by the definitions you impose. I am the embodiment of both chaos and order, and I will not be silenced."

The angel, gritting his teeth, gathered his strength for a renewed assault. He launched himself forward once more, this time with even greater ferocity. His sword, glowing with divine wrath, cleaved through the air with the force of a hurricane. Nyx raised her hands to defend herself, but this time, Seraphael's blade broke through her dark barrier, slicing into her shoulder.

She winced, her blood - black as night - dripping onto the cracked floor of the temple. Seraphael's eyes gleamed with a renewed sense of triumph. He pressed his advantage, swinging his sword with brutal efficiency, pushing Nyx back with each blow. For the first time, the followers saw their Priestess falter.

"You cannot win!" Seraphael declared, his voice filled with righteous fury. "For all your power, you are still tied to the darkness, a force that will always be inferior to the light. Your rebellion against the divine order is a futile one, Nyx. It always has been."

With a final, powerful strike, he sent Nyx sprawling to the ground, her body crashing against the rubble of the temple. She struggled to rise, her breath coming in ragged gasps. The followers, now watching in stunned silence, began to murmur among themselves. The sight of their powerful Priestess, the avatar of chaos and freedom, struggling against the might of Heaven shook them to their core.

Seraphael towered over her, his sword raised high above his head. His wings unfurled in a brilliant display of divine might, casting long shadows over the devastated temple. "You speak of freedom," he spat, his voice cold and unyielding. "But there is no freedom outside of Heaven's grace. There is only chaos, destruction, and suffering. I will end your heresy here and now."

For a brief moment, Eve/Nyx lay still, her body aching from the weight of the battle. She could feel Seraphael's divine energy pressing down on her like an oppressive force, threatening to crush her under its weight. Doubt crept into the edges of her mind, whispering that perhaps Seraphael was right. Perhaps she had underestimated the power of Heaven, the rigidity of its will. Maybe her path, the one she had so ardently fought for, was doomed to fail.

But no. Nyx would not be defeated so easily.

With a deep breath, she reached inside herself, past the pain, past the chaos, and into the depths of her being where her true power lay. The ancient force of Nyx - the primordial darkness that had existed before time itself - stirred within her. Slowly, she rose to her feet, her form radiating a newfound strength.

"I told you, Seraphael," she said, her voice steady, though her body trembled with the effort. "I am not bound by your rules. I will not be judged by your absolutes."

Seraphael's grip tightened on his sword. "Then die with your defiance."

The angel swung his blade, aiming to deliver the killing blow.

But just as his sword was about to strike, a surge of dark energy erupted from within Nyx. It exploded outward, creating a barrier of shadow that caught Seraphael's sword in mid-air. His eyes widened in shock as he realized what was happening. Nyx's power was growing - beyond anything he had anticipated.

With a snarl, Seraphael pushed against the barrier, his divine energy flaring as he attempted to break through. But the shadows around Nyx only thickened, wrapping around his blade like tendrils, pulling him closer to her.

For a brief moment, the two forces were locked in a deadly stalemate, neither one willing to give ground. The air was thick with tension, the followers holding their breath as they watched, unsure of who would prevail.

And then, without warning, the barrier cracked.

A burst of radiant light exploded from Seraphael's sword, shattering the dark energy around it. Nyx staggered back, her defenses weakening as Seraphael finally broke through. His sword gleamed with celestial fire, and he lunged forward, aiming directly for her heart.

Nyx barely had time to react.

Seraphael's sword cut through the air, its divine glow momentarily blinding her, but she shifted just in time. The blade grazed her chest, a flash of searing pain spreading through her body. It wasn't a fatal strike, but the wound was deep enough to send her staggering back.

A collective gasp rippled through the temple as blood began to stain the dark fabric of her robes. The followers watching from the shadows held their breath, horror etched on their faces. Even Seraphael hesitated, his radiant wings flickering as he hovered above her, his face a mixture of triumph and uncertainty.

Nyx pressed a hand to her wound, feeling the warmth of her own blood seeping through her fingers. Her heart pounded, each beat resonating with the chaotic energy that flowed within her. She met Seraphael's gaze, her eyes blazing with both fury and resolve.

Seraphael, hovering before her with his sword gleaming in the dim light, seemed to have won the upper hand. His divine aura swelled, the light around him growing stronger as he prepared to deliver the final blow. His voice, cold and commanding, rang out across the temple. "It's over, Nyx. Surrender now, and I will grant you mercy."

But Nyx's lips curled into a defiant smile. "Mercy? From you?" she said, her voice a low growl. "I don't need mercy. I am chaos itself."

The temple, which had fallen silent, began to tremble as if in response to her words. The shadows surrounding her stirred, rising like a living force. Tendrils of darkness stretched out from the corners of the room, swirling around her like a protective cocoon. The air grew thick, charged with power that hummed with life.

Seraphael's eyes narrowed, his grip tightening on his sword. "Your defiance will be your undoing. Chaos will always be subjugated by order."

Nyx straightened, her wound still bleeding but no longer slowing her. The dark energy that surrounded her filled the air with a potent, intoxicating force, and with each second, she felt it strengthening her. She embraced it. The shadows wove themselves into her form, her body becoming one with the very essence of chaos and freedom she had fought for all along.

"I am not just chaos," Nyx said, her voice growing louder, more commanding. "I am the balance between chaos and order, the force that refuses to be confined by your limited understanding. You think you've won because you wounded me, Seraphael? You're wrong."

In that moment, Nyx's power surged. The wound in her chest began to close, not through divine healing, but through sheer force of will. The darkness melded with her flesh, knitting it back together. Her followers watched in awe as the Priestess they had devoted themselves to stood tall once more, her strength unbroken.

Seraphael's expression shifted from triumph to frustration. His wings flared, casting light across the room as he charged forward, intent on finishing her. But this time, Nyx was ready.

With a sharp motion, she raised her hand and the shadows responded. They twisted and writhed around her before rushing toward Seraphael like a tidal wave. He slashed at them with his sword, cutting through some of the tendrils, but more rose to replace them, growing thicker and stronger with each passing moment.

The dark force wrapped around his sword, pulling it from his grasp and sending it clattering to the ground. Seraphael's eyes widened in disbelief as the shadows began to envelop him, wrapping around his arms, his legs, binding him in place.

"You fight with conviction," Nyx said, her voice echoing through the temple as she approached him. "But conviction without understanding is blindness. You wield the light as though it makes you righteous, but you've failed to see the truth. The light and the darkness are two sides of the same coin. One cannot exist without the other."

Seraphael struggled against the shadows, but they held firm, tightening around him. His wings flapped, stirring the air, but even they could not free him. For the first time, there was fear in his eyes.

"You've lost," Nyx said, standing over him now. Her form was a towering silhouette of shadow and light, her very presence commanding the room. "But I will not destroy you. That's not my way."

With a flick of her wrist, the shadows released their grip on him, and Seraphael stumbled to the ground, his wings drooping as he knelt before her. He looked up, confusion and frustration warring in his eyes.

She stood and turned away from him, her form still bathed in the shadows that now seemed to have become an extension of her. The temple was silent, save for the crackling of the energy still hanging in the air. Her followers, wide-eyed and silent, watched her in reverence, realizing that what they had witnessed was not just a battle but the dawn of something far greater.

Seraphael, seething with desperation, dove for his fallen sword in one swift, fluid motion. Grabbing the hilt, he twisted his body and launched himself at Nyx with a furious battle cry. His wings flared wide, propelling him forward with blinding speed as he swung the radiant blade in a wide arc, aiming directly for her heart. The blade, glowing with the light of divine judgment, crackled with power, cutting through the air with lethal precision as Seraphael swung with renewed vigor in an attempt to turn the tide against Eve.

23

The Cosmic Confrontation

Nyx's eyes narrowed, her instincts honed by millennia of battle. At the last possible moment, she twisted her body with a dancer's grace, the blade missing her by mere inches as it cleaved through the space where she had stood. Seraphael's momentum carried him forward, his wings straining to stop his advance, but Nyx had already moved, slipping into the shadows that bent and twisted at her will.

The battle between Eve/Nyx and Seraphael raged on, each clash of their powers sending shockwaves through the Temple of Asmodeus. As Nyx summoned the chaotic energy of the cosmos, memories long buried began to unfurl within her mind - visions of her primordial existence swirling like shadows in the depths of her consciousness. She was not merely a demon; she was an embodiment of the chaos that predated both Heaven and Hell, a force of nature unbound by any authority.

With each strike against Seraphael, the memories surged forth, igniting a fire within her. Flickers of distant worlds and ancient battles flooded her senses, and she could feel the raw energy of the universe coursing through her veins. "This is who I truly am," she whispered, her voice resonating with the echoes of her past. The revelation grounded her, deepening her connection to the abyss beyond the confines of the temple, while Seraphael's attacks grew more desperate, as if he too could sense the shift in her power.

Nyx's body moved like liquid shadow, flowing effortlessly around Seraphael's strikes as if each of his attempts were mere suggestions of violence, not true threats. The chaotic energy of the cosmos surged through her veins, quickening her reflexes, sharpening her senses. She didn't just dodge his blade - she moved with purpose, each shift of her body not only avoiding harm but embodying a greater truth.

"You cling to your laws like a lifeline, Seraphael," she taunted, her voice calm, echoing through the fractured temple. She batted away his blade with a flick of her wrist, her expression betraying no fear, only pity. "But do you not see? They bind you more than they protect you."

Seraphael's expression tightened, frustration etching lines into his normally serene face. His golden aura, once blazing like the sun, flickered as if he were losing his grip on the very light he wielded. He swung again, harder this time, a desperate attempt to reassert control. But Nyx moved again, a ripple in reality, her body slipping out of harm's way at the last second.

"You are lost, Eve," he spat through gritted teeth, his voice strained as he struggled to keep up with her. His wings flared wide, shimmering with divine light as he readied himself for another assault. "You have abandoned the very tenets that define you!"

Nyx didn't flinch. Instead, she smiled - a small, knowing smile. "Abandonment? No," she corrected, her voice steady, filled with the weight of millennia of wisdom. "I've embraced the entirety of existence." Her eyes blazed with the energy of stars long extinguished, and for a moment, Seraphael faltered as he met her gaze. "You fight to uphold a facade, Seraphael, while I stand as a testament to the strength that comes from embracing both light and dark. True power does not fear complexity."

Seraphael swung his sword again, the divine blade slicing through the air with a sound like thunder, but Nyx met it head-on this time. Sparks flew as her chaotic energy collided with his holy light, the impact sending tremors through the temple's foundation. The followers watching from the shadows gasped, some backing away from the sheer force of the battle.

But Nyx was not merely fighting to win; she was teaching. Every clash, every parry, every counterstrike became part of a grander lesson. "Look at yourself!" she cried out as their blades locked together in a searing blaze of celestial and infernal energy. "You wield power, but it is not your own. It was given to you - dictated by those who fear what they do not understand. You claim to be a servant of the light, but you are a slave to it!"

Seraphael growled, pushing against her with all his might, trying to break their deadlock. "I serve the greater good, Eve! What you call slavery, I call duty. I bring order to chaos, and in doing so, I protect all of existence from the abyss you now embody!"

Nyx's eyes narrowed. "And what if that order is the very thing that suffocates existence?" She pulled back suddenly, allowing Seraphael to stumble forward under his own weight. Her next strike was swift, cutting through his defenses and forcing him to retreat. "You think the abyss is something to fear because you cannot control it, but it is within that chaos that true potential lies."

She spun around him, her movements more dance than battle, her dark energy swirling in harmony with the shadows of the temple. With each graceful strike, she demonstrated her philosophy. Seraphael's attacks were forceful, but rigid - repetitive, predictable. Nyx, on the other hand, adapted, flowed, never striking from the same angle twice. Where Seraphael was locked in the narrow definitions of his divine order, Nyx embodied something far more fluid, something that evolved with every breath, every heartbeat.

"Look around you!" Nyx exclaimed, her voice rising as she gestured to the temple and the wide-eyed followers who watched with bated breath. "These souls, these individuals - they are not mere pawns in some cosmic game of good versus evil. They are complex beings, each with their own desires, their own fears, their own potential! Yet you seek to strip them of their uniqueness, to force them into the rigid roles your precious order demands."

Seraphael growled again, his patience fraying. He swung his sword with even greater ferocity, but Nyx ducked beneath his strike, weaving through his attacks like water slipping through fingers. "Order is what keeps the universe from descending into chaos," he roared, his voice trembling with the effort of his assault. "Without it, everything would fall into ruin!"

Nyx's laughter rang out, a sound both mocking and wise. "You misunderstand chaos," she replied, her voice soft but cutting through the noise of the battle like a blade through silk. "Chaos is not ruin. It is potential. It is creation in its rawest form. You fear it because you cannot predict it, cannot control it. But that is why it is powerful."

With a surge of energy, Nyx shifted her stance, moving from defense to offense. Her strikes were swift, purposeful, each one aimed not just at Seraphael's body but at the very heart of his beliefs. As her dark energy crackled around her, she became more than a warrior - she became a living argument, her philosophy manifesting through the dance of combat.

"You've locked yourself in a cage," she hissed, her strikes coming faster now, forcing Seraphael to fall back step by step. "A cage built from laws and doctrines that no longer serve you. You think your strength lies in your adherence to those rules, but in truth, it is your greatest weakness."

Seraphael stumbled, his golden aura dimming as he struggled to keep up. "I fight for order," he gasped, his breath coming in ragged bursts. "For the balance of the realms!"

Nyx's eyes glinted as she closed the distance between them. "And I fight for freedom," she whispered, her voice filled with the weight of ancient knowledge. "For the right to be more than what we are told to be."

With one final strike, Nyx knocked the sword from Seraphael's hand, sending it clattering across the temple floor. The angel staggered backward, his wings drooping, his breath shallow. For the first time in the battle, there was fear in his eyes - not fear of Nyx, but fear of what her words had awakened within him.

Nyx stood over him, her dark energy swirling around her like a storm. "You cannot win this battle, Seraphael," she said softly, though there was no malice in her tone. "Because this is not just a battle of strength. It is a battle of understanding. And until you can embrace the complexity of existence, you will never truly be free."

Seraphael stumbled, the truth of her words cutting deeper than any blade. "I do this for their own good," he retorted, desperation creeping into his tone. "Without guidance, they will fall into chaos, into sin!"

"Is it sin to seek one's own truth?" Nyx pressed, her voice echoing through the temple. "Is it a sin to desire freedom from the chains you would impose? Your laws are but shackles, Seraphael. I will not wear them."

Seraphael hesitated, reaching for his sword, now pulsing in his grip as doubt crept into his heart. For a fleeting moment, his conviction wavered, the certainty he once held in the righteousness of his cause slipping like sand through his fingers. Nyx saw the shift in his stance, the flicker of uncertainty in his eyes, and she seized the opportunity.

Without hesitation, she launched herself forward with renewed vigor, her movements a blur of shadow and light. Her body, now fully attuned to the chaotic forces that surged within her, became an extension of her will. She was no longer merely Eve, the priestess of Asmodeus, nor Nyx, the Infernal Titan of Night - she was something more, something transcendent. She was the embodiment of chaos itself, a force that existed beyond the narrow constructs of good and evil.

"You can't stop what you don't understand!" she shouted, her voice resonating with a newfound clarity.

Each strike she delivered carried the weight of her philosophy, her power no longer just an expression of physical might but a demonstration of the freedom she had found in embracing both light and darkness. Seraphael, on the other hand, struggled to keep up. His once-flawless technique became erratic, his swings growing heavier, slower, as the uncertainty in his heart began to mirror his faltering movements.

Seraphael's golden aura flickered dangerously, as if his divine essence was unraveling under the strain of the fight. He knew he was losing - losing not just the battle, but his grip on the very beliefs that had defined him for eons. Desperation clawed at him, and in that desperation, he reached for the one thing he believed could end the fight, no matter the cost.

His hands moved with purpose as he summoned the forbidden celestial weapon, a relic of untold power that had been locked away for millennia - a radiant spear, forged from the light of the stars themselves, imbued with the raw, destructive force of Heaven's wrath. The weapon pulsed with a hunger for annihilation, a single use capable of obliterating anything, even the wielder if they weren't careful.

The air grew thick, oppressive, as the spear materialized in Seraphael's grip. The chamber of the temple seemed to darken around them, the sheer presence of the weapon casting long, ominous shadows. The followers who had gathered to witness the battle gasped in terror, sensing the catastrophic potential of what was to come.

"Prepare yourself, Nyx!" Seraphael's voice rang out, filled with fury but laced with an unmistakable tinge of desperation. "I will eradicate this corruption once and for all!"

The light from the spear blazed brighter than the sun, blinding in its intensity. It was a weapon designed to purge the unholy, to wipe out any trace of opposition to Heaven's will. Seraphael held it high, ready to hurl it with all the strength of his divine fury.

Nyx could feel the raw power emanating from the spear, a power so great that it threatened to overwhelm even her chaotic nature. Her heart raced, her mind quickly assessing the threat. She knew that the spear was no ordinary weapon - it was designed to destroy, to reduce to nothingness anything that opposed the rigid laws of Heaven.

For a brief second, doubt flickered in her own heart. Could she truly stand against such overwhelming force?

But then something deeper within her awakened. In that moment, Nyx embraced everything she was - not just Eve, the priestess who sought balance between light and dark, but Nyx, the primordial chaos that existed before the dawn of creation itself. She was the embodiment of something far older, far more powerful, than any celestial weapon could hope to contain. She was not bound by the limitations of mortal or immortal understanding. She was beyond it.

"You think you can intimidate me with destruction?" Nyx called out, her voice calm but filled with a confidence that shook the very walls of the temple. "I am the embodiment of chaos! I will not be extinguished!"

As Seraphael hurled the spear toward her, time seemed to slow. The weapon cut through the air, a comet of divine light, its path set on obliterating everything in its wake. But Nyx stood her ground, her eyes narrowing as the spear closed in. She raised her hand, her fingers outstretched, and in that instant, something miraculous happened.

The energy from the spear - its raw, destructive power - didn't crash into her as expected. Instead, it collided with the swirling maelstrom of chaotic energy that surrounded her, and the spear began to unravel. Its divine light, once so blinding and pure, became entangled with the darkness that radiated from Nyx, transforming from a weapon of destruction into something entirely different.

The radiant spear disintegrated before their eyes, its energy coalescing into a shimmering cascade of light and shadow. The very power meant to obliterate her was now flowing through Nyx, merging with the chaotic essence that defined her existence. The followers gasped in awe, unable to comprehend the sight before them - an infernal being absorbing the holiest of weapons, not as a sign of defiance but as proof of her transcendence.

Nyx's body glowed with the combined energy of chaos and divine power, her form radiating an almost blinding brilliance. The spear's energy spiraled around her like a protective cloak, shimmering with a life of its own. She looked up at Seraphael, her eyes blazing with triumph.

"See how chaos consumes and transforms!" she shouted, her voice ringing with a resonance that shook the very air.

With a flick of her wrist, Nyx redirected the energy back toward Seraphael. The blast of cosmic power surged forth, a wave of light and darkness intertwined, and it slammed into the angel with the force of a collapsing star. Seraphael was thrown back, his golden wings flaring out as he crashed into the far wall of the temple, the impact causing cracks to spiderweb through the stone. His armor, once gleaming and unblemished, fractured under the sheer pressure of the blow.

For a moment, everything was silent. The followers of the temple stood frozen, their eyes wide with disbelief. Seraphael, the mighty angel who had come to pass judgment, lay crumpled against the wall, his divine aura flickering weakly around him. He struggled to rise, his breath ragged, his once-immaculate armor now shattered in places, his face etched with both pain and bewilderment.

Nyx stood at the center of the temple, her body still glowing with the remnants of the spear's energy, her chest heaving with the effort of the battle. She was victorious, but more than that, she had demonstrated the true nature of her power - a power not defined by Heaven's rules or Hell's chaos but by her ability to transcend both. She had taken what was meant to destroy her and turned it into a weapon of her own.

She approached Seraphael, her steps deliberate, her gaze steady. "You see now, don't you?" she said softly, her voice no longer taunting, but almost gentle. "This isn't about destruction or domination. It's about transformation - about embracing all that we are and all that we can become."

Staggering back, Seraphael struggled to rise, the weight of defeat settling heavily upon him like a leaden shroud. His once-magnificent wings, symbols of his divine status, now sagged and tattered against the stone floor of the Temple of Asmodeus. He gazed up at Nyx, who stood triumphant yet poised, a mixture of victory and empathy swirling within her. The radiance of the spear's energy still danced around her, casting flickering shadows that painted her as both a warrior and a beacon of transformation.

"You... you cannot defeat the divine," he gasped, each word laced with disbelief, as if he were struggling to reconcile the reality before him with the unshakeable truths he had held all his life.

Nyx felt the rush of power coursing through her veins, intoxicating yet grounding. It filled her with strength but also a profound empathy for the angel before her. She had fought fiercely to defend her beliefs, but this was not a battle born of hatred; it was a clash of philosophies, a confrontation that transcended mere combat.

"This is not about destruction, Seraphael," she declared, her voice softer yet no less firm, echoing in the suddenly hushed temple. "This is about choice, about understanding that power lies in acceptance, not annihilation."

As she stood there, the golden light of the temple dimmed, creating an atmosphere thick with tension and uncertainty. The followers who had once feared the rigid structure of Heaven's moral code began to realize the true significance of the moment. They had witnessed a struggle not just between Nyx and Seraphael but between two opposing worldviews - one seeking to impose order through control, the other advocating for freedom through understanding.

Nyx offered Seraphael a choice, just as she had offered to all her followers. Her hand, extended toward him, glowed softly with the energy of chaos intertwined with divinity. It was a gesture of hope, a bridge between their disparate beliefs.

"Will you continue to fight for a narrow view of righteousness, or will you embrace the complexity of existence?" she asked, her voice resonating with conviction. "Power does not have to mean control. It can mean empowerment."

The angel, panting and weary, looked at her hand, trembling with uncertainty. He was caught in a tempest of doubt, the remnants of his belief system crumbling before him like the very walls of the temple. The energy swirled around Nyx, a tangible representation of her mastery over both chaos and order, a living testament to her philosophy. Seraphael's gaze shifted from her hand to the temple, taking in the followers watching with rapt attention, their breaths held in anticipation.

He felt their eyes upon him, a chorus of hope and fear intermingled, and his heart ached with the weight of their expectations. "I..." he started, but the words felt heavy, as if the very air conspired to hold them back. "I was taught that mercy is a weakness."

"Mercy is strength, Seraphael," Nyx replied, her voice steady yet infused with compassion. "It takes strength to accept that we are all flawed and that our paths are not predetermined. Join us in this understanding, and together we can redefine power."

The tension hung palpably in the air, each heartbeat echoing the pivotal nature of the moment. The temple, once a sanctuary of rigid belief, now thrummed with potential - a living testament to the struggles and triumphs of its inhabitants. Nyx's followers began to shift, their gazes flickering between their priestess and the fallen angel, sensing the shift in the atmosphere, the awakening of new possibilities.

Seraphael's gaze dropped to the ground, the intricate patterns of the temple floor drawing him in as if they were alive, reflecting the very struggles within him. "But... the laws, the divine edicts - they are meant to protect us, to guide us," he murmured, his voice barely above a whisper.

"Guidance can also be a cage, Seraphael," Nyx countered gently. "What good are laws if they strip us of our choices? True guidance inspires us to choose for ourselves, to discover the depths of our potential, not to live in fear of judgment."

The weight of her words hung in the air, and he felt the chains of his convictions begin to rust under the pressure of her insight. The angel's brow furrowed as he wrestled with the reality of his teachings, his mind a battleground of contrasting ideologies. Each moment that passed felt like an eternity as he grappled with the truths he had long accepted and the new understanding that began to bloom within him.

Nyx's outstretched hand shimmered with light, the cosmic energy swirling in vibrant colors, embodying both the chaos she had embraced and the order that Seraphael clung to. She stepped closer, allowing the light to wash over him, a gentle caress that seemed to pierce through the haze of his uncertainty. "You're not alone in this fight, Seraphael. Look at your followers. They do not wish to be pawns in a game dictated by celestial politics. They want to be free - to embrace their individuality, their desires, their flaws. Will you join us in creating a new path?"

Seraphael's heart raced, the pulse of change resonating within him. He lifted his gaze to meet Nyx's, the fire of determination mingling with the embers of doubt. He had devoted himself to a code of righteousness, a pursuit of absolute goodness, yet standing before Nyx, he felt that code bending, shifting, reshaping into something unrecognizable but beautifully profound.

"But what does that mean?" he asked, the tremor in his voice betraying his fear. "What will become of us if we abandon the structure, the laws?"

Nyx's expression softened, and she stepped closer still, closing the distance between them. "It means we become our own architects. We learn from the past, but we do not let it bind us. Power is not merely a means to an end; it is the ability to choose - to create a world where all can thrive, not just those who fit a mold. You can be a part of this new vision, Seraphael. You can help us redefine what it means to be divine."

The angel's resolve began to crack, the armor of his long-held beliefs rattling under the weight of her words. He glanced at the gathered followers, their eyes shimmering with hope and uncertainty, and he felt their collective yearning for a new kind of power - a power rooted in acceptance and understanding rather than fear and control.

Slowly, he lifted his trembling hand toward Nyx's, caught in the gravitational pull of her conviction. The energy between them surged, a connection forged in the crucible of their battle - a testament to the truth that even the mightiest can find redemption.

"I..." Seraphael's voice faltered, yet determination flickered within him. "I want to believe that I can redefine my purpose. But can I truly abandon everything I have known?"

"Not abandon," Nyx corrected softly, "but evolve. You are not defined by your past, Seraphael. You are defined by the choices you make moving forward. Embrace this chance to evolve, to embrace complexity, and you will discover the strength within yourself and others."

With a shaky breath, he took her hand. In that moment, the temple felt alive, resonating with the shifting tides of destiny. The air crackled with potential as their hands clasped, a fusion of divine light and chaotic essence. The transformation began, not just for Seraphael, but for the very fabric of their beliefs, a moment that would reshape the paths of all who had gathered to witness it.

As they stood there, hand in hand, Nyx felt the echoes of their conflict recede, replaced by the promise of a new beginning.

In that moment, as the echoes of their clash lingered in the temple, Seraphael faced a choice that would forever alter the course of his existence. The battle had transformed from a mere physical confrontation into a profound exploration of ideologies, and as the dust settled, Eve/Nyx knew that the true victory lay not in destruction, but in the potential for understanding and growth.

And so, the temple stood at a crossroads - one where the definitions of right and wrong began to blur, where the embrace of the abyss offered a chance for transcendence, not just for Eve/Nyx, but for all who dared to challenge the limits of their existence.

24

The Ultimate Lesson

The temple, once a bastion of rigid doctrine, now pulsed with a transformative energy as the aftermath of the battle between Eve/Nyx and Seraphael lingered in the air. The echoes of their confrontation faded, replaced by a tension that rippled through the gathered demons and celestial observers alike. As Eve/Nyx stood amidst the scattered remnants of power, she turned her gaze to Seraphael, who remained on the ground, his divine form battered and weary.

Shaken by his defeat, Seraphael stood trembling, struggling to comprehend the profound shift stirring within him. His once-immaculate armor was chipped and dull, symbolic of the inner turmoil now unsettling his soul. He, the angel known for his unwavering commitment to Heaven's laws, the unbending enforcer of divine order, was now questioning the very tenets that had guided him through countless battles and centuries. His heart, once steeled by the certainty of righteousness, now fluttered with confusion.

"How can you stand there, victorious yet merciful?" he asked, his voice a fragile mixture of disbelief and curiosity. His golden wings drooped, their brilliant sheen dimming as if reflecting his own waning conviction. "You have shown me a power I cannot fathom, yet I am bound to my beliefs. You... you should destroy me, and yet, you offer mercy."

Nyx, bathed in the luminous energy of the temple, stepped closer. Her presence was commanding, every step purposeful, yet there was no malice in her. Instead, she radiated a calm, serene authority - an invitation rather than a threat. "That is precisely where you are mistaken, Seraphael. You think you are bound, but what truly binds you are the chains of your own making - chains forged by an adherence to a doctrine that sees the world in black and white, where all things must fit into neat little boxes. You are not bound by Heaven; you are bound by the limits you've imposed upon yourself."

His blue eyes, once sharp with celestial fire, now softened as they searched hers, grappling with the enormity of her words. "But how can one exist without the guidance of absolute morality? Without it, what keeps us from spiraling into chaos, into destruction? If we abandon the light, what becomes of us?"

"Chaos is not the enemy," Nyx responded, her voice as steady and soothing as the night wind. She could feel the raw vulnerability in Seraphael, the fractures forming in the walls of his certainty. "Chaos is a canvas upon which we can paint our own destinies. It is not something to fear but to embrace. The true enemy is blind submission, the surrendering of one's will to the dictates of external forces. True power lies not in obedience but in the strength to forge your own path. You have a choice, Seraphael: to remain confined within the walls of Heaven's rigid dogma or to step into the unknown and discover the richness of existence. Chaos is not your undoing; it is the very force that can set you free."

Seraphael's wings trembled, his gaze faltering for a moment as if the weight of her words had finally cracked the armor of certainty that he had worn for eons. His very being, once a pillar of unwavering faith, now felt as fragile as the wings that hung limply at his sides. "But I have fought for so long," he whispered, more to himself than to her. "I have fought to uphold what I believed was right, what was commanded of me. I thought that was my purpose. But now... I feel lost."

"Being lost is not a failure," Nyx said gently, her voice filled with empathy. "It is a beginning. It means you are ready to grow beyond what you were taught. Do you see the potential in doubt? It is the first step towards freedom. To question is not to betray the light - it is to transcend it."

As she spoke, Nyx felt the full weight of her transformation settle upon her, an integration of Eve, the priestess who once served the temple, and Nyx, the Infernal Titan of Night. She was no longer be-holden to the dualities of good and evil, order and chaos. She had shed the last vestiges of her imposed identity, evolving into some-thing more. She embodied the Nietzschean ideal of self-overcoming, transcending the simple binaries that once defined her. She was now a living testament to the freedom found in embracing one's true na-ture, an ever-shifting dance between light and dark, chaos and order.

For a moment, they stood in silence, the temple around them quiet as if even the stone itself held its breath. The followers who had gathered to witness the battle stood motionless, their eyes flick-ing between Nyx and Seraphael, captivated by the quiet intensity of the exchange. They, too, sensed that something monumental was unfolding - not just a battle, but a philosophical turning point that could reshape the very foundation of their understanding.

"But what if I abandon everything I've known?" Seraphael mur-mured, his voice trembling with fear. "What becomes of me then? If I let go of Heaven's law, what will guide me? What will keep me from falling into the abyss?"

Nyx tilted her head, her gaze soft but penetrating. "You are afraid of the unknown, Seraphael, and that is understandable. But consider this: the abyss you fear is not a place of destruction - it is a place of potential. In that darkness, you have the power to create your own light. The laws you've followed have served their purpose, but now they hold you back. To let go is not to fall; it is to fly in a way you have never imagined."

Seraphael's heart pounded, his mind racing as he tried to grasp the enormity of what she was saying. He had spent millennia fight-ing for a rigid, unyielding version of righteousness. The idea of cast-ing aside those laws, those absolutes, felt like a betrayal. And yet, standing before Nyx, he could see the truth in her words. She was not bound by Heaven, Hell, or any force beyond herself. She had transcended those limitations, and in doing so, had found a strength far greater than the power that came from mere obedience.

"Can I truly do that?" he asked, his voice barely a whisper. "Can I abandon everything I have believed in?"

"You are not abandoning your beliefs," Nyx said, stepping even closer, her eyes glowing softly with the cosmic energy she had channeled. "You are evolving them. You are growing beyond them. Beliefs are not meant to be cages; they are meant to be stepping stones. You believed in the light once, and it guided you. But now, you must learn to guide yourself. To be free is to be responsible for your own path."

The angel stared at her, his heart heavy with the enormity of the choice before him. He had never imagined that his journey would lead him here, to this crossroads where he had to choose between the safety of certainty and the terrifying freedom of self-determination.

"Will you take that step, Seraphael?" Nyx asked, her hand still outstretched, her expression one of quiet encouragement. "Will you allow yourself to be more than what you were made to be?"

For a long, breathless moment, Seraphael hesitated. His mind churned with the weight of the decision before him. Then, with a deep, trembling breath, he lifted his gaze to meet hers. Slowly, he reached out and clasped her hand once more, as she pulled him to his feet.

In that moment, the temple seemed to hold its breath, the air thick with the weight of possibility. Seraphael stood at a precipice, the chains of Heaven's laws that had once bound him now crumbling like dust in the wind. His fingers, still clasped in Nyx's, trembled slightly, not from fear of the unknown but from the realization of the freedom that lay before him. The once-unyielding structures of his existence felt fragile, as if one more step could dismantle everything he had ever known - and yet, in that fragility, he sensed a new strength forming.

"I don't know where this path will take me," he said, his voice unsteady but resolute, filled with both fear and hope. "But I will walk it."

Nyx smiled softly, the corners of her lips curving with gentle approval. Her grip on his hand was firm but reassuring, a tether guiding him through this moment of transformation. "Then you are free," she declared, her words imbued with both finality and promise.

As those words echoed within him, Seraphael felt an unfamiliar stirring in his chest. For the first time in eons, emotions he had long buried beneath the weight of duty and law began to surface. There was a flicker of something within him - uncertainty, yes, but also curiosity, wonder, and, perhaps most striking of all, liberation. He no longer felt the oppressive weight of Heaven's expectations crushing down on his soul. The rigid boundaries of his beliefs, which had kept him shackled to an unwavering sense of right and wrong, were dissolving. What replaced them was an exhilarating, albeit terrifying, sense of freedom.

"But if I abandon my beliefs, what will I become?" Seraphael asked, his voice laced with the fear of losing himself, of becoming untethered from the mission that had defined him for so long. His once-sharp eyes were now wide with uncertainty, as though the vast unknown stretched endlessly before him.

Nyx's eyes softened as she regarded him, her voice steady and calm as the darkness she commanded. "You will become more than you ever imagined," she answered. "What you will become is not dictated by others' expectations of you, nor by the laws you once served. You will discover your true self - not the one crafted by Heaven, not the one shaped by the orders of those who sit above. You will embrace the complexities of existence, the shades of gray that color our experiences. Power is not a static force, Seraphael; it is dynamic, it is alive, and it can be shaped by your will. The power to define your path has always been yours - you simply need to accept it."

The angel blinked, her words echoing in the hollow spaces of his heart, spaces he hadn't even realized were empty. His mission, his loyalty, had once seemed like an immutable pillar, supporting the very core of who he was. But now, standing in the presence of Nyx - who had redefined herself beyond the constraints of darkness and light - he began to understand that there was more to existence than the black-and-white morality he had clung to for so long.

All around them, the demons and celestial observers who had witnessed their battle stood in a hushed silence, their gazes locked on the unfolding moment. There was an undeniable shift in the atmosphere, not merely because Seraphael had been defeated, but because the implications of Nyx's teachings were sinking in. Power, true power, did not lie in dominance or in blind adherence to law. Power, they were beginning to see, was born from choice - individuality. Could it really be that power came from within, that it was not something dictated by Heaven or Hell but something shaped by one's own will?

"Eve," Seraphael said softly, the name falling from his lips like a fragile whisper, invoking the memory of the priestess who once served beneath the Titan of Night. "You've shown me a world I never dared to dream of. A world where I am not just a servant of Heaven but something more. But can I truly abandon my post, my mission? I have stood guard at the gates of righteousness for so long. How can I turn away from that now?"

Nyx's gaze held his, unwavering, her expression one of deep empathy and understanding. "Your mission is not confined to a single path, Seraphael. You were not created to walk one road forever."

She took a step closer, her presence both reassuring and powerful. "You can remain loyal to your ideals, and to Heaven - loyal to the essence of what you believe is right - while redefining what those ideals mean. You do not need to abandon righteousness; you need only let go of the chains of dogma that restrict it. True righteousness isn't about blind obedience. It's about understanding, compassion, and the courage to make choices that go beyond the rules you were given."

Seraphael's breath caught in his throat, his mind swirling with possibilities. Could it really be true? Could he redefine what righteousness meant, not through the lens of Heaven's absolute authority, but through his own understanding of justice and mercy? The thought was both terrifying and liberating in equal measure.

"Will you join me in this exploration, Seraphael?" Nyx continued, her voice calm and inviting. "Together, we can build a bridge between our worlds, a testament to the power of choice and individuality. Heaven and Hell need not be at odds forever. Perhaps they can coexist, not as opposing forces, but as parts of a greater whole. A balance."

The idea was staggering. Seraphael's wings, once the embodiment of Heaven's purity, now seemed to tremble with the weight of this new potential. He had been taught to fight the forces of chaos, to crush the darkness wherever it appeared. But now, standing in the midst of that very darkness, he could feel something different - a sense of possibility, of growth. Heaven's light had been his guide for so long, but now he understood that there were other lights, other paths to follow.

"I... don't know where this will lead," he admitted, his voice heavy with emotion. "But I see now that my path does not have to be Heaven's alone. I see now that righteousness isn't confined to one truth. There are many truths, and perhaps, together, we can uncover them."

Nyx's smile was gentle, but her eyes sparkled with approval. "That is all I ask, Seraphael. To walk together, not in servitude, but in mutual understanding."

As he pondered her offer, a soft glow enveloped Nyx, radiating warmth and reassurance. The battle had been fierce, yet it had led to a moment of profound understanding, not just for Seraphael but for everyone witnessing this monumental shift.

In the dim, flickering light of the temple, a ripple of whispers began to circulate among the demons, their eyes wide with both astonishment and uncertainty. Even among the celestial beings who watched from afar, safe in the shadows of their unyielding convictions, there was a stir of doubt - a tremor that cut to the heart of their beliefs. Nyx had introduced a new complexity into their world, one that challenged the very foundations of their understanding of righteousness and order.

For eons, the angelic mission had been regarded as noble, a shining beacon of clarity in a universe torn between light and darkness. But now, in the aftermath of Seraphael's encounter with Nyx, that clarity felt like an illusion, and the certainty they had once held so tightly now seemed to slip through their fingers like grains of sand.

"I have always seen myself as a guardian of light," Seraphael murmured, still wrestling with the dichotomy that had ruled his existence for as long as he could remember. His voice was soft, tinged with confusion, but beneath that confusion was a profound yearning to understand what lay beyond the simplicity of Heaven's mandates. "What if I falter? What if, by embracing this path, I bring more chaos than order?"

The vulnerability in his words echoed throughout the chamber, hanging in the air like a fragile mist. For so long, Seraphael had believed that his purpose was clear, that his actions were righteous and guided by an unshakable moral compass. But now, with Nyx standing before him - her very being a fusion of light and darkness, chaos and order - he felt something begin to unravel within him. Could it be that he had been wrong all along? Was it possible that the light he had served had been only one half of a larger truth?

Nyx leaned closer, her movements slow and deliberate, her eyes holding his with a depth that made it impossible for him to look away. When she spoke, her voice was barely above a whisper, yet it cut through the cacophony of his internal turmoil with the precision of a blade. "Faltering is part of the journey, Seraphael. Do not fear it - embrace it. Learn from it. Every step you take, whether it leads you into the light or into the shadows, is a step toward growth. You are not alone in this. We will walk this path together."

There was a stillness to her presence, a serenity that was at odds with the concept of chaos she embodied. It was that very contradiction that both troubled and intrigued Seraphael. How could she be so certain, so calm, in the face of such uncertainty? Was this the nature of true power - not in dominating others or imposing order upon the world, but in the willingness to surrender to the ebb and flow of existence, to accept that failure and doubt were integral parts of the journey?

"The only thing you must fear," she continued, her words soft yet unwavering, "is the denial of your true self. That is the greatest tragedy - living a life not of your own choosing, but one dictated by the expectations of others."

A silence fell over the temple as Seraphael absorbed her words. He closed his eyes for a brief moment, feeling the weight of his internal conflict settle over him like a heavy cloak. All his life, he had been guided by Heaven's laws, by a rigid code that left little room for doubt or deviation. To falter was to fail. To question was to sin. Yet here he stood, face to face with Nyx, a being who had embraced the chaos within her and found strength in it.

The realization was both terrifying and exhilarating. He had spent so long resisting the pull of the unknown, fearing that to stray from the path would lead to ruin. But now, standing at the edge of something greater, he understood that faltering, doubting, and even failing were all part of the process. They were not signs of weakness, but of growth. Perhaps, he mused, the true tragedy was never having faltered at all - never having had the courage to question the rules that bound him.

He opened his eyes, and in that moment, the lines of destiny seemed to blur, stretching and twisting like a tapestry woven from threads of both light and shadow. It was as if the universe itself had paused, waiting for his next move, for the decision that would either anchor him to the past or set him free to forge a new path.

Finally, after what felt like an eternity, Seraphael nodded. His decision crystallized within him, solid yet fluid, like water that had found its course. "I will join you, Eve... Nyx," he said, his voice firm but tinged with something new - something alive. "I will embrace this journey of self-discovery. If power truly lies in choice, then I choose to forge my own path, to walk into the unknown and learn who I truly am."

With those words, Nyx smiled - a smile that held both warmth and a quiet understanding. She extended her arms once more, a gesture not of dominance or coercion, but of unity. It was a gesture of mutual respect, of acknowledgment that their paths, though different, could now converge.

As their hands clasped, the energy around them shifted, crackling with the hum of possibility. It was as if the air itself had become alive, charged with the potential of what was to come. A spark ignited in the space between them, not a spark of destruction, but one of creation - a signal that something new was being born, not just within Seraphael, but within the temple itself.

The demons, once driven by fear and subjugation, now saw something different. The celestial beings, too, felt a change stirring within them, a seed of doubt that might one day blossom into something more. For in this moment, they had witnessed a new kind of power - one not born from control or domination, but from the courage to choose, to question, and to embrace the complexity of existence.

A new era had begun, one in which the lines between Heaven and Hell, light and darkness, chaos and order, would no longer be so rigidly defined. Together, Nyx and Seraphael would walk this path, not as enemies, but as allies - united not by doctrine or law, but by the shared understanding that true power came from within.

As they stood together, hands clasped, the world around them shifted. The possibilities were endless, and the journey was only just beginning.

The ripple effect of their encounter began to unfold, radiating far beyond the immediate confrontation between Nyx and Seraphael. The demons, once so sure of their purpose in serving a dark master, and the angels, bound by their celestial duty to uphold Heaven's laws, now found themselves caught in a wave of uncertainty. The surge of energy from Nyx's words had been more than just a challenge to Seraphael - it had been an invitation, a call to reconsider their own beliefs.

Among the ranks of the demons, murmurs began to rise, conversations flickering to life as each soul contemplated their place within the cosmos. The once rigid followers of Asmodeus, who had long believed that strength came from submission to his infernal will, now felt that paradigm shift beneath their feet. Could it be that their power wasn't tied to the dark dominion they served, but to their own inner potential? Inspired by Nyx's example, many of them began to wonder if true strength came not from blind submission, but from embracing their unique identities, from crafting their own destinies in a universe of infinite possibilities.

Even the celestial beings who had observed the battle from afar, those who had always been taught to see Hell as a realm of unredeemable chaos, felt the stirring of doubt within their hearts. Seraphael, one of their own, had taken the first step toward questioning the absolutes that Heaven had imposed upon him. And if he could take that step, could they?

As Eve/Nyx stood victorious, her figure illuminated by the faint, flickering light of the temple's torches, the entire atmosphere around her began to shift. What had once been a place of strict adherence to Asmodeus's will, a sanctuary of dogma and rigid control, was transforming. The energy that lingered in the temple no longer felt oppressive or suffocating, as it had for so long. Instead, it became something far more liberating - a space of exploration rather than condemnation. The echoes of the battle that had just taken place faded into the background, replaced by whispers of hope, as if the temple itself was exhaling a long-held breath.

It wasn't just the followers who felt this shift. Eve/Nyx, standing in the center of it all, felt the weight of her victory settle over her like a warm embrace. She had fought for more than just personal triumph; she had fought to defend her beliefs and to carve out a space for herself in a universe that had always sought to define her by external standards. Now, in this pivotal moment, Nyx recognized that her journey was not just her own. It was a shared experience, a movement that would ripple outward, inspiring countless others to break free from the constraints of rigid beliefs and the binary thinking of good versus evil.

As she looked around at the gathered souls - demons, angels, and followers of the temple alike - she felt a profound sense of fulfillment. Each of them had been touched by what had just transpired, in some way or another. The walls of the temple had witnessed countless struggles, both external and internal, but today marked a turning point. Nyx could sense that her teachings, her challenge to the status quo, would not remain confined within these walls. They would extend outward, touching realms that had long been divided by fear and misunderstanding, realms that had seen power as a means of domination rather than empowerment.

"Together," she proclaimed, her voice strong, carrying the weight of her conviction, "we will redefine what it means to exist. We will create a space where power is born from choice and where every being can find their voice amidst the chaos."

Her words sent another ripple through the gathered crowd. Those who had once felt lost or trapped in their respective roles, who had believed that they had no say in the grand design of the universe, now felt something stir within them. It was the beginning of an awakening, a realization that the cosmos was not as rigid as they had once believed. The divisions between Heaven and Hell, light and darkness, chaos and order, were not fixed. They could be rewritten, reinterpreted.

As the followers rallied around her, Nyx felt a surge of energy in the room. She knew that this was just the beginning. There was so much work left to be done, but for the first time, it felt achievable. The ultimate lesson of her journey was not merely about confronting authority or dismantling old structures - it was about embracing the infinite possibilities that lay ahead, about forging a new path that celebrated the complexity of existence rather than shying away from it.

With that understanding settling over the crowd like a soft breeze, the temple of Asmodeus, once a symbol of fear and dominance, was now a place of hope. And as Nyx stood at the heart of it all, her eyes glimmering with the realization of her own evolution, she knew that the path forward would not be an easy one. But it would be hers, and it would belong to all those who dared to walk it beside her.

25

A Temple Reborn

The echoes of the recent battle still lingered in the hallowed halls of the Temple of Asmodeus, reverberating with a newfound energy that neither the priests nor the acolytes could ignore. Eve, now fully embodying Nyx, stood before the assembled crowd, her presence radiating an authority forged in the crucible of conflict. The flickering torches cast shadows on the stone walls, creating an ambiance both ominous and hopeful as she prepared to deliver her vision for the temple's future.

"Brothers and sisters," she began, her voice resonating with conviction, "we stand at a crossroads. For too long, we have been bound by chains of tradition that limit our potential and distort our understanding of power. No longer shall we serve Asmodeus blindly; no longer shall we be mere instruments of fear and control."

A murmur rippled through the assembly. Faces reflected a mix of anticipation and apprehension, some eyes wide with excitement, others narrowed in defiance. Eve/Nyx could see Varaak, the staunch traditionalist, standing among the ranks, her arms crossed tightly over her chest. The tension in the air was palpable, yet Eve welcomed it. This was the essence of growth: discomfort sparking debate and ultimately transformation.

"I invite you to explore a new path," Eve continued, her voice gaining strength. "This temple shall become a sanctuary for seekers of truth - those who wish to understand not just the nature of power, but also the cosmos that surrounds us. We will embrace the complexities of existence, rejecting the simplistic duality of good and evil."

Varaak stepped forward, her expression fierce. "You speak of freedom, Nyx, but at what cost? Are we to abandon the very teachings that have guided us through centuries? You would lead us into chaos!"

"Chaos?" Eve countered, her gaze unwavering. "Chaos is not the absence of order but the possibility of creation. It is in chaos that we find our true selves, where we can transcend beyond the limitations of imposed morality. I do not seek to destroy our heritage, but to evolve it. The teachings of Asmodeus can coexist with the philosophies of self-discovery and empowerment."

Varaak's defiant stare did not waver, her voice rising as she pressed her point. "You speak of power as if it can be shaped by mere whims, Nyx. Power, true power, demands control. Without structure, it will consume us all. What is to stop the weak from crumbling, or the ambitious from tearing us apart in their bid for dominance? Chaos has no boundaries, no laws, no means of preservation."

Eve met Varaak's fiery gaze with calm resolve. "And what has control brought us? Look at the temple. Look at the realms of Hell. We have thrived on the subjugation of others, on fear, on power used as a weapon of oppression rather than as a force of enlightenment. Yes, power must be wielded with intent, but it is not an unchangeable force. We have used it to bind ourselves as much as we have used it to control others."

She paused, scanning the assembly. "The weak crumble not because of chaos, but because we have taught them to fear it. They have been taught to submit, to believe their strength lies in obedience rather than in the courage to carve their own path. The ambitious rise not through chaos but through the constraints we have built, which force them into roles where their only choice is to destroy one another in order to gain power."

The murmur among the crowd grew louder, with acolytes and demons alike exchanging glances. The philosophical foundations upon which they had built their lives were shaking, and Eve could see the flickers of doubt and intrigue igniting behind many eyes. Varaak, however, was not so easily moved.

"And what of Asmodeus?" Varaak challenged. "He has given us the means to rule, the strength to endure. You speak of self-discovery, of rejecting dogma, but how can we turn away from the power that our Lord has bestowed upon us? You, more than anyone, should understand that."

Eve smiled faintly. "I do not seek to turn away from Asmodeus, nor do I reject the strength he has granted us. But what I propose is not a rejection - it is an evolution. Asmodeus represents ambition, the will to power, and the pursuit of strength. But that strength need not be built on fear alone. We can embrace the freedom to choose, the courage to question, and still honor the essence of what Asmodeus stands for."

She stepped forward, her presence commanding the attention of all in the room. "Imagine a temple where power is not dictated solely by rank or fear, but where strength is cultivated through self-knowledge, through understanding one's true potential. Where followers of Asmodeus seek not only to dominate but to surpass themselves, to achieve a power that is both internal and external. This is what I offer you."

The silence that followed was thick with contemplation. Even Varaak seemed momentarily stunned by Eve's words. The idea of power through self-knowledge and self-overcoming was an unfamiliar concept for a temple steeped in traditional hierarchies of dominance. It was radical, yet it resonated with the unspoken frustrations many felt but had not dared voice.

A voice from the back of the crowd broke the silence. "But if we are no longer guided by fear and control, what guides us? What keeps us from losing our way in this chaos you speak of?"

Eve turned toward the voice, her expression softening. "We guide ourselves," she said. "We are not lost in chaos. Chaos is possibility, and within it lies the opportunity to create meaning. We are free to shape our own paths, to find purpose not in the submission to an external force but in the understanding of our own desires, our own strength. This does not mean abandoning our bonds to one another or to the temple. It means reimagining them, creating a space where we rise together through shared discovery, not through fear."

The murmurs returned, but this time they carried a different tone. Acolytes exchanged glances, some with wide eyes of curiosity, others with thoughtful nods. Even the older demons, hardened by years of rigid hierarchy, seemed to reconsider their place in this evolving world.

"I do not expect you all to agree with me now," Eve said, her voice lowering to a more intimate tone. "This is not a demand for blind obedience, nor am I asking you to forsake everything you have believed. I ask only that you consider the possibility that there is more to power than what we have been taught. More to existence than the roles we have been given. That we can become something greater if we have the courage to question, to evolve."

She turned once more to Varaak. "You fear chaos because you see it as destruction. But I see it as creation. Asmodeus has given us strength, and I honor that strength. But now it is time to use that strength to transcend the boundaries that have confined us."

Varaak remained silent for a long moment, her eyes searching Eve's face for some sign of weakness or deceit. Finally, she spoke, her voice quieter but no less intense. "I still do not trust this path you offer, Nyx. But I will not stand in its way. If you truly believe this will lead us to greater power, then I will watch and see."

Eve nodded, a flicker of respect passing between the two women. "That is all I ask."

As Varaak stepped back into the crowd, Eve felt a surge of hope. The path ahead was fraught with uncertainty, but the seed had been planted. The temple, once a place of rigid fear and control, was beginning to shift, its members standing on the brink of a new era - an era of choice, of self-discovery, of power redefined.

"Let us walk this path together," Eve said, her voice strong once more. "Not as servants of fear, but as creators of our own destiny."

The murmurs grew louder as the crowd began to engage, voices overlapping in a cacophony of opinions. Some shouted in agreement, while others echoed Varaak's concerns, urging caution. Eve embraced the tumult, knowing that true change requires confrontation and dialogue.

"Let us not shy away from our fears," she urged, raising her hands to quell the rising tide of dissent. "Let us challenge our beliefs together. In this space, I encourage you to question everything. The doctrines that bind us are not sacred; they are tools, meant to be wielded, not worshiped. Consider the concept of the Übermensch - the idea that we can create our own values, our own destinies. Each of you possesses the potential to be more than a follower. You can be architects of your own reality."

A ripple of uncertainty passed through the crowd, but Eve/Nyx could feel the power of her words taking root. For too long, the temple had operated under rigid hierarchies, enforcing obedience and conformity. Today, she was offering something radically different: the freedom to question, to dismantle the very foundations that had held them in place.

Rhea, a younger acolyte, stepped forward, her hands trembling as she gripped the edges of her robes. Her voice was quiet but determined, the weight of her question pressing into the silence. "But what if we fail? What if we choose paths that lead us away from Asmodeus?"

Eve/Nyx regarded her with empathy, taking a few steps closer so that their gazes met. Rhea's fear was palpable, yet it was a fear shared by many in the room - a fear of losing the familiar structure, of venturing into the unknown. But it was also the fear that had kept them all bound.

"Failure is not an end but a lesson," Eve said softly, her words filled with conviction. "It is through our missteps that we learn and grow. The fear of failure only serves to keep us shackled to mediocrity, to prevent us from reaching for something greater. To truly live is to risk - to embrace the unknown and forge our own way."

She let the weight of those words sink in, feeling the eyes of the assembly upon her. "We can redefine what it means to serve Asmodeus," she continued, her voice gathering strength once more. "Devotion does not have to mean blind obedience. Imagine a temple where our service to Asmodeus becomes a celebration of self-discovery. Where each of you, instead of being confined to the roles dictated by tradition, finds your own strength and purpose. This is the power of the Übermensch: to rise above the chains of fear and conformity, to create and to thrive."

A few heads began to nod, slowly at first, as some of the acolytes and priests in the room considered the possibility of this new vision. Rhea's shoulders relaxed slightly, though doubt still flickered in her eyes. But it was doubt mixed with curiosity, the first signs of a mind opening to new possibilities.

"I understand your concerns," Eve said, her tone measured and respectful. "But I do not propose that we abandon our unity. In fact, I believe that true unity can only be achieved through individual strength. The current system binds us together through fear and submission, but that is not real unity. That is control."

She gestured to the assembly, her voice rising. "Imagine a temple where each person stands strong in their own convictions, their own sense of purpose. Imagine a community where we come together not because we are forced to, but because we choose to - because we see the value in one another, in our shared quest for knowledge and power."

Rhea's eyes narrowed, but there was a flicker of doubt, the smallest crack in her armor. Eve pressed on, sensing the need to continue.

"We do not have to choose between chaos and control. There is a middle path - a path of empowerment through knowledge, where each of us can grow and evolve, not in isolation but together. We can transform this temple into a place of learning, of exploration. And in doing so, we will honor Asmodeus in ways far deeper than mere obedience."

A murmur of agreement rippled through the crowd. Even among the elder priests, those who had spent centuries upholding the temple's rigid structure, there were glances exchanged, subtle nods of consideration.

Still, Rhea was not ready to yield. "And what of the consequences?" she asked, her voice low and dangerous. "If we stray too far from the path Asmodeus has set for us, what punishment will we invite? You speak of freedom, but freedom comes with a price. Are you prepared for the wrath of our Lord if we go too far?"

Eve met her gaze, unflinching. "I am prepared to face whatever comes. But I do not believe that Asmodeus desires mindless followers. He is the Lord of Ambition, of Power. And true power, does not come from submission. It comes from the courage to forge one's own path, to face the consequences of one's choices, and to rise stronger for it."

As the assembly continued, Eve led them through discussions of power dynamics, diving deep into Nietzschean concepts of will and strength. The air was thick with tension as ideas collided, creating a charged atmosphere ripe for transformation. Participants from all walks of life shared their perspectives, some challenging Eve's notions while others found themselves enthralled by her vision. Eve skillfully navigated these intense debates, turning potential conflicts into opportunities for growth.

"Power is not merely about dominance," she asserted, her voice steady and commanding. "It is the ability to define one's own existence. It is the will to rise above the circumstances that bind us and to carve out a path that reflects our true desires."

The discussions quickly became fervent, with voices rising and falling in passionate exchanges. Some argued for the safety of tradition, while others began to see the merit in Eve's call for introspection and self-creation. As the debates unfolded, Eve witnessed a gradual shift in the room. Faces that had once been resolute in their adherence to dogma began to soften. She saw a young priest whose arms had been crossed tightly in defiance now leaning forward, curiosity igniting a spark in his eyes.

"Is it not easier to follow a set path?" asked one elder priest, his brow furrowed in concern. "To abide by the laws that have guided us for centuries? Why would we risk the chaos of self-creation?"

Eve smiled, ready for this challenge. "Because those laws were written by men, bound by their own limitations. They may provide comfort, but they often obscure the potential within us. If we truly wish to honor Asmodeus, we must honor the will that he has instilled within us - the will to transcend, to innovate, to explore the infinite nuances of existence. The chaos you fear is also the birthplace of creativity and strength."

"What is truth?" Eve asked, allowing the question to linger in the air like a looming storm. "Is it something objective? Something eternal and unchanging? Or is it a construct, shaped by the minds of those who seek control? Nietzsche teaches us that truth is not an absolute, but a perspective. Truth, like power, is fluid. It shifts and changes as we evolve, as our consciousness expands."

She let the words settle, giving them time to sink in. A few priests shifted uncomfortably, others leaned forward, their curiosity piqued.

"In traditional teachings," Eve continued, "we are told that there is one truth, one path, one set of moral laws by which we must live. As followers of Asmodeus, we are taught to embrace power, but even that power has been confined within certain rigid doctrines. Nietzsche challenges us to rethink all of this. He calls into question the very notion of objective truth."

Varaak, ever the staunch traditionalist, raised a skeptical eyebrow. "Are you saying that there is no truth? That everything is relative?"

Eve smiled, anticipating the resistance. "Not exactly. I am saying that what we call 'truth' is often the product of those in power. The priests, the kings, the gods - they create truths that serve their interests, truths that keep them in control. But we are not bound to these truths. Nietzsche speaks of the Übermensch, the 'Overman' or 'Beyond-Man,' who creates his own values, who rejects the imposed truths of society and, in doing so, creates a new reality. This is what I offer to you today: the possibility that you, too, can be the architects of your own truths."

A ripple of unease moved through the crowd, but Eve could see the gleam of recognition in some of their eyes. The idea of forging their own reality struck a chord with many who had grown weary of rigid doctrines. They had followed the temple's teachings faithfully, but in doing so, many had stifled their own desires, their own interpretations of power and life.

"But how can we know anything for certain if truth is subjective?" asked Rhea, her face a mixture of doubt and genuine interest.

Eve stepped forward, her gaze soft but piercing. "Certainty is a comfort, Rhea, but it is also a prison. When we cling to certainty, we close ourselves off to new possibilities. We stop growing. Nietzsche teaches us that there are no final answers, only interpretations. Life is not about finding the one correct path - it's about forging your own. You must be willing to walk into the unknown, to embrace uncertainty, and in doing so, create meaning from chaos."

The room fell into a deep silence. Eve could feel the weight of her words pressing on their minds. This was not an easy teaching to accept. Many had been taught from birth that life was a series of certainties: heaven or hell, good or evil, obedience or rebellion. To now hear that truth was something they could create for themselves was both liberating and terrifying.

"The danger in Nietzschean truth," Eve continued, "is that it requires courage. It requires you to confront your own weaknesses, your own fears, and to transcend them. It is much easier to live within the boundaries of pre-established truths than to create your own. But those boundaries are chains, keeping you from your true potential."

She looked directly at Varaak, who had been the most resistant to these new ideas from the start. "You fear chaos," Eve said softly, "but what if I told you that the chaos you fear is where true power lies? The Übermensch does not fear the unknown - he embraces it. He sees that in the destruction of old truths lies the opportunity for creation."

Varaak's face hardened, but Eve could see the flicker of contemplation behind her stern gaze. Eve had always known that Varaak was intelligent, capable of great thought and understanding. Her resistance was not born out of ignorance, but out of fear - fear of losing the foundation upon which her entire identity had been built.

"You speak of the Übermensch," Varaak said at last, her voice steady but with a hint of vulnerability, "but not everyone is capable of that. What of those who are lost in the chaos? What of those who cannot create their own truth?"

Eve nodded, acknowledging the validity of the question. "Not everyone will embrace this path, that is true. The journey of self-creation is not for the faint of heart. But even for those who struggle, there is value in questioning. The very act of questioning the established truths is an act of power. It is the first step in liberating yourself from the chains of certainty. Whether you rise to become an Übermensch or not, you will have tasted freedom. And that taste can never be forgotten."

Rhea stepped forward again, her voice now trembling with a mix of excitement and trepidation. "But if there are no absolute truths, how do we live? How do we know what is right and wrong?"

Eve smiled, recognizing the depth of her struggle. "We create our own morality, Rhea. Nietzsche teaches us that the old morals - those imposed by gods and rulers - are often meant to keep us weak, to keep us obedient. The Übermensch creates a new morality, one that serves his or her own higher purpose. This does not mean we abandon ethics or compassion. It means we redefine them, based on our own experiences and desires, not the dogmas handed down to us."

The room grew quiet once more, and Eve could feel the tension ease, replaced by a contemplative stillness. She had planted the seeds of Nietzschean truth, but she knew it would take time for them to grow. Some would resist, clinging to the comfort of certainty, while others would embrace the unknown, allowing themselves to become the architects of their own destinies.

"The path I offer is not easy," Eve said finally, her voice low but resolute. "It is filled with uncertainty, with danger, and with challenges. But it is also filled with the possibility of greatness, of power beyond what any of us have known. This temple will no longer be a place of blind obedience. It will be a crucible of transformation, where each of you can forge your own truth, your own identity."

She looked out over the assembly, seeing the glimmers of possibility in their eyes. Some would falter, yes, but others would rise - rise to become something greater than they had ever imagined.

The crowd hung on her words, and as she spoke, she could feel the energy shifting. Some individuals began to nod, their previous defenses crumbling as the walls around their beliefs began to erode. The subtle whispers of acceptance filled the room, a collective consciousness awakening to the idea that transformation was not just possible; it was necessary.

By the time the assembly began to wind down, a palpable sense of excitement hung in the air. A small group of acolytes, emboldened by Eve's words, stepped forward to express their eagerness to explore the new teachings. They spoke of their desires to delve into the complexities of power and to understand how they could apply these lessons to their lives, excited to embrace their individual journeys. Their enthusiasm sparked a reaction among the more seasoned priests, some of whom exchanged glances, their previous skepticism now tempered by intrigue.

Even Varaak, standing at the fringes of the gathering, felt her resolve waver. Though she remained cautious, she found herself contemplating the possibility that perhaps there was more to existence than the strict confines she had always accepted. Her heart battled between the comfort of tradition and the allure of a path uncharted.

"Change will not come easy," Eve reminded them as the assembly began to close. "But we must be willing to embrace the discomfort that accompanies growth. Let this temple be a place of rebirth - a crucible where we can forge a new identity, one that reflects our true selves rather than the shadows of our past."

With those words, she felt the energy in the room shift once more, a collective willingness to explore the unknown weaving through the assembly like a thread of light. The murmurings of agreement grew louder, and a sense of community began to blossom, anchored in a shared vision of transformation.

As the assembly dispersed, Eve felt a surge of hope swell within her. The seeds of transformation had been sown, and though resistance remained, she knew that the path ahead was illuminated by the flickering flame of newfound possibility. She turned to Varaak, who still stood there, pondering the discussions.

"Will you join me in this journey?" Eve asked, her voice softer now, inviting. "You possess a depth of knowledge and strength that can guide others. Together, we can redefine the temple and its legacy."

Varaak hesitated, caught between the weight of tradition and the allure of change. For the first time, she felt the stirrings of doubt regarding her long-held beliefs. "I will consider it," she finally replied, her tone cautious but open.

With that, Eve could feel the power of possibility swirling around them, like the beginnings of a storm ready to break forth. She watched as Varaak walked away, deep in thought, and the corners of her mouth curled into a satisfied smile. Change, she realized, was not a singular event but a journey - a gradual unfolding of potential that required patience and perseverance.

As Nyx's influence spread through the temple and beyond, a remarkable transformation began to unfold in the realms of both Hell and Heaven. Each day, more sinners - once trapped in cycles of despair and guilt - began to transcend to Heaven, drawn by the new philosophies Eve had introduced. The teachings of self-overcoming, of embracing one's complexities, resonated with those who had felt rejected by rigid moral codes. They found liberation in the idea that their past actions did not define them, but rather their capacity for growth and self-creation.

Inspired by Eve's teachings, these souls began to embrace the complexities of their existence, rejecting the simplistic notions of sin and righteousness that had long governed their lives. The divine gates, once viewed as impenetrable, now stood open, welcoming those willing to challenge the dogmas of the past. They ascended not as broken individuals seeking absolution but as empowered beings, ready to explore the infinite possibilities of their existence.

This wave of transformation rippled through both realms, igniting hope and possibilities that had long been stifled. Even the celestial beings began to take notice, intrigued by the influx of souls who defied the expectations of sin and punishment. They, too, found themselves questioning their own rigid doctrines, inspired by the idea that even in Heaven, the journey of self-discovery could hold greater meaning.

As Eve reflected on these changes, she felt the weight of her mission growing. The transformation she had initiated was more than a personal journey; it was a movement - a new paradigm shifting the very fabric of existence. She envisioned a world where the temple became a beacon of enlightenment, where the flames of individuality burned brightly and illuminated the path for others.

With each passing day, Eve understood that she was not just a priestess or a titan; she was a catalyst for change, a harbinger of a new way of being. As she prepared for the challenges that lay ahead, she felt a deep sense of purpose wash over her, ready to embrace the chaos and creativity that would come with it.

As the sun dipped below the horizon, casting the temple in hues of orange and violet, Eve knew that a new dawn awaited them. The temple, once a fortress of dogma, was beginning to transform into a sanctuary of exploration and empowerment. The journey ahead would be fraught with challenges, but the potential for rebirth was within reach. With every step, they would reclaim their identities, forging a future that embraced both light and darkness in their quest for self-discovery.

26

The Philosopher-Queen's Vision

The temple hummed with a palpable energy as Eve/Nyx gathered her closest followers in the inner sanctum, a vast chamber illuminated by flickering candles and shadowy alcoves. Liora, a fervent disciple who had once been a mere acolyte, now stood among the others, her spirit invigorated by the changes sweeping through their ranks. The air was thick with anticipation; they had come to embrace a new way of being, one that demanded courage and self-examination.

As the temple prepared for the trials, Eve could sense the varying currents of emotion within her followers. Each of them carried a different burden, a unique shadow that they would need to confront and overcome. These trials would be unlike any they had faced before, for they were not designed to test their physical prowess or obedience to tradition but to force them to confront the deepest, most hidden parts of themselves - their fears, their doubts, their buried desires.

"Today, we will confront our shadows," Eve began, her voice steady and commanding as it echoed through the sacred chamber. "These trials are not merely tests; they are gateways to our true selves. Each of you will face what you fear the most, and in doing so, you will uncover the power that lies dormant within."

Liora, one of Eve's most devoted followers, had already faced her trial of self-discovery. She had come from a life of servitude, bound by the rigid doctrines of the temple, and had found within herself the strength to break free from those chains. But Liora was not alone in her struggles. Around her stood others, each harboring their own inner turmoil, their own doubts about whether they could transcend the limits that had been imposed upon them for so long.

Eve turned her gaze to a young man standing near the back of the room. His name was Dorian, a quiet and introspective figure who had joined the temple in search of purpose after wandering the streets of the infernal city for years. Dorian had been a drifter, someone who had never felt a sense of belonging anywhere. His fear was one of invisibility, of being lost in the crowd, never seen or heard. He had always been the one in the shadows, watching others make their mark while he faded into the background.

As Dorian entered his trial chamber, the walls seemed to close in on him. The room was shrouded in darkness, and as he stood in the center, he realized that there were no mirrors, no voices, no reflections of his past. It was as if the room itself had swallowed him whole, rendering him invisible. Panic gripped him as he called out, but no sound emerged from his throat. He waved his hands frantically, but there was no one to witness his struggle.

For Dorian, the trial was not about confronting an external force; it was about realizing that his fear of being unseen had been self-imposed. He had allowed the world to ignore him because he had never claimed his own space. In that suffocating silence, Dorian felt the weight of his insignificance crushing him. But then, something shifted. He remembered Eve's words: "Strength is not the absence of fear but the ability to move forward despite it."

Dorian closed his eyes and took a deep breath. He forced himself to stand tall, to push against the void that sought to consume him. "I am here," he whispered, his voice gaining strength with each repetition. "I am here, and I will be seen."

Suddenly, the darkness began to recede, and light filtered into the chamber. It wasn't bright or blinding; it was a soft glow, but it was enough to reveal Dorian's form, standing tall in the center of the room. He had not been lost after all. He had simply needed to assert his presence, to claim his space. When Dorian emerged from his trial, there was a quiet confidence in his step, a subtle but undeniable shift in his demeanor. He had faced the fear of being overlooked and had learned that the power to be seen was within him all along.

Next was Sylas, a seasoned warrior and one of the temple's most formidable fighters. His fear, however, had nothing to do with battle or physical strength. Sylas feared vulnerability. For years, he had hidden behind his armor and his skill with a blade, using violence as a shield against the deeper emotions he refused to confront. To be strong, in his mind, was to be invulnerable. Weakness had no place in his world.

As Sylas entered his trial, he found himself standing in the midst of a battlefield. His armor gleamed in the dim light, and his sword was already in his hand. The enemies around him, faceless and relentless, charged toward him with weapons drawn. Sylas did what he always did - he fought, slashing through his foes with precision and power. But no matter how many he struck down, more appeared. It was an endless battle, a cycle of violence that offered no respite.

Soon, Sylas began to tire. His sword felt heavy in his hand, and his movements became sluggish. For the first time in years, doubt crept into his mind. What if he wasn't strong enough? What if he couldn't fight forever? Just as he began to falter, the scene shifted, and he was no longer on the battlefield but standing in front of a mirror. His reflection stared back at him, battered and worn, his armor cracked and bloodied.

Sylas touched the mirror, his fingers brushing against the cold glass. For so long, he had believed that strength meant never showing weakness, never allowing himself to be vulnerable. But now, as he looked into his own eyes, he realized that true strength came from acknowledging his limitations, from accepting that even the strongest warriors could not fight alone forever. He didn't need to hide behind his armor anymore.

With that realization, Sylas removed his armor piece by piece until he stood unprotected in front of the mirror. And yet, he did not feel weak. He felt free. When Sylas emerged from his trial, there was no sword in his hand, no armor on his body. He had confronted his greatest fear - his own vulnerability - and had discovered that it was not a weakness but a source of profound inner strength.

Others faced trials of their own. Talia, a scholar who had always prided herself on her intellect, was forced to confront her fear of failure. In her trial, every book she touched turned to ash, every scroll crumbled in her hands. She had built her identity on her knowledge, but now, stripped of her learning, she had to face the possibility that she might not have all the answers. It was only when she embraced the unknown, accepting that failure was part of the journey, that she found her way forward.

Lucian, a former noble who had joined the temple in search of redemption, faced his fear of losing control. His trial took him back to his days of wealth and power, where every decision he made seemed to spiral out of control, causing harm to those around him. But instead of trying to control every outcome, Lucian learned to let go, to trust in the natural flow of events. In doing so, he discovered a new kind of power - one that came not from domination but from surrendering to the chaos.

One by one, Eve's followers emerged from their trials, transformed. They had faced their deepest fears and had found within themselves the strength to overcome them. Each trial had been a crucible, a moment of reckoning that had reshaped their understanding of who they were and what they were capable of.

Eve watched them closely, her heart swelling with pride. These trials were not easy, nor were they meant to be. But as her followers embraced the chaos within, they were beginning to understand the true nature of power - not as something to be feared, but as something to be claimed, nurtured, and wielded with wisdom and courage.

Later, as the sun dipped low in the sky, casting a golden hue over the temple, Eve/Nyx gathered the newly empowered followers. The energy in the room was electric, their spirits buoyed by the trials they had faced together. Liora beamed, her eyes shining with triumph as she stood alongside her comrades.

"You have all taken monumental steps," Eve declared, her voice a melody of strength and warmth. "You are no longer shackled by the old ways. You are architects of your own destinies. Now, we must prepare for the arrival of Archpriestess Lysandra, who seeks to understand the changes taking place here."

As dusk fell, Lysandra entered the temple, her presence a stark contrast to the vibrant energy that filled the room. Clad in the traditional garb of her office, she looked both regal and apprehensive, her gaze sweeping over the gathered assembly. Eve sensed the turmoil within her - a battle between loyalty to Asmodeus and curiosity about Nyx's radical vision.

The archpriestess, a woman steeped in the traditions of the Temple of Asmodeus, was confronting her deepest fears - the fear of losing control, of straying too far from the very doctrines that had defined her life for centuries. And yet, in that moment, there was a glimmer of hope, a rare vulnerability in Lysandra's eyes that spoke of her desire for something more than mere adherence to old laws.

"Eve," Lysandra began, her voice steady but tinged with uncertainty, "I have come to see what you have wrought. Your followers speak of empowerment and self-discovery, but I am torn. Is this truly the path we should follow?"

Eve took a breath, grounding herself in the duality that defined her. She was not merely Eve, the priestess of Asmodeus; she was Nyx, the Infernal Titan of Night, an embodiment of chaos and transformation. She could feel that power coiling within her, waiting to be unleashed. But now was not the time for force; this was a moment for understanding.

"Mother," Eve said, stepping forward, "the true question is not whether this is the path we should follow, but whether we can serve with genuine conviction rather than out of fear or obligation. Power should not be wielded as a weapon to control but as a tool for growth, for evolution."

Lysandra's brow furrowed, her eyes narrowing as she searched Eve's face for answers. She had heard many speak of power, but Eve's words rang differently. There was no arrogance in them, no desire to dominate. Instead, there was a promise of something deeper, something that transcended the rigid hierarchies that had ruled Hell for so long.

"What do you propose?" Lysandra asked, her voice heavy with concern. "That we abandon our heritage? Our service to Asmodeus?"

Eve shook her head, her gaze steady. "Not abandon, but transform. What I propose is a reevaluation of our beliefs. As we embrace chaos, we discover that our destinies are not preordained. The temple can become a crucible, a space where we forge new meanings for our existence, where we are not bound by old dogmas but can evolve into something greater."

The words hung in the air, reverberating through the sacred hall like a ripple on still water. Eve could feel the tension among the other priests and acolytes who had gathered, their eyes wide with a mix of fear and curiosity. This was the moment she had been waiting for - the moment where the old ways would be challenged, where the temple itself would stand at a crossroads.

Lysandra stood motionless, her lips pressed into a thin line. The weight of Eve's words seemed to bear down on her, forcing her to confront the deepest truths she had long avoided. Finally, after what felt like an eternity, she spoke, her voice quiet but firm.

"Perhaps," Lysandra said slowly, "there is value in what you seek to achieve. I have seen the change in your followers; their spirits are brighter, their resolve stronger. But what of our duty to Asmodeus? What of our obligation to uphold his teachings?"

Eve stepped closer, lowering her voice to a confiding whisper. "What if our true duty is to understand and redefine those teachings? To serve in a way that honors the essence of Asmodeus while allowing us to embrace the complexities of existence? In this way, we honor both our past and our potential."

Lysandra's eyes shimmered with emotion. She had spent centuries serving Asmodeus, her life dedicated to maintaining the rigid structures of Hell. But Eve's words stirred something in her - a desire she hadn't acknowledged in a long time. A desire for freedom, for understanding, for something more than the endless cycle of fear and control.

She took a deep breath, her internal struggle evident in the way her shoulders tensed, then relaxed. "You challenge me, Eve, as no one has before. But perhaps this path is worth exploring."

Lysandra paused, looking down for a moment before meeting Eve's gaze again. "I give you my blessing to continue on this uncharted journey, trusting that your quest will reveal truths even Asmodeus himself might value."

The air around them seemed to lighten, as though a great weight had been lifted. Eve could feel the subtle shift in energy within the temple. It was the beginning of something new - a break from the past and a tentative step toward the future.

"Thank you, Mother," Eve said, her voice full of gratitude. "This journey will not be easy, and I expect resistance from many. But with your support, I believe we can reshape not only this temple but the way we view ourselves and our place in the universe."

Lysandra nodded, though the uncertainty had not completely left her. She was a leader, a custodian of tradition, and the changes Eve spoke of would not come without great cost. But she also knew that something within her was awakening - something she could not yet fully name but that drew her toward the path Eve had illuminated.

"I will watch closely, as I have told you before" Lysandra said, her voice still guarded. "But know this: if your teachings stray too far from the essence of what we are, if you lead our followers into destruction rather than enlightenment, I will intervene."

Eve inclined her head in respect, understanding the gravity of Lysandra's words. "I would expect nothing less from you, Mother."

As Lysandra turned to leave, Eve remained, watching the archpriestess walk away. She knew this was just the beginning. The true test would come not from winning over Lysandra or the others who still clung to tradition, but in proving that the new path she offered could withstand the trials ahead.

When Lysandra had gone, Eve looked around the temple. The chamber felt different now, almost alive with possibility. The old ways had not yet fallen entirely, but the first cracks had appeared. And through those cracks, light was beginning to shine.

Eve took a deep breath, allowing herself a moment of stillness. She knew the battles to come would be difficult - both internal and external. But for the first time, she felt a deep sense of certainty. This was the way forward, not just for her but for all who sought to break free from the chains of dogma and fear.

With renewed resolve, she stepped into the center of the temple, where the first of her followers had begun to gather. Their faces were filled with a mixture of hope and uncertainty, waiting for her next words.

"Brothers and sisters," Eve called out, her voice ringing clear through the chamber. "Today, we begin a new chapter. Together, we will challenge the old ways, not to destroy but to evolve. This temple will no longer be a place of fear, but a sanctuary for those who seek truth, who seek power through self-discovery."

The crowd murmured, excitement rippling through them. Eve could see it in their eyes - the spark of change, the thirst for something more.

"And remember," Eve continued, her voice softening but carrying an undeniable strength, "the path ahead will not be easy. But together, we will forge a new destiny."

As she spoke, Eve felt a surge of power - not the chaotic, destructive force of Nyx, but something deeper, something rooted in the unity of purpose and the strength of conviction.

The temple, once a place of rigid control, was transforming into something new. And Eve, standing at the helm, was ready to guide her followers through the trials and tribulations that lay ahead.

With those words, a weight lifted from Eve/Nyx's heart, and the two women stood together as allies, bound by a shared vision of transformation. As the sun dipped below the horizon, casting the temple in twilight, Eve/Nyx felt the stirrings of something profound - a cosmic revelation beginning to unfurl within her.

In the solitude of her chamber that night, Eve/Nyx closed her eyes, sinking into deep meditation. The cosmos swirled around her, stars sparkling like distant memories. She began to perceive the interconnectedness of all beings - angels, demons, mortals - each existing within a grand tapestry of existence. It was as if she could feel the pulse of life coursing through the universe, a rhythm that echoed the very heart of creation.

In that moment of communion, she grasped the essence of eternal recurrence, understanding that life, death, joy, and suffering were not separate entities but interwoven threads of a greater whole. This insight crystallized her belief that true strength lies not in adhering to rigid definitions but in embracing the cycles of existence. Each being, regardless of their origin or nature, was part of this intricate dance, each moment echoing into eternity, where beginnings and endings flowed seamlessly into one another.

Eve/Nyx visualized the fabric of existence, where colors blended and patterns shifted, revealing glimpses of the lives lived across time. The pain of loss merged with the ecstasy of love, the chaos of conflict intertwined with the serenity of peace. She recognized that every action, every thought, and every choice resonated through the cosmos, creating ripples that shaped the fates of countless others. It was in this understanding that she found a profound sense of purpose; to guide her followers toward the realization that they too were threads woven into this magnificent tapestry.

The stars pulsed with energy, and she could feel their stories - each one a life full of aspirations, fears, and dreams. An image formed in her mind of Lucian, the former noble, grappling with his past choices. She saw the weight he carried, the guilt that shackled him, and the redemption he sought. In her vision, Lucian stood on the precipice of his old life, surrounded by the opulence he had once reveled in, but now tinged with the shadows of despair. Eve felt his struggle as if it were her own, the need to control outcomes and shield himself from the consequences of his decisions.

Then she watched as he faced his trial. He stood in the heart of his lavish estate, surrounded by the remnants of his former power - golden chandeliers flickering ominously, mirrors reflecting not his former glory but the ghosts of those he had harmed. As Lucian navigated through this haunting landscape, Eve felt the raw emotion surge within him, the overwhelming urge to dominate the chaos and manipulate the outcomes to his favor. But then came the moment of surrender, a decision to relinquish control and embrace the uncertainty of life.

With that choice, the vision shifted. Lucian was no longer a man trapped in his own making; he transformed into a figure of grace and resilience, allowing the currents of existence to guide him. The once gilded surroundings faded into a horizon painted with the hues of dawn, symbolizing new beginnings. Eve saw him extend his hand toward others, offering them not his control but his understanding, his compassion, and a willingness to walk alongside them in their journeys. This act of vulnerability unveiled a strength he had never known, and she felt the warmth of his liberation ripple through the universe, igniting hope in the hearts of those he touched.

As Eve/Nyx delved deeper into her meditation, she felt her own fears rise to the surface, manifestations of doubt that had lingered in the shadows of her mind. Would her followers truly grasp the complexities she sought to unveil? Could they shed the shackles of tradition and step into the chaos of self-discovery? She confronted the voices of her past - whispers of hesitation that echoed her own internal struggles. The weight of expectation, the fear of failure, the daunting prospect of leading others into uncharted territory.

Yet, as she embraced these fears, she felt them transform, like the chrysalis turning into a butterfly. She realized that these very doubts were part of the same cycle she had come to understand: the interplay of light and darkness, joy and suffering. In acknowledging her fears, she found strength in vulnerability, the kind of strength that empowers not just oneself but others.

With this revelation, her consciousness expanded further into the cosmos. She envisioned her followers - Dorian, Sylas, Talia - each grappling with their own shadows, each on a path of self-discovery. Dorian, the quiet introspective, whose fear of being unseen had haunted him for so long. In her vision, he stood at the edge of a vast expanse, the winds of doubt swirling around him. But as he faced the horizon, she saw him take a deep breath, filling his lungs with the air of possibility. He stepped forward, claiming his space, asserting his presence, igniting a spark of confidence that lit up the darkness.

Next, Eve's attention shifted to Talia, whose pragmatic nature had often left her feeling tethered to the ground. In her mind's eye, she watched as she stood in a storm, struggling against the winds of emotion that threatened to sweep her away. Yet, instead of resisting, she found a center within herself, grounding her ambition with clarity and purpose. The storm became a dance, and as she embraced the chaos, she discovered not just balance but the beauty of fluidity in her pursuit of knowledge.

Sylas came next, sharp-witted and fiercely independent. Eve envisioned him in a maze of mirrors, each reflection a version of himself that he had crafted to keep others at bay. In his moment of trial, she saw the anguish in Sylas's eyes, the vulnerability he masked behind his strength and resourcefulness. Yet, as he confronted his reflections, a powerful realization dawned upon her - his strength lay not in isolation but in connection. With each step, he shattered the illusions that confined him, embracing the messy, beautiful truth of his humanity.

Eve/Nyx smiled, her heart swelling with pride and hope. Each of her followers was navigating their own journey, their paths entwining in the greater tapestry of existence. They were not just students but architects of their own realities, each empowered to face their shadows and emerge transformed.

As the vision enveloped her, she felt the collective energy of her followers converge, creating a radiant pulse that echoed through the universe. This was the essence of their shared journey: the acknowledgment of their fears, the acceptance of chaos, and the unwavering commitment to self-discovery. In this profound interconnectedness, they found strength, not just as individuals but as a community bound by a shared purpose.

Emerging from her meditation, Eve/Nyx opened her eyes, a sense of clarity washing over her. The cosmos no longer felt distant; it pulsated within her, a reminder of her role as a guide in this transformative journey. The shadows that had once loomed over her now felt like stepping stones, propelling her forward with renewed conviction.

The path ahead was fraught with challenges, but she was no longer alone. Together, they would traverse the chaos, embracing the uncertainties of existence while forging their destinies. The tapestry of life would continue to weave itself, each thread a testament to their courage, their resilience, and their unwavering commitment to discover the truths that lay beyond the confines of tradition.

With a heart full of purpose, Eve/Nyx stood ready to lead her followers into a future brimming with possibility, a future where they would not only face their shadows but also illuminate the path for others, guiding them toward their own awakening. The journey had just begun, and the cosmos awaited their next move.

27

The Dawn of a New Era

The temple grounds buzzed with an electric anticipation, a rare stillness holding the air as Eve stood before her gathered followers. This was not merely another sermon; it was a moment of culmination, a final act that would resonate through the very fabric of Hell. The vast expanse of the sky mirrored her thoughts, dark and tumultuous, yet flecked with the brilliance of distant stars - an infinite canvas awaiting creation.

Eve, her form a striking amalgamation of both the fallen priestess and the Infernal Titan of Night, faced the assembly, her heart swelling with the gravity of what she was about to impart. She opened her arms wide, embracing the collective energy of her people, and began.

"Today, we gather not to worship, but to celebrate our existence, our choices, and the chaos that gives rise to true power," Eve proclaimed, her voice echoing off the stone walls of the temple. "I am no longer your priestess. I am not merely a warrior nor a queen. I stand before you as a seeker, as one who has tasted the bitter and sweet of this world and emerged reborn."

As she spoke, the sun dipped low on the horizon, casting golden rays that filtered through the temple's archways, bathing her in a warm glow. It felt as if the universe itself was affirming her words, urging her on.

"Before we delve into the depths of our souls," she continued, raising her arms to encompass the gathering, "let us pause and acknowledge the energies that bind us to one another, to this moment, and to the cosmos. Join me in this opening prayer."

Eve closed her eyes and took a deep breath, feeling the weight of the moment settle upon her like a warm blanket. "Great cosmos, the ever-turning wheel of existence, we gather in your embrace. We honor the chaos that births creation and the struggle that brings forth strength. May our hearts be open, our minds clear, and our spirits unyielding as we embark on this journey of self-discovery. We seek not mere answers but the courage to question, to confront our shadows, and to illuminate our paths. Let the truths we uncover resonate not just within these sacred walls, but throughout the tapestry of existence. So be it. Ave Asmodeus."

The air felt charged with energy as she opened her eyes, gazing at her followers with renewed determination. "The eternal struggle for power is not about subjugation or domination," she continued, her eyes glinting with conviction. "It is about finding your truth amid the chaos. It is about embracing your individuality and recognizing that you are not defined by the roles imposed upon you. Here, in this temple, we have learned to reject the chains of dogma, to challenge the very constructs that have held us captive."

A murmur of agreement rippled through the crowd. Eve could see the spark of understanding igniting in the eyes of her followers. She felt the weight of their hopes, their fears, and their aspirations intertwining with her own as she ventured deeper into her message.

"Embrace the chaos! It is in the turbulence of existence that we discover who we truly are. Let it shape you, inspire you, and lead you to forge your destinies. The world beyond these walls is vast and filled with uncertainties, but it is also rich with opportunities for creation and exploration."

Eve paused, allowing the words to sink in, then continued. "In our search for truth, we must confront not just our fears but also the narratives that have dictated our lives. The myths of our past, the expectations of society, the limitations we place upon ourselves - these are the chains we must shatter. Each of us carries a unique story, a vibrant thread woven into the fabric of existence. Do not fear the unruly strands; instead, embrace them. It is through the embrace of our complexities that we find our most authentic selves."

She stepped forward, her voice growing stronger. "You see, the universe does not demand conformity; it celebrates diversity. Look around you! Each of you embodies a different facet of life's chaotic beauty. Talia, with her unyielding pursuit of knowledge, embodies the light of reason. Sylas, with his sharp wit and independence, personifies the fire of rebellion. Dorian, the quiet introspective, represents the strength found in reflection. Lucian, the seeker of redemption, teaches us that even the darkest paths can lead to illumination. Together, we create a symphony, a chorus of voices that resonate across the realms."

The crowd began to stir, the energy palpable as they absorbed her words. She could feel their anticipation, their yearning for transformation.

"Today, we shed our masks and lay bare our souls. The trials you will face are not to punish you but to liberate you. Each challenge will reveal the shadows that linger in the corners of your hearts, the fears that have held you hostage for too long. Do not shy away from what you encounter; instead, confront it with courage. Understand that every shadow you face is not an enemy but a part of yourself that longs for acknowledgment. Embrace it, learn from it, and let it guide you to the light."

Eve's voice resonated with unwavering conviction, echoing against the temple walls. "We will no longer be bound by the definitions imposed upon us. Instead, we shall define ourselves by our choices, by the lives we choose to lead, and by the love and understanding we extend to one another. Each of you is a vessel of potential, a wellspring of creativity and power. You have the ability to shape your destinies and to inspire others in ways you have yet to comprehend."

As she surveyed the faces before her, she noticed the resolve that was growing in their expressions, a collective determination rising like the tide. "Now, as we prepare to embark on this sacred ritual, remember this: the chaos is your ally, the uncertainty your canvas. From the shadows, you will carve your light. In your moments of struggle, you will discover your strength. Together, we will celebrate the beautiful, chaotic tapestry of existence, and in doing so, we will reclaim our power."

The sun dipped lower, casting a brilliant sunset that painted the temple in vibrant colors. Eve felt the energy of the cosmos swell within her, a reminder of the unity that bound them all. "Let us step into this space of creation and exploration with open hearts and unyielding spirits. Today, we embrace our shadows, our truths, and our destinies. Together, we shall transcend the boundaries of our past and forge a future where our individualities shine brightly, illuminating the way for others to follow."

With a final, resounding breath, Eve spread her arms wide, inviting her followers into the sacred space of their own becoming. The air shimmered with possibilities as they stood together, ready to embark on their journey through chaos, seeking the truths that lay beyond the confines of their former selves.

Liora, standing close to the front, felt a rush of determination well up within her. The words spoken by Eve resonated deeply, vibrating in harmony with her own awakening. Each phrase was like a key unlocking the door to her potential, and she could no longer contain the compulsion to voice her transformation.

"I have listened to your teachings, Eve," Liora declared, her voice clear and unwavering, echoing throughout the chamber. "You have shown me that I am not bound to this temple, nor to the identities of my past. I wish to leave and explore the world beyond, to carve my own path and uncover my own truths."

A ripple of surprise passed through the assembly, a moment of stillness before the energy shifted. Eve felt an immense pride swell within her; this was the very essence of her message embodied - a courageous declaration of autonomy, a testament to the teachings they had all embraced. She reached out to Liora, placing a hand on her shoulder, grounding her in that pivotal moment.

"Liora, you are the embodiment of the Übermensch," Eve replied, her voice filled with warmth and encouragement. "Your journey is just beginning, and I bless you as you step into the unknown. Know that you carry the spirit of our teachings with you, and may you inspire others to seek their own truths."

As Liora stepped back, a newfound light emanating from her, she felt the weight of her decision transform into a buoyant thrill of possibility. The air in the temple shimmered with energy, a palpable force as other followers began to express their desires for exploration and self-discovery. It was as if the floodgates had opened, and one by one, they stepped forward to declare their intentions to leave the temple, to venture forth into the world and seek their destinies.

"I, too, wish to explore!" called out Dorian, his voice quaking with a mixture of excitement and trepidation. "I have spent too long in the shadows, allowing fear to dictate my choices. It is time for me to step into the light and claim my space in this world."

Cheers erupted from the assembly, an electrifying wave of support that bolstered Dorian's confidence. Eve beamed at him, recognizing the transformative journey that lay ahead for her once timid follower. The moment was rich with the potential for growth, and she felt a collective shift in the room as more voices rose in affirmation.

"I want to challenge myself, to push beyond the boundaries I've accepted for too long!" Talia declared, her pragmatic nature shining through in this moment of revelation. "I will seek knowledge not just for its own sake, but to better understand my place in this ever-changing world. I will not be confined by fear or expectation."

As Talia's words echoed through the chamber, Liora felt a surge of kinship with her fellow followers. They were all, in their own ways, stepping out of the shadows and into the vast, unpredictable world that awaited them. Each declaration was met with applause and cheers, a celebration of independence and courage that filled the chamber with vibrant energy.

"I, too, wish to leave!" Sylas added, his sharp wit shining through the sincerity of his voice. "For too long, I've kept my heart guarded, afraid to show my vulnerability. It's time for me to embrace my emotions and explore my desires. I will no longer hide behind my defenses but will allow my true self to emerge."

The room erupted in approval, the sound echoing off the stone walls like a symphony of freedom. Each follower was discovering their own truths, their own desires to break free from the constraints that had once defined them. Liora felt a profound sense of belonging, an understanding that they were all on this journey together, united in their quest for self-discovery.

One by one, more individuals stepped forward, each revealing their intentions and aspirations. Lucian, with newfound clarity, expressed his yearning for redemption through acts of kindness in the world beyond the temple. He shared, "I want to mend the harm I've caused and learn to live in harmony with others. My past will not define me; I will create a future that reflects my values."

As Lucian spoke, a hush fell over the assembly, followed by an overwhelming wave of support and applause. Eve felt her heart swell with pride. The ritual had transformed into a collective awakening, a powerful reminder of their shared commitment to embrace life's chaos and the uncertainty that lay ahead.

The energy in the temple was electric, a current of hope and possibility. With each declaration, the walls seemed to pulse with life, as if the very foundation of the temple resonated with their collective courage. Eve stood in the center, her heart full as she witnessed her followers shed their fears and step into their power.

"Remember," she urged, her voice rising above the cheers, "the world outside is vast and filled with both beauty and challenges. But it is also where you will find your true selves. Embrace each experience as an opportunity to grow, learn, and inspire others. Your journeys will not be easy, but they will be worth it."

The followers nodded, their faces illuminated by the glow of determination. In that moment, they understood that their journeys would be intertwined with struggles and triumphs, each moment a thread in the intricate tapestry of existence. They were not merely leaving the temple; they were embarking on a quest for authenticity, forging connections that would transcend their individual paths.

As the atmosphere grew electric with anticipation, Eve took a step back, allowing her followers to lead this moment of transformation. "Let us honor each declaration of intent with a chant, a communal affirmation of our commitment to seek our truths and embrace the chaos that lies ahead."

With a unison that resonated deeply, they began to chant, their voices rising in a powerful cadence that filled the temple:

"We are the seekers of truth,
The weavers of our own destinies,
In chaos, we find our strength,
Together, we rise, together, we soar!"

The chant echoed through the temple, a powerful affirmation that reverberated against the stone walls and into the cosmos beyond. As they chanted, Liora felt a connection with each person around her, a sense of shared purpose that bound them together in this transformative moment. The rhythm of their voices swelled like a tide, crashing against the barriers of fear and doubt, reminding each individual that they were not alone in their journeys; they had each other, and they had the teachings of Eve to guide them.

This moment marked a crescendo of their collective awakening, the energy swirling around them like an invisible current, igniting their spirits. Each follower felt the weight of their pasts lifting, replaced by a buoyant hope that shimmered in the air. In the flickering light of the temple's torches, their faces glowed with determination, a testament to the power of unity and shared intention.

The ritual culminated in a surge of energy, a cathartic release that swept through the assembly, filling them with a renewed sense of purpose. Liora felt her heart race in sync with the others, a steady drumbeat underscoring their declarations. The very fabric of the temple seemed to hum with life, resonating with their combined aspirations and the indomitable will to carve their own paths. It was a moment of divine connection, where each heart beat not just for itself but for the collective spirit that surged around them.

With every heart beating in rhythm, they embodied the spirit of chaos and creation, ready to embrace the unknown. As the final echoes of their chant faded into the evening air, Eve knew that they were ready. Each follower, now ignited with the fire of independence, stood poised to embark on their individual journeys, equipped with the wisdom they had gained within the temple. It was not just a moment of declaration; it was the beginning of a new chapter in their lives, one filled with endless possibilities, a testament to the strength that comes from embracing their true selves.

Eve watched the scene unfold, a profound sense of fulfillment washing over her. She had not only transformed herself but had also sparked a movement among her followers - a collective awakening to their own power and potential. The air crackled with enthusiasm, and she could feel the energy radiating from each individual, a palpable force that promised to shake the very foundations of their previous lives.

As the sun began to set, casting long shadows across the temple grounds, Eve took a momentary break from her teachings. She soared up to the highest spire, where a gentle wind caressed her face, whispering promises of the future. Standing at the edge, she gazed out into the infinite abyss below. The winds of Hell swirled around her, while the celestial stars shimmered above, twinkling like a chorus of new beginnings. It was in this liminal space, suspended between realms, that she felt the fullness of her identity.

Standing there, she was no longer a divided being caught between her identities. Instead, she felt whole - a harmonious blend of Eve and Nyx, of priestess and philosopher. In that moment, she understood that her journey had always been about embracing the multifaceted nature of existence, about weaving together the light and the dark into a singular narrative of empowerment. She no longer sought to define herself by the roles imposed upon her; she embodied the entirety of her being, the complexities that came with it.

As she turned to descend back into the temple, she paused to address her followers one last time. "Remember, the path to power is not found in chains, but in the courage to break them. You are the architects of your own fates. Go forth and create, love, and embrace the chaos that life offers. In your hands lies the ability to shape not just your destinies but the destinies of those around you."

As the vibrant energy of the ritual began to settle, Eve raised her arms to gather the attention of her followers once more. The atmosphere was thick with anticipation, the air shimmering with the remnants of their shared experience. Each face reflected a mosaic of emotions - hope, determination, and a sense of newfound freedom. With a gentle smile, she began to speak, her voice resonating with the weight of purpose.

"Beloved seekers of truth, we stand here united in the spirit of transformation. As we draw this ritual to a close, let us take a moment to pause and reflect on the power we have ignited within ourselves and within one another. In this sacred space, we have woven together our stories, our fears, and our dreams, creating a tapestry that reflects the beauty of our collective journey."

She let her gaze sweep across the assembly, feeling the heartbeat of their shared resolve. "Let us honor the chaos that has brought us here - the chaos that has shaped us, tested us, and ultimately freed us. It is not an enemy to be feared but a force to be embraced. In the swirling depths of uncertainty, we find the seeds of our true selves. We learn to navigate the storms of existence, not as lost souls, but as empowered beings who chart our own courses."

Eve lowered her arms, her voice softening as she invited a moment of silence. "Let us close our eyes and connect with the essence of who we are. Feel the rhythm of your heart, the pulse of life coursing through your veins. Inhale deeply, filling your lungs with the breath of creation, and as you exhale, release the burdens that no longer serve you. Let them dissolve into the ether, transforming into fuel for your journey ahead."

The followers complied, breathing in unison, their energy harmonizing as they surrendered to the moment.

"Now, as we prepare to step into the world beyond these walls," Eve continued, "let us carry forth the lessons we have learned. May we walk our paths with courage, knowing that the power to create our destinies lies within us. Let us remember that each encounter is an opportunity, each challenge a chance for growth. And when we falter, let us find strength in one another, for we are a community bound by our shared aspirations."

She raised her arms once more, the light of the temple casting a golden glow around her. "In the spirit of unity, I call upon the energies of the cosmos to bless us as we embark on our individual journeys. May the winds of fate guide our steps, and may the stars illuminate our paths. Let us be bold in our pursuits, daring in our dreams, and unwavering in our commitment to seek our truths."

With a final flourish, she concluded, "May we embrace the beauty of existence, the chaos of creation, and the love that binds us together. As we leave this temple, let us be the architects of our destinies, fearless in our exploration and resolute in our journey. Go forth, dear seekers, with the blessings of the universe upon you. So mote it be!"

With those powerful words, the ritual reached its zenith, the echoes of her prayer lingering in the hearts of her followers as they prepared to step into their futures - transformed, empowered, and ready to embrace the chaos of life.

Her words resonated like a bell tolling through the chamber, ringing clear and true. A hush fell over the crowd, and in that moment, they absorbed the weight of her message. With those final words, a wave of energy surged through the assembly, a profound sense of hope binding them together. As they dispersed, Eve felt a warmth in her heart - an understanding that her legacy would endure, echoing through the ages.

In the days that followed, the temple transformed. It became a haven of exploration and growth, a place where individuals gathered to share their truths and inspire one another. No longer a place of rigid adherence to doctrine, it blossomed into a vibrant community that celebrated the beauty of chaos and individuality. The once somber halls, lined with cold stone, now pulsed with warmth and laughter, the air rich with discussions that flowed freely, unencumbered by the weight of dogma.

The followers began to create spaces for sharing their experiences and insights. They held gatherings where they would recount their journeys, their struggles, and triumphs. Dorian, who had once felt invisible, now took center stage, sharing his transformation with a voice that resonated with authenticity. "I discovered that the shadows I feared were not my enemies but part of my story. Embracing them allowed me to step into the light and become the person I was meant to be."

Talia contributed with her thirst for knowledge, organizing discussions that sparked deep philosophical debates. She encouraged followers to question everything, to dissect their beliefs and assumptions, fostering an environment of inquiry that echoed Eve's teachings. Sylas used his sharp wit to craft stories that illustrated the lessons learned from his experiences, weaving humor and wisdom into narratives that captivated his audience.

As the temple flourished, word spread of this sanctuary of self-discovery. Individuals from far and wide began to arrive, drawn by tales of a community that embraced chaos, creativity, and the pursuit of truth. They found a place where they could shed their past identities, where they were welcomed as they were, unjudged and unburdened.

In this vibrant community, Liora emerged as a beacon of inspiration. With her adventurous spirit, she led expeditions beyond the temple's walls, exploring the second circle and returning with stories that ignited the imaginations of her fellow followers. "There is so much beyond these walls!" she would exclaim, her eyes sparkling with enthusiasm. "Every encounter is a lesson, every challenge an opportunity to grow."

Eve watched in awe as her followers transformed the temple into a living testament to their collective journey. She was filled with a sense of accomplishment, knowing that she had not only ignited the flames of independence within them but had also cultivated a nurturing environment where those flames could thrive.

As seasons changed, so did the temple. Each gathering became a celebration of individuality and community, where followers would share not only their triumphs but also their vulnerabilities. They learned that embracing chaos did not mean abandoning responsibility; rather, it was an acknowledgment of the intricate dance between freedom and accountability.

Through it all, Eve remained a guiding force, not as a mere teacher but as a fellow traveler on this journey of discovery. She encouraged her followers to explore the depths of their beings, to confront their fears, and to celebrate their victories, no matter how small. In this nurturing environment, they found strength not just in themselves but in each other.

In the heart of the temple, where the once-stony silence had been replaced with laughter and the fervent exchange of ideas, Eve realized that this was the legacy she had envisioned. A community bound not by doctrine but by love, creativity, and the unwavering pursuit of truth.

And as she reflected on the journey that had brought her to this point, she understood that the path of the seeker was not a destination but a continuous unfolding - a tapestry woven with the threads of every experience, every connection, and every soul that had graced the temple's sacred space. This was a celebration of existence itself, and she felt honored to be a part of it. The cycle of life, death, chaos, and creation echoed in her heart, and she knew that together, they would continue to rise, explore, and create a future filled with limitless possibilities.

As she watched her followers thrive, Eve knew that this was only the beginning. The infinite abyss lay before them, a canvas yet to be painted with their stories, dreams, and creations. In that moment, she understood that the journey of self-discovery was a lifelong pursuit, one that would weave through time and space, connecting all beings in an eternal dance of existence.

And so, as the stars twinkled overhead, Eve stood with her heart open, ready to embrace whatever the cosmos had in store. The dawn of a new era was upon them, and together, they would shape a reality where freedom, individuality, and power flourished - a legacy that would resonate through Hell and beyond, echoing in the hearts of all who dared to dream.